Children's Literature

Criticism and Response

Mary Lou White

Wright State University

Charles E. Merrill Publishing Co.
A Bell & Howell Co.
Columbus, Ohio 43216

Published by Charles E. Merrill Publishing Co.
A Bell & Howell Co.
Columbus, Ohio 43216

This book was set in Optima and Palatino.
The production editor was Laura Harder.
The cover was designed by Will Chenoweth.

For my father and mother
Bryan and Mary Usery

International Standard Book Number:
0–675–08621–3

Library of Congress Catalog Card Number:
75–39319

1 2 3 4 5 6 7 8 9 19—80 79 78 77 76

Printed in the United States of America

Preface

Literary criticism has a long history and a large body of contributions. In fact, it is common to speak not of literary criticism in general, but of the various schools of theoretical viewpoints concerning criticism. The criticism of children's literature, however, is relatively young and sparse by comparison. The intent of this book is to draw examples of criticisms of children's literature, from the larger body of literary criticism using the frameworks of four theories: psychological, sociological, archetypal, and structural criticism. Critical essays representative of a variety of views within each of the theories are included in the first four chapters. Following these are comments drawn from the essays and suggestions for ways in which the adult reader might respond to the critical statements. Hopefully, a broadened perspective for viewing children's literature will result from the reading of this collection of essays and commentaries. Adult readers tend to bring their own experiences to children's books and, unless stimulated by other readers with different sets of experiences, they interpret books from a limited range. The field of literary criticism offers ways for interpreting children's literature that can pique the curiosity, shed new light on the story, or irritate the reader to the point of stoutly supporting the original interpretation!

It is possible that literary criticism can offer added ways in which children can respond to their literature. The final chapter presents a framework of ideas usable for developing activities for children. A variety of teaching suggestions related to the various critical theories are offered.

The initial idea for this book grew out of a project done under the advisorship of Alexander Frazier at The Ohio State University. His vision and earnest help encouraged me to develop the concept.

Thanks are given to Charlotte Leonard, Director of Children's Services of the Dayton and Montgomery County Public Library, and her staff for their help in finding children's books; to Barbara Trinkle, my secretary who helped in countless ways; and to Nanette Anderson, who typed the bulk of the manuscript. The final word of thanks is for my liberated husband, Tom, whose patience and good humor have supported me to the completion of another major task.

Acknowledgments

The author gratefully acknowledges permission to reprint the following material:

From "The Artistry of 'Blue Willow'" by Jon C. Stott in *Elementary English*, May 1973. Copyright © 1973 by the National Council of Teachers of English. Reprinted by permission of the publisher.

From "Lad as a WASP in Dog's Clothing" by Gaddis Smith in *The New York Times Book Review*, November 7, 1971. Copyright © 1971 by The New York Times Company. Reprinted by permission.

From "e. e. cummings and the Young Reader: A Celebration" by Michael L. Lasser in *Elementary English*, November/December 1973. Copyright © 1973 by the National Council of Teachers of English. Reprinted by permission of the publisher.

From several poems by e. e. cummings: "sweet spring is your," "if everything happens that can't be done," and "when faces called flowers," from *Complete Poems 1913–1962* published by Harcourt Brace Jovanovich, Inc., 1972. Reprinted by permission of the publisher.

From "The Nonsense of Edward Lear" by Warren J. Barker in *The Psychoanalytic Quarterly*, October 1966. Reprinted by permission of the author and the publisher.

From "The Real Tod Moran" by Shirley Jennings and Dewey Chambers in *Elementary English*, April 1969. Copyright © 1969 by the National Council of Teachers of English. Reprinted by permission of the publisher and the authors.

From "Lionni's Artichokes: An Interview" by Rose Agree in the *Wilson Library Bulletin*, May 1970. Reprinted by permission from the May 1970 issue of the *Wilson Library Bulletin*. Copyright © 1970 by the H. W. Wilson Company.

From "Ferdinand the Bull" by Martin Grotjahn in *American Imago*, June 1940. Reprinted by permission of the Association for Applied Psychoanalysis.

"From "Jack and the Beanstalk" by William H. Desmonde in *American Imago*, September 1951. Reprinted by permission of the Association for Applied Psychoanalysis.

From "Old and New Sexual Messages in Fairy Tales" by Diane Wolkstein in the *Wilson Library Bulletin*, October 1971. Reprinted by permission from the October 1971 issue of the *Wilson Library Bulletin*. Copyright © 1971 by the H. W. Wilson Company.

From "What Chinese Children Read: A Morality Tale" by Phyllis Krasilovsky in *Publishers Weekly,* February 26, 1973. Reprinted by permission of Curtis Brown, Ltd. Copyright © 1973 Xerox Corporation. Reprinted from the February 26, 1973 issue of *Publishers Weekly,* published by R. R. Bowker Company, a Xerox company. Copyright © 1973 by Xerox Corporation.

From "Ideologies in Children's Literature: Preliminary Notes" by Ruth B. Moynihan in *Children's Literature: The Great Excluded,* 1973. Reprinted by permission of the author and the publisher.

From "Mary Poppins Revised: An Interview with P. L. Travers" by Albert V. Schwartz in *Interracial Books for Children,* 1974. Reprinted by permission of the Council on Interracial Books for Children.

From "A New Look at Old Books: *The Bronze Bow"* by Phyllis Cohen in *Young Readers' Review,* October 1966. Reprinted by permission of L. R. Stolzer.

From "The Second Sex, Junior Division" by Elizabeth Fisher in *The New York Times Book Review,* May 24, 1970. Copyright © 1970 by The New York Times Company. Reprinted by permission.

From "Values in Popular Literature for Children" by David C. McClelland in *Childhood Education,* 40, November 1963, pp. 135–138. Reprinted by permission of David C. McClelland and the Association for Childhood Education International, 3615 Wisconsin Avenue, N.W., Washington, D.C. Copyright © 1963 by the Association.

From "Science Fiction: Impossible! Improbable! or Prophetic?" by M. Jean Greenlaw in *Elementary English,* April 1971. Copyright © 1971 by the National Council of Teachers of English. Reprinted by permission of the publisher and the author.

From "Acceptance Speech: Hans Christian Andersen Award" by Scott O'Dell in *The Horn Book Magazine,* October 1972. Reprinted by permission of Scott O'Dell.

From "Classic Hero in a New Mythology" by Marion Carr in *The Horn Book Magazine,* October 1971. Reprinted by permission of the publisher.

From "Fantasy and Self-Discovery" by Ravenna Helson in *The Horn Book Magazine,* April 1970. Reprinted by permission of the publisher.

From "Finding God in Narnia" by Charles A. Brady in *America,* October 27, 1956. Reprinted with permission of AMERICA 1956. All rights reserved. Copyright © 1956 by America Press, 106 West 56th Street, New York, N.Y. 10019.

From *"The Legend of Sleepy Hollow: A Mythological Parody"* by Marjorie W. Bruner in *College English,* January 1964. Copyright © 1964 by the National Council of Teachers of English. Reprinted by permission of the publisher and the author.

From "To Seek and To Find: Quest Literature for Children" by June S. Terry in *The School Librarian,* December 1970. Reprinted by permission of the School Library Association.

From "Use Wordless Picture Books to Teach Reading, Visual Literacy and to Study Literature" by Patricia Cianciolo in *Top of the News,* April 1973. Reprinted by permission of the American Library Association from *Top of the News,* April 1973, pp. 226–234.

From "Style in Children's Literature" by Jean Guttery in *Elementary English,* October 1941. Reprinted by permission of the National Council of Teachers of English.

From "Power of Picture Book to Change Child's Self-Image" by Naomi Gilpatrick in *Elementary English,* May 1969. Copyright © 1969 by the National Council of Teachers of English. Reprinted by permission of the publisher.

Acknowledgments

From "A Structural Approach to the Study of Literature for Children" by Peter F. Neumeyer in *Elementary English,* December 1967. Copyright © 1967 by the National Council of Teachers of English. Reprinted by permission of the publisher and the author.

From "The Owl Service: A Study" by Eleanor Cameron in *Wilson Library Bulletin,* December 1969. Reprinted by permission from the December 1969 issue of the *Wilson Library Bulletin.* Copyright © 1969 by the H. W. Wilson Company.

From "Notes: Longfellow's Motives for the Structure of Hiawatha" by Cecelia Tichi in *American Literature,* 1970. Reprinted by permission of the Duke University Press.

Contents

Three: Archetypal Criticism   **108**

Four: Structural Criticism   **159**

Introduction

Children's literature is enjoyed by nearly everyone who touches on it in even the most casual way. Sharing with a classroom group of children the sorrow of the spider's death in White's *Charlotte's Web,* laughing about the zany adventures of Kraus' *Milton the Early Riser,* or recalling a memorable incident from one's own childhood reading of Alcott's *Little Women* are experiences that bring great pleasure to people in teaching roles as well as in private, personal capacities. The joy of children's literature is fundamental to all its discussions.

The pleasure gained from children's literature is the primary objective of using literature with children. This book goes beyond that objective, however; it deals with the criticism of children's literature and the implications for teaching that can be drawn from critical studies of children's books.

Issues about Children's Literature

Difficult issues are raised when children's literature is critically studied from varying points of view. A few examples will introduce some of the controversies.

Does reflection upon or even a second reading of a children's book stir thoughts of deeper meanings than those gained initially? Consider the book, *Blue Willow,* and the fuller meanings of its symbolism made explicit by the critic who wrote the following:

> The final symbolic setting, the Anderson farm, represents the security which the Larkins once possessed and to which they wish to return. . . . However, the farm, like the promised land in many fairy tales and romances, is guarded by the evil ogre who must be defeated if it is to be achieved. Bounce Reyburn defies Janey, suggesting to her that she is a thief, and silently but threateningly enjoining her not to tell Nels Anderson about the Larkins' rental arrangements. When the family is faced with eviction, Janey goes to the Anderson

1

farm and, in asking to see the willow plate, tells Mr. Anderson about Reyburn and, in a sense, defeats the ogre. Moving to the farm, Janey and the family achieve permanence. The foreman's house which is built for them symbolizes the security they have found.[1]

Is it possible that children would benefit from discussing this symbolism within the book? Would children be able to extrapolate the notion of slaying the dragon—perhaps by dramatizing and discussing the actions of the main character in Galdone's version of "Jack and the Beanstalk," *The History of Mother Twaddle and the Marvelous Achievements of Her Son Jack,* or one of the Arthurian legends, such as Hieatt's *Sir Gawain and the Green Knight*—and understand that the same archetype recurs in *Blue Willow* with its adult bully?

One concern being raised about children's books is that they may be a source for subliminal learning. Although hard data are not available concerning the possibility of subliminal learning through children's books, many persons are operating on the hunch that such learning takes place. If the notion of the cruel stepmother is inherent within "Snow White and the Seven Dwarfs," as one critic has pointed out in the following excerpt, what are the implications for teachers?

> The queen dies, or rather, begins to undergo a profound change, when the daughter is born, and this change is completed in a year when she reappears in the form of the jealous stepmother. This echoes the sinister note struck by the black of the window frame. The stepmother who so frequently appears in fairy tales seems to be the child's fantasy of the "bad," cruel or jealous mother. It also expresses the real mother's unconscious hatred of her children. A mother tends to be jealous of her children and to hate them because she must now share with them her husband's love. But they are her own children, and this provides a real compensation which is denied to the stepmother. They are aliens to whom her husband is often more attached than he is to her, and if she is childless, they are constant reminders of her frustrations.[2]

Would it be worthwhile for a teacher, being aware of the kinds of psychological implications possible within children's literature, to guide children into a discussion activity focusing on quite personal problems? For example, the students mght make a chart of the family structures in books such as Sachs' *The Truth about Mary Rose* or Donovan's *I'll Get There. It Better Be Worth the Trip* and move into a discussion of their own personal family relationships and concerns. If such an activity would be considered beneficial, then how might a teacher go about becoming aware of the psychological implications pertinent to the students' needs within the bulk of children's books?

Do some children's books carry subtle stereotypes? In the following quotation, the critic notes that a WASPish attitude of Albert Payson Terhune, author of *Lad, A Dog* and other dog books, is not explicit but implied. Is this just another instance of the work of critics who can find fault with anything?

---

1. Jon C. Stott, "The Artistry of Blue Willow," *Elementary English* 50, no. 5 (May 1973): 764–65.
2. A. S. Macquisten and R. W. Pickford, "Psychological Aspects of the Fantasy of Snow White and the Seven Dwarfs," *The Psychoanalytic Review* 29, no. 3 (July, 1942): 237.

The analogy between thoroughbred dogs and human aristocrats is implicit in all Terhune's stories. If his villains are not black, they may have a mysterious Oriental strain like the slant-eyed Dr. Phager in "Unseen!" Half-breeds are the worst, as in "Grudge Mountain." Terhune did sympathize, however, with the American Indian. He has one character explain, 'You see, I am leaving not only California but America as well. America is no place for us aboriginal Americans. In France I shall probably be received in fairly good society . . . I may even acquire the title of *le beau sauvage* or something equally flattering.' The "blue-eyed Niggers" of "Treasure" are a sorry and dangerous group—alleged descendants of Hessian soldiers who took slaves and Indians as wives.[3]

If such sociological implications in books are not to be lightly dismissed, then what should be done with the books? Should they be withdrawn from the shelves? Censored? Or is it the responsibility of teachers and librarians to raise social issues, to teach children how to observe implicit connotations, and to contrast these books with others that offer different treatments? Could teachers, for example, effectively use a book that contains a black stereotype, such as Lofting's *The Story of Dr. Doolittle*, as a basis for contrasting the positive treatment of blacks in a book such as *The Empty Schoolhouse* by Carlson? Both books show black racism but one is racist in its treatment of characters and the other shows the effects of racism on the main characters.

Is it possible that the structure of a piece of children's literature— the very words, phrases, and punctuation with which it is created—give deeper meaning to the literature? The following discussion of some of e. e. cummings' poems suggests that the form the poet used adds to the meaning of the poems. Are these comments simply a scholarly exercise?

Few poets sing more beautifully than cummings, and children who have had experience with rhythmics or pantomime or dance love to move to his music alone:

(all the merry little birds are
flying in the floating in the
very spirits singing in
are winging in the blossoming)

we're anything brighter than even the sun
(we're everything greater
than books
might mean)
we're everyanything more than believe
(with a spin
leap
alive we're alive)
we're wonderful one times one

when more than was lost has been found has been found
and having is giving and giving is living—

---

3. Gaddis Smith, "Lad as a WASP in Dog's Clothing," *The New York Times Book Review* sec. VII, November 7, 1971: 10.

but keeping is darkness and winter and cringing
—it's spring (all our night becomes day) o, it's spring!
all the pretty birds dive to the heart of the sky
all the little fish climb through the mind of the sea
(all the mountains are dancing; are dancing)

His songs are filled with the language of movement and the liveliness that comes from it; they are inherently dramatic—flying, floating, winging, blossoming, everything, spin, leap, times; dive, climb, dancing, dancing. He relies heavily on the present-participial form of the verb, a word in motion. He creates movement through repetition of words and word patterns:

"when more than was lost has been found has
been found"

through word progressions:

"and having is giving and giving is living—"

and through assonance:

"but keeping is darkness and winter and cringing"

He then breaks his rhythm only for the great discovery, the grand announcement:

"it's spring (all our night becomes day) o,
it's spring!
all the pretty birds dive to the heart of the
sky
all the little fish climb through the mind of
the sea
(All the mountains are dancing; are dancing)"

It is a moment of ecstasy so pure that the hyperbolic imagery becomes not merely impossible but necessary. We read the lines with disbelief yet we are forced to say, "Yes, that's the way it is, not for the birds or the fish or the mountains, but for us." The music carries us into the meaning so that we may make it our own.[4]

Could children use the medium of dance to discover meaning beyond the words of the poem? If so, would dancing the poem be just as didactic as beating out the rhythm and nothing the breaks in rhythm in the various measures? Would the whole poem be best left untampered with other than just reading it?

The series of questions raised here are not included for their easy answers. They represent some of the issues that are central to the criticism of children's literature and the implications of that criticism for teaching.

Organization of the Book

Children's literature is increasingly understood to be worthy of serious criticism on much the same terms as adult literature. A growing body of criticism dealing with children's literature supports this contention. Within this book

4. Michael L. Lasser, "e. e. cummings and the Young Reader: A Celebration," *Elementary English* 50, no. 8 (Nov./Dec., 1973): 1182–83.

are critical articles, both historical and current, exemplifying the variety of views of children's literature.

The intent of the book is not solely to support children's literature as an area of literature worthy of analysis in its own right, however. Of greater importance is the viewpoint that there are implications for teaching stemming from this body of criticism. The thesis is that if children are given opportunities to reflect on literature from a wide variety of points of view, it is likely that their responses to literature will be varied and will grow in depth both rationally and nonrationally. The suggestions in this book for ways of responding to literature are offered as a means of using and testing this idea.

The first four chapters are based on four major types of criticism prevalent in the study of adult literature: psychological, sociological, archetypal, and structural criticism. Although other forms of criticism exist and, in fact, may have permeated some facets of the four types discussed in this book, the four selected types are common to the field of literary criticism. They serve as a basis for bringing together adult and children's literary criticism. Each of the four chapters contains a discussion of the type of criticism and examples of criticisms of children's literature. The readings are drawn from varied sources and, in some cases, were written primarily as psychological or sociological commentaries rather than as literary discussions. Following the readings of each chapter are suggestions for ways in which teachers and librarians might respond to the literature. Adult awareness and experience with responding to literature through the use of the various critical methodologies are fundamental to using literature with children within these same frameworks.

Selected readings related to the specific forms of criticism are annotated in each of the four chapters under the heading, "For Further Reading." A listing of all children's books cited in the preceding text is placed at the close of each chapter.

The Four Types of Criticism

Psychological criticism deals with an analysis of the emotions related to the literature. It takes the forms of biographical studies of the author and analyses of the characters within the fiction itself. The earlier excerpt concerning "Snow White and the Seven Dwarfs" is an example of psychological criticism. The article from which the excerpt was drawn was written by a psychologist who used literature as a focus for describing actual psychological responses of persons.

Sociological criticism is concerned with the view of society that is reflected in literature. It explains literature in terms of social, economic, and political views of the time. The discussion of *Lad, A Dog* is an example of sociological criticism. The excerpt from the article is representative of articles that appear concerning social issues that are current at any one time.

Archetypal criticism is concerned with the theme of the literary work. The themes or motifs have symbols that recur in all great literature over time and space. Thus, these symbols represent man's relationship with himself, other men, and the universe. Archetypal criticism draws from anthropology, psychology, and religion. The discussion of the security of the farm setting within *Blue Willow* shows the use of archetypal criticism. Great themes that recur in world literature—historical as well as current—recur in children's literature also, although sometimes in more simplified styles.

Structural criticism is concerned with the form of the literary work. It uses an analysis of the structure of the work to understand the meaning of the literature. The fields of semantics and linguistics are basic to structural criticism. The discussion of the use of e. e. cummings' poetry with children is based on principles of structural criticism. Advocates of this form of criticism stress that it is the one form that is central to the literature itself, not more pertinent to outside forces.

Implications for Using Literature with Children

The final chapter draws on the preceding chapters for the theories and methodologies of the four types of literary criticism and develops those ideas for use with children. The suggested activities are intended to be used as guides or samples on which teachers and librarians can draw as they adapt the plans for particular children. The activities provide opportunities for children to respond to the literature individually or in groups independently, or by teacher direction. Some of the activities are based on cognitive thinking while others are planned to develop affective responses. Attention is also given to providing for various ways of responding through writing, speaking, or movement. Emphasis should be given here to the fact that these are suggestions, not set formulas for teaching literary criticism. The intent of this book, and especially the final chapter, is to set forth an idea, support it with examples, and offer implications for using literature with children.

The concept is growing, not static; it is meant to encourage adaptation and experimentation with the ideas, not to dictate a style of literary use.

Intended Outcomes

Adapting the methodologies of literary criticism for use with children is not advocated as an exclusive method or as the one way for using books with children, nor is it suggested as a replacement for current methods of teaching literature. Instead, it offers another framework for working with children and books. The concept is based on the supposition that employing some of the techniques of literary criticism will broaden and deepen children's ability to respond to literature. Too often, the activities proposed for use with children's literature lead to merely surface responses. Games and arts and crafts projects are frequently tangential to the literature but do not enable children to make any in-depth responses to books. Activities of this nature are worthwhile for the motivation for reading they provide, but teachers and librarians should realize their limitations. The activities suggested within this book are intended to foster more thoughtful and more meaningful responses to literature through the use of methods long used in the criticism of adult literature.

REFERENCES

Alcott, Louise M. *Little Women*. Illus. Barbara Cooney. New York: Thomas Y. Crowell, 1955.

Carlson, Natalie Savage. *The Empty Schoolhouse*. Illus. John Kaufmann. New York: Harper & Row, 1965.

Donovan, John. *I'll Get There. It Better Be Worth the Trip*. New York: Harper & Row, 1969.

Galdone, Paul. *The History of Mother Twaddle and the Marvelous Achievements of Her Son Jack*. New York: The Seabury Press, 1974.

Gates, Doris. *Blue Willow*. Illus. Paul Lantz. New York: The Viking Press, 1940.

Grimm, Jacob and Wilhelm. *Snow White and the Seven Dwarfs*. Freely trans. and illus. Wanda Gàg. New York: Coward, McCann & Geoghegan, 1938.

Hieatt, Constance. *Sir Gawain and the Green Knight*. Illus. Walter Lorraine. New York: Thomas Y. Crowell, 1967.

Kraus, Robert. *Milton the Early Riser*. Illus. Jose and Ariane Aruego. New York: Windmill Books, 1972.

Lofting, Hugh. *The Story of Dr. Doolittle*. Philadelphia: J. B. Lippincott, 1920.

Sachs, Marilyn. *The Truth About Mary Rose*. Illus. Louis Glanzman. Garden City, New York: Doubleday, 1973.

Terhune, Albert Payson, *Lad, A Dog*. Anniversary edition. Illus. Sam Savitt. New York: E. P. Dutton, 1959.

White, E. B. *Charlotte's Web*. Illus. Garth Williams. New York: Harper & Row, 1952.

chapter one

Psychological Criticism

Psychological criticism tries to give a greater understanding of the literary work through an analysis of the emotions. Methods of analysis adapted from the areas of psychology and psychoanalytic theory have been used to find explanations in authors' lives for their use of certain literary allusions. These same analytic techniques have been applied to the study of characters within the literary work and to the responses that the literary work evokes on the part of the reader.

The development of the new field of psychoanalysis in the early twentieth century provided a vast new core of ideas from which literary critics began to draw. Sigmund Freud, himself a devotee of literature, was the key figure of the psychoanalytic movement. Psychological criticism is characterized by many of the concepts attributed to Freud. Some of these include the use of symbols, the many references to unconscious acts and dreams, infantile sexuality, references to psychic maladies such as the Oedipus complex, allusions to the phenomenon of repression, and the use of psychoanalytic language to describe situations appearing in the literature.

Types of Psychological Criticism

The use of psychoanalytic methods in studying literature has developed into studies of the biography of the author and studies of the fictional characters.

Biographical Criticism. Biographical criticism presents an analysis of the author's life. Wilson's essay on Sophocles' drama *Philoctetes* asserts the notion that the greatest of artists have something abhorrent and something marvelous —a wound and a bow—and that the two are necessary in order to produce greatness. Using this idea, Wilson analyzed Dickens' work in relation to Dickens' life. He noted that it was necessary to understand the personality of Dickens, the person, in order to fully appreciate Dickens, the writer.[1]

Wilson described the humiliating six months the child Dickens spent in the blacking warehouse, noting his neurotic illnesses and quoting from Dickens' autobiographical notes his despair with ever forgetting those terrible days. Wilson asserted that Dickens tried throughout his career to use those early physical and mental abuses in his writing to give a true picture of the times in which those hardships took place.[2] Thus, the abhorrent childhood realities became the basis for several marvelous fictional tales.

The biography of Edgar Allan Poe depicts from childhood the evolution of a neurotic man. The child Poe was abandoned by his father, and, soon after, his beloved mother died. He was taken into the family of his uncle but never adopted by this cold and psychologically cruel man—a situation that caused embarrassment and insecurity for the young Poe, thrust into aristocratic Southern society without the proper credentials. Krutch studied Poe's life and books and validated Poe's neuroses and made a case with a strong factual basis for Poe's writings being influenced by his early life.[3]

Character Analysis. Another type of literary study that makes use of psychoanalytic methods is the study of the characters within the work of art itself. Critics who use this form of analysis base their judgment on the idea that fictional characters can be studied as if they were real. Using this assumption, the characters would make use of the same symbols, would repress the same wishes within their unconscious, and would have the same conflicts among the psychic forces as real life persons. Interpretations of characters through the application of psychoanalytic theory would thus give a deeper understanding of literary works.

An example of character analysis as a form of criticism is Rosenfield's study of Golding's *Lord of the Flies*. Rosenfield drew heavily on Freud for symbolic meanings—the use of the two leaders, Ralph and Jack, as God and the Devil, the characterization of Piggy as the father, and the cannibalistic rituals of death.[4] Rosenfield stayed closely with the text in the analysis, using psychoanalytic theory to explain depth meanings of the novel. Golding's private life was not entered into, nor was there any attempt to explain meanings that were personal to the critic as an individual reader. The emphasis was on the combined use of the text and psychoanalytic theory.

A comparison between Prince Hal's moral dilemma in Shakespeare's *Henry IV* and *Henry V* and the similar problem that occurred in a clinical case offered an interesting intertwining of literature and psychology. Kris, a psychologist, presented a careful psychoanalytic study of Shakespeare's character, drawing information from history as well as the plays. He discussed Prince Hal's imposition of an ideal greatly superior to his own father that created problems in

1. Edmund Wilson, *The Wound and the Bow: Seven Studies in Literature* (New York: Oxford Univ. Press, 1947), p. 9.
2. Ibid., p. 8.
3. Joseph Wood Krutch, *Edgar Allan Poe: A Study in Genius* (New York: Knopf, 1926).
4. Claire Rosenfield, " 'Men of a Smaller Growth;' A Psychological Analysis of Golding's *Lord of the Flies*," *Literature and Psychology* 11 (Fall 1961): 93–101.

their father-son relationship. The second problem Kris detailed was the prince's adoption of a father substitute, Falstaff, who was just the opposite of his father. Both problems are common in the clinical studies of young males, according to Kris.[5]

Pros and Cons of Psychological Criticism

Psychological criticism offers the reader insights into the literature from the field of psychology. It is the form of criticism that is most closely related to the mind and emotions. When the reader peruses a critical essay based on a psychoanalysis of the literary work, he is offered ideas that do not necessarily represent the author's meaning; instead he receives ideas that could possibly extend the personal meaning he finds within the work.

Psychological criticism has been attacked for its oversimplification of the complexities of life. Too often, literary works are labeled as castration tales or the character is written off as having an Oedipus complex when much more insightful commentaries could be given. Symbol-mongers are rampant among psychological critics, a situation that causes many readers to discount any psychoanalytic study as being a ridiculous hunt for sexual implications.

Another weakness of psychological criticism is its use of terminology that seems, at times, vulgar to the reader. Lesser used the example of the term anal-erotic as the most accurate description of a quality in *Robinson Crusoe,* at the same time noting concern about the use of the term for such a revered book in the realm of children's fiction.[6] The use of clinical terms may also create barriers between the reader and critic due to a lack of technical understanding.

A third weakness results from the inability of most psychological critics to be top-rate specialists in both fields. Generally the critic is either a psychologist or a literary scholar; seldom does he bring expertise in both fields to his criticism. Thus, there is the tendency of the psychologist to use the literature as an embellishment of his clinical experiences while the literary scholar's analyses suffer from the problem of "a little knowledge is a dangerous thing." The psychologist offers sparse insight into the literary form of the work while sometimes going so deeply into the psychological aspects as to suggest a priori causes for the characters' actions. On the other hand, the literary scholar tends to use old, sometimes outdated ideas, to confuse the notions of writers in the field, specifically Freud and Jung, and to operate with a partial understanding of the psychoanalytic theory being applied.

Finally, the tendency of much psychological criticism to dwell on the artist, not on the artist's work, is considered a weakness by many opponents to this approach. Biographical analysis based on psychoanalytic theory is counted by many critics as being external to the work of art and of little value in understanding the literature per se.

---

5. Ernst Kris, "Prince Hal's Conflict," *Psychoanalytic Quarterly* 17 (1948): 487–06.
6. Simon O. Lesser. *Fiction and the Unconscious* (Boston: Beacon Press, 1957), p. 306.

Psychological Criticism of Children's Literature

Psychological criticisms of children's literature are found primarily in psychiatric journals. Most of the articles deal with literary classics, nursery stories, and folk tales.

Biographical Criticism

Biographical criticisms are abundant, particularly studies of the authors of children's literary classics, such as Robert Louis Stevenson, Lewis Carroll, James Barrie, etc. One article written by a psychiatrist is included as representative of the abundance of psychoanalytic studies of the authors through their works. Barker's commentary on Edward Lear uses factual information from family history and draws ideas from Lear's nonsense verses and pictures. Barker combines this information to build several hypotheses concerning Lear's impressive childhood experiences that led him to write with his particular style and content.

Jennings and Chambers use a combination of interview, diary extrapolation, and analysis of a novel to present a criticism of the writings of Howard Pease. The most unique feature of this article is the account of Pease's discovery through psychoanalysis of the resemblance of his personal life to that of his hero.

Agree's interview with Leo Lionni affords the opportunity of seeing how this children's novelist personally analyzes his own works. The simplicity with which this is done is in distinct contrast to the complexity of the psychiatrists' analyses in terminology, allusion, and symbolism.

Character Analysis

The second set of four articles deals with character analysis. Critics have studied characters within the novels as if they and their actions were real. Grotjahn gives a thorough analysis of the bull Ferdinand, drawing upon Freudian methodology for studying the character of this modern story.

Desmonde gives a brief but highly clinical psychonalytical criticism of the hero of "Jack and the Beanstalk." The story is representative of the numerous studies that have been done of folk tales.

Wolkstein touches upon several characters in her discussion of the sexuality and sensuality apparent in children's literature. She discusses the differences in sexual allusions between older folk tales and modern stories.

READINGS

The Nonsense of Edward Lear

Warren J. Barker

A study of the work and life of Edward Lear, in addition to other benefits and pleasures, holds promise of revealing something of the psychological nature of nonsense. I refer now to nonsense as a form of the comic—a playing with words, with form, and with line—intended, more or less, by its creator to amuse and entertain others, while surreptitiously serving more important, sometimes deep-seated, emotional needs of his own. An examination of these highly personal needs of the creator of nonsense—Edward Lear specifically—will constitute the main effort of this inquiry. I will not attempt a comprehensive and exhaustive treatise on nonsense in general, nor will I undertake a systematic investigation into the nature of talent, of creativity, or of taste.

Moss (*II*) points out that nonsense is by no means the same as *no* sense. "The senseless," he writes, "is merely irrational, but nonsense holds the plausible and the implausible in tension and makes of the absurd an entertainment, a release, and a form of criticism." Greenacre says of nonsense that, "It leaps the barriers of apparent similarities and exists seemingly in its own incomparable realm and independent right, denying even relationships by contrast and comparison which are implicit in exaggeration and simile. Nonsense is not only the lack of reason or loss of expected order, but it is the defiance of reason which men value most, and it is achieved by apparent isolation, inconsequence and generally heedless disconnection. There is a quality of (generally quiet) explosive destructiveness about sheer nonsense—an unannounced nihilism—which is never absolutely achieved, but is felt in its subtle implication" (3, p. 271).

I will proceed now by reviewing some of the facts and the myths pertaining to Lear's life. Following this I will attempt to describe some of his pictorial and verbal productions. Finally, with special reference to his nonsense, I will attempt some reconstructions which may show connections between Lear's life experiences on the one hand and his work on the other.

Reprinted from *The Psychoanalytic Quarterly* 25, no. 4 (October 1966): 568–86.

. . . We come at last to the difficult and hazardous task of attempting some meaningful inferences about the determinants of Lear's nonsense. In spite of the fact that the available material is fragmentary, there are a number—too many for present study—of promising pathways that beckon to be explored. One might put emphasis on the ego aspects of his nonsense, or concentrate on an analysis of the content of his limericks or his nonsense poems. Alternatively, one could investigate in detail the manifestations of Lear's orality or anality as they might bear on his artistic career. The possibilities are numerous.

Some important feelings that go a long way in explaining the content of Lear's tragicomic poems are related to the fact that he was turned over to the care of his sister Ann at an early age. Most likely this occurred at the time of the birth of his sister Charlotte, an event which brought about his weaning and eviction from the parental bedroom. The theme of abandonment, desolation, and a hoped-for reunion is worked and reworked in these poems. These are feelings, by the way, which were painfully reactivated by the dissolution of the Lear family when Edward was thirteen years of age. One important mitigating factor in the alienation from his mother lies in the fact that sister Ann seemed to have given him a full measure of attention, devotion, and love.

In his haunting poem called "The Dong with the Luminous Nose," fragments from which I quote, Lear refers to the "Jumblies" who

> . . . . danced in circlets all night long,
> To the plaintive pipe of the lively Dong
>
> * * *
>
> For day and night he was always there
> By the side of his Jumbly girl so fair
>
> * * *
>
> Till the morning came of that hateful day
> When the Jumblies sailed in their sieve away,
> And the Dong was left on the cruel shore
> Gazing–gazing for evermore,–
>
> * * *
>
> But when the sun was low in the West,
> The Dong arose and said,—
> —"What little sense I once possessed
> Has quite gone out of my head!"—
> And since that day he wanders still
> By lake and forest, marsh and hill,
>
> * * *
>
> "For ever I'll seek by lake and shore
> Till I find my Jumbly girl once more!"

The yearning expressed in this poem is for a chance to relive those supposedly blissful days and nights when he was secure in the midst of his family and at the side of his mother.

Granted that weaning, separation, and the consequent frustration and loneliness (with implicit rage) are themes that are pertinent to his nonsense, especially the poems, it seems to me that there must have been other early experiences to account more adequately for Lear's emotional and artistic fate. I am inclined to believe, for reasons which will be elaborated below, that Lear suffered an additional, sharp, and overwhelming psychic trauma during early childhood—before exile from the parental bedroom—which materially influenced his life and work.

There are hints—but, alas, there is no direct and irrefutable evidence—that the young Lear witnessed the primal scene. What is the basis for such an assumption? First, let us take another and a closer look at the poem, "The Dong with the Luminous Nose." In addition to the theme that we have already considered, it seems likely indeed that Lear was also describing a primal scene experience. The Jumblies dancing in circlets all night refers quite probably to the parents in the act of sexual intercourse. The plaintive pipe of the lively Dong alludes to Lear's own sexual excitement. When the morning came he was still gazing, still trying to cope with what he had seen, heard, and felt. Yet he was left dumbfounded; what little sense he once possessed, he tells us, had now quite gone out of his head. In rage and desolation he felt obliged thenceforward to repudiate his mother—the bad mother—and to search forever for the good mother, the asexual one. Even the men he loved subsequently seemed mainly mother figures.

Another hint pointing to an unintegrated primal scene experience was his recollection from childhood, "my imperfect sight in those days . . . formed everything into a horror." Why a "horror" instead of, say, a "blur"? Lear's way of putting it strongly suggests that something he had seen was terrifying.

Also, there is his statement that 'I feel woundedly like a spectator all my life on what goes on amongst those I know. . . . ' I suspect that this represents one of Lear's most poignant feelings at the time of the primal scene experience.

To continue with our clues, there is Lear's first memory. This, you may recall, was of "being taken out of bed to see the illuminations after the Battle of Waterloo." In general, this memory undoubtedly refers to an intense sensory experience. More specifically, it has all the earmarks of a screen memory. It contains allusions to the bedroom; to being awakened from sleep; to looking; to his own immobility, that is, of having been wrapped in a blanket; and to a battle, perhaps not mainly to Waterloo but to a "struggle" that went on in front of his very eyes—and ears.

There is a great deal of mystery surrounding Lear's so-called epilepsy. No description of the attacks comes down to us, although Lear recorded their frequency. Could it be that, in part, the seizures were periodic affect-storms, desperate, unconscious, attempts to regurgitate the incorporated but undigested primal scene experience, reenactments of it without affect-awareness? Greenacre observes that "many children have some fabled ogre, often in animal form . . . with which they scare each other and themselves." She goes on to say that "psychoanalysis reveals that it is generally some representation of the primal scene, in which the sexual images of the parents are fused into a frightening or awe-inspiring single figure." (3, p. 240).

Another one of Lear's lifelong physical complaints must come under suspicion. One might wonder if his respiratory difficulties—asthma and bronchitis—served as an expression of his breathless excitement as the observer of the primal scene; and of the loud and distinctive breathing of the principals as well. It has already been noted that Lear had an intense aversion to noise—"people noises," especially.

In one of his illustrated stories (8), Mr. Lear, a parrot, and a cat are out strolling. Various misadventures occur. The climax comes when they fall into a ditch and each is broken up into several sections—quite bloodlessly, of course. Some well-intentioned person comes along and puts them back together again but in so doing, puts Mr. Lear's head on the body of the parrot, the parrot's legs on the body of the cat, and so on. Where once there had been three distinct characters with distinct identities, there were now three figures which were each a mixture and a conglomeration of one another. This is, I think, more than a warning that "togetherness" can be overdone. This imagery was made possible by his having had a primal scene experience, and reflects an aspect of it. It poses the specific question of where, in the sexual act, the body of one parent leaves off and that of the other begins; and, it betrays Lear's guilt-laden wish to have been a part of what went on in his parents' bed. The story suggests, too, that Lear was quite reluctant to separate himself from his parents, and this reluctance seems relevant to the fact that Lear could easily shift his identification from man, to woman, to child, and back again, depending upon whose company he was in, and at the same time be basically confused about who he was, as well as confused about the role and function of both parents. Somewhat related to this identity diffusion was Lear's propensity to distort the body-image (13) in his comic drawings, depicting many of the figures, variously, with greatly elongated noses or chins, with swollen torsos or with enormous heads. What is predominantly reflected here, I think, was not only a projection of the erotic tumescence of Lear's penis and of the body parts which symbolically represent it, but in a more general way the distortion felt by the whole body in a state of dammed-up libido.

From the standpoint of affect, the primal scene was painfully intolerable; in terms of its perceptual and ideational content its fascination was exceeded only by its shocking incomprehensibility. His eyes, his ears, and his sexual excitement pushed him toward a true assessment of what was going on between his parents. His strong wish to deny his parents' sexuality and his own disturbing erotic sensations, his jealous rage, and his fright, forced him to try to deny its implications. Result—a tormenting and unshakable doubt. The primal scene experience brought about a sudden and overwhelming flood of sexual excitation, far too intense to be successfully repressed or adequately integrated. Lear was obliged to resort to unstable defenses, and unstable identifications, and to suffer a number of other distortions in his character structure. One can presume the emergence of a whimsical and arbitrary superego, sometimes harshly critical, sometimes overindulgent. Lear's psychosexual development was arrested at a pregenital level, enhancing his narcissism, his exhibitionism, and scopophilia, and in general giving his erotic drives an oral—and anal—sadistic coloring. Greenacre (4) is of the opinion that the libidinal organization of the artist is more like that of the perverse individual than that of the neurotic one. I would be inclined to conclude, by the way, that it is unlikely that the desperately inhibited Lear ever had any kind of overt sexual experience with either sex.

Lewin (9) points out that a not uncommon reaction to the primal scene is an oral one, i.e., it is conceived of as a cannibalistic feast, and that it is often the event that gets reproduced in adult depressions and elations—moods quite prominent in Lear's life. Many of his limericks concern eating, while a lesser number refer to being eaten, and a few to sleep. Others, Kanzer (6) for example, stress paranoid or persecutory trends in the making of the clown.

If an influential primal scene did indeed take place in Lear's infancy, what relevance might it have had for his creative work in general and his nonsense in particular? I have suggested that this traumatic experience was neither successfully repressed nor successfully integrated. It will come as no surprise at this juncture to learn that I now offer the hypothesis that Lear's nonsense represents a reenactment of the primal scene experience. This is not to say, of course, that his nonsense had no other determinants, or, on the other hand, that there were no other important manifestations of the primal scene experience. Admittedly, the social nature of the comic—of nonsense—is important. Through it, Lear could relate more easily than otherwise and even attract favorable attention.

As a reenactment of the primal scene, the nonsense production served two main purposes. In the first place, it was a way of expressing—of reliving—something forbidden, something traumatic, but which nevertheless had a considerable mischievous pleasurable component. This aspect can be thought of as a contribution of the id. Secondly, the nonsense served a defensive function by blunting the original, raw affect, and by modifying the ideational content in such a way as to make it unobjectionable, even pleasurable—an ego contribution. The creation of his nonsense was an active, purposive, controlled reliving of an event which originally had overwhelmed him in a state of passivity and helplessness. Aside from merely neutralizing anxiety, rage, or other strong affect, Lear got a bonus of pleasure from two ego sources,—the pleasure experienced in mastery, and the pleasure arising from the sudden release of tension by an economic expenditure of thought. Kris (7) comments that the enjoyment of the comic entails a feeling of security from danger; what was feared yesterday is made to appear funny today.

Lear's nonsense appears to have had another, more generalized function—to divert him from the awareness of any painful affect, or even from boredom. We are reminded, in this connection of Lord Westbury's complaint that Lear "forcibly introduced ridiculous images in order to distract the mind from what it is contemplating." Greenacre (3) sees a direct connection between Lewis Carroll's nonsense and the primal scene. She considers the last stanza (or as Carroll himself called it, the last 'fit') of his poem, "The Hunting of the Snark," to have been a reenactment of the primal scene.

In Lear's nonsense the sexual impulses, pregenital as they are, are much less apparent than are the hostile and aggressive ones. In spite of the fact that the aggression in the manifest content of the limericks seems so irrational and so irrelevant as to appear almost innocent, in the latent content of the limericks it is not hard to discern that Lear is protesting violently against the status quo, and that in his nonsense he turns the conventional world—the world of the adults who "wounded" and confused him—into a shambles. Greenacre so aptly characterized this subversive quality of nonsense as "an unannounced nihilism."

Reference has been made previously to Lear's facility in transmuting himself from the realm of sense to the realm of nonsense and back again at will. We recognize this as an excellent example of regression in the service of the ego. In line with Greenacre's thinking, it is probably also correct to think of this shift of being at times in the nature of a dissociative episode, "but of less ominous prognostic significance than would be true in a less gifted person" (4). Kris (7) reminds us that in the production of the comic, the ego remains in control of the primary process while in dreams, in neurosis, and psychosis, the ego is overwhelmed by the primary process.

If Lear's nonsense is predominantly a direct expression of primary process, albeit under ego control, then his landscapes can be looked upon mainly as reflections of secondary process activity. While Lear seemed to enjoy the conception and execution of his comic drawings and of his hasty sketches, his painting in oil was more often than not experienced as drudgery. He once confided to a friend, "Yes, I do hate the act of painting and although day after day I go steadily on, it is like grinding my nose off" (2, p. 181).

If much of Lear's nonsense can be looked upon as a disguised reproduction of the primal scene, then his serious landscapes can be considered as attempts to negate the primal scene altogether. His nonsense was a "doing," his painting an "undoing." The content of these large canvases betrays a determined need to picture a world ruled by order where immobility and serenity held sway. In them and through them it is as if Lear is periodically declaring: "See, nothing frightening is happening; nothing is amiss." Since his oil painting was something that had an unconscious negating and, most likely, an atoning and restorative intention as well, it did not lead to release of pentup feeling. Rage and frustration mounted during this serious and onerous activity so that sooner or later there was an eruption from below, often taking the form of nonsense. Like the primal scene itself, the hapless characters in the illustrations for the limericks make the point that, in Lear's view, there is little reason, order, or gentleness that prevails in the relationship between and among human beings. When nonsense failed as a sufficient release or defense, it is not improbable, as I have already suggested, that intense affect may have been discharged by way of the so-called epileptic seizures.

In closing I want to comment that Lear, having once learned the complex techniques of nonsense and having learned that it was not only mind-saving but socially applauded, tended to invoke it to handle a variety of affects from a variety of sources. It became, in effect, a final common pathway through which painful tensions could be optimally discharged. Most fortunately what was good for Lear was also good for the world.

REFERENCES

1. Chesterton, G. K. "How Pleasant to Know Mr. Lear." In *A Handful of Authors.* New York: Sheed & Ward, 1953.

2. Davidson, Angus. *Edward Lear: Landscape Painter and Nonsense Poet (1812–1888).* New York: E. P. Dutton & Co., 1939.

3. Greenacre, Phyllis. *Swift and Carroll. A Psychoanalytic Study of Two Lives.* New York: International Universities Press, 1955.

4. ————."The Childhood of the Artist." In *The Psychoanalytic Study of the Child,* *Vol. XII.* New York: International Universities Press, 1957.

5. Jackson, Holbrook, ed. *The Complete Nonsense of Edward Lear.* New York: Dover Publications, 1951.

6. Kanzer, Mark. "Gogol—A Study on Wit and Paranoia." *J. Amer. Psa. Assn.* III (1955): 110–25.

7. Kris, Ernst. "Ego Development and the Comic." In *Psychoanalytic Explorations in Art.* New York: International Universities Press, 1952.

8. Lear, Edward. "Mr. Lear, the Polly, and the Pussybite." In *Teapots and Quails and Other New Nonsenses.* Edited by Angus Davidson and Philip Hofer. Cambridge, Mass.: Harvard University Press, 1954.

9. Lewin, Bertram D. *The Psychoanalysis of Elation.* New York: The Psychoanalytic Quarterly, 1961. (Orig. c. W. W. Norton & Co., Inc., 1950.)

10. McCarthy, Desmond. "Thurber and Lear." In *Memories.* New York: Oxford University Press, 1953.

11. Moss, Howard. Foreword to *The Nonsense Books of Edward Lear.* New York: New American Library of World Literature, 1964.

12. Murphy, Ray, ed. *Edward Lear's Indian Journal.* New York: Coward-McCann, 1954.

13. Reitman, F. "Lear's Nonsense." *J. Clin Psychopathology* VII (1946): 671–78.

14. Untermeyer, Louis. *A Treasury of Great Poems.* New York: Simon & Schuster, 1942, p. 852.

15. Van Thal, Herbert, ed. *Edward Lear's Journals.* New York: Coward-McCann, 1952.

The Real Tod Moran

Shirley Jennings
Dewey Chambers

Tod Moran, the youthful hero of sixteen of the highly successful novels for adolescents by Howard Pease, has already begun to settle down in the selective company of American, junior literary folk heroes. Like Tom Swift, the Hardy Boys, Nancy Drew, Mark Tidd and Jack Armstrong, Tod belongs to a genre of American fictional heroes for children that have thrilled generations of youthful readers and will likely thrill generations to come. His "All-American-type" physique and personality, have been prototypes of an American dream familiar to all whose interests skirt the folk hero. Tod Moran's romanticized and dramatic sea adventures remain in print, and successfully so, forty-three years after his literary birth.

Tod Moran first tasted the printer's ink when he came to life in Howard Pease's *The Tattoed Man* (Doubleday) in 1926. His appetite for ink has lasted through sixteen novels, translated into eight European languages, and selling into the millions. Tod's first adventures, as lived in the pages of *The Tattoed Man*, are still for sale in the newest editions from the original publisher. His appeal, according to the sales statements, is still formidable, for despite his age—nearing sixty—this character is still able to arouse the blood of young readers as the ghost of Douglas Fairbanks would like to do after his "heyday," many years ago in another literary form.

Projected Image

Tod Moran, like many creations of highly imaginative people, is a projected image of his creator. Howard Pease, now a lively seventy-three years of age, still lives and works in Central California, near the place of genesis of his novels, and the home of Tod Moran. Even today, this children's author still reflects the masculine, idealistic, forward-looking hero he created so many years ago. Tod

Reprinted from *Elementary English* 46, no. 4 (April 1969): 488–91.

19

Moran springs to life when Howard Pease speaks. The artistic creation and the creator are inseparably wedded in the personality of Howard Pease.

Tod Moran really lived! His roles are fictional, but his fiber was taken from the truth of the life of Howard Pease. Even his name is a combination of the familiar from the early childhood of his creator. Howard Pease describes how he chose this name for his hero in the following manner:

> . . . Sometimes I'm asked, where did I get the name Tod Moran? Well, it came from two families I knew. Tod Cosley of Stockton went through high school with me, and I used his name, Tod. Across the street was the Moran family and the daughter played with my little sister. So I think we took the Moran family name and Tod's name and I had my Tod Moran.[1]

Similarly, Tod Moran's adventures are taken from the life of his creator. Howard Pease, for example, like Tod Moran, grew up in Stockton, California, and watched the barges and ships slip quietly down the San Joaquin River, then brace to meet the first deep swell of the great Pacific Ocean. He, like Tod, tramped through fields and along dusty roads in France, lived for three months in Tahiti, and during a number of ocean voyages, watched the mighty oceans roll under the fierce onslaught of the storm, saw islands swimming on the horizon, and relished the bitter-sweet growth to maturity.

From Personal Diary

Shipping out on an old tramp steamer while still a youth in college, Howard Pease sweated in the stifling engine rooms as oil wiper, bathed in sticky salt water, and, with limbs often numbed in utter weariness, kept a day-by-day journal record of one of his trips through the Panama Canal on the S.S. "K. I. Luckenbach." Leafing through it, one is impressed by the immense similarity between Pease's actual adventures and experiences recorded therein, and those experienced by Tod Moran in such books as *The Jinx Ship*, *The Tattoed Man*, *Wind in the Rigging*, and *Ship Without A Crew*. A few excerpts may illustrate. The following is taken from his entry dated Wednesday, June 30, 1926:

> . . . Today the sun shone for first time since we left S.F. This p.m. the little Chilean and I began chipping or washing the white paint of engine room sky-light. Placed planks, two by two, across beams and took 2 buckets of water each—one with powdered soap and other clear fresh water. Slow work washing around white-painted rivets which must be kept spotless. At first I was afraid I couldn't do it so far—60 feet above floor plates, but by 4 o'clock I was nonchalantly washing and humming far above the heat and hum of engines.

And again, on Wednesday, July 7, 1926, we find the following account:

> . . . Worked in corner of engine room this a.m. Hot, dead, stale air . . . I drank too much of the ice water, came up to the fountain in the starboard passage-way. As a result, by noon I was weak, unable to lift my arms. A cold sweat and chills swept thru my body. My dungarees and singlet wringing wet. I took a sticky salt water shower, changed and feel better now . . .

Both of the foregoing, of course, may be found as incidents befalling Tod Moran.

In the Black Gang's foc'sle where Howard Pease actually lived on a voyage, he encountered those swaggering, tough seamen who cursed loudly, drank mightily and fought fiercely through the pages of his books. They were men who could eat the weevil-infested food served for mess with grim but determined faces—for their survival depended on their stoicism. Remembering what it was like, Pease stated recently:

> . . . In the old days a life was not so important. Really! And the owners of ships didn't give a goddamn for the men on board . . . They gave them the worst food, the cheapest of everything, and the cheapest of wages. So from that . . . time when I sailed as a wiper I became a union man. And even though the union men go to extremes at times, I'm still a union man because most people do not now know what it was like to work in the days where there were no unions and you were at the mercy of any kind of boss.[2]

Yet, through it all, Howard Pease could look up into that often distant heaven and record its changing, softened mood as night slipped down:

> . . . Tonight the sun, a round disc of red, sank below the horizen (sic) to starboard and aft of our ship . . . One hour later twilight gave way to night. How close the stars seem—millions of them. The big dipper is directly overhead.[3]

Or, again, with imagination winging into the fathomless depths—where eyes no longer served any purpose, and great grey shapes swept blindly on—Howard Pease reached out and touched these formless shadows, encapsulating the vastness of the sea and the insignificance of man for millions of readers.

A Subconscious Hero

While undergoing psychoanalysis after the death of his wife, Howard Pease was told by a Dr. Kowalski that he was the hero of all of his books—that he was the "real" Tod Moran.[4] Somewhat shocked at the idea, yet fascinated, Pease went home and reread some of his books. Indeed, he found the parallels striking.

Those familiar with *The Tattoed Man*, for example, will remember that herein Tod Moran searches for and eventually finds his brother in France, dissipated by drugs. If we think of Howard Pease as Tod Moran, his comments concerning this book are most interesting. In a tape-recorded interview dated November 18, 1967, he stated:

> . . . I had used my brother in reverse form in *The Tattoed Man*, but I had done it unconsciously. I didn't realize it until I reread it twenty years after I wrote it that I'd used my own brother and made him exactly opposite to what he was, because I had been as a young fellow very jealous of my brother's success when I was very slow in getting going.

Even when the central character bears the name other than Tod Moran, we find the indelible stamp of Howard Pease. In *Shipwreck*, for example, the author symbolically portrays his own period of chaos and despair—a period during which he found it impossible to write. In *Heart of Danger*, when Rudy Behrens loses his arm in a Nazi concentration camp and is thus unable to play his beloved violin, it symbolically represented to Pease the deliberate and rather ruthless manner in which he turned away from his own violin playing, with which he had been intimately involved for over twenty years, in order to allow more time for his writing.

The examples which could be offered are numerous. From them, one conclusion appears to stand out rather clearly: Howard Pease assumes the role of the central character in the majority of his books. He wrote from first-hand experiences, and fused his personal feelings into these experiences. As a consequence, his works draw validity and vitality from the fact that his life and literary career are inextricably woven.

It is interesting to note that just as Tod Moran springs to life when Howard Pease speaks, quite the reverse is also true. Through Tod we encounter the author, Howard Pease, again and again, and learn to know his philosophy quite well. This is most apparent in the recurrent theme running throughout *The Tattoed Man*—Tod's search for reality and values upon which to base his life. The opening paragraph of this book, for example, emphasizes the fact that as a young boy, Tod, and thus Howard Pease, had been living in a "dream world" created in and existing only between the "rose-tinted covers . . . of a book." Pease writes:

> . . . Sea fog hazed like spindrift along the San Francisco water front. Tod Moran, coming from the echoing halls of the Ferry Building to the Embarcadero, paused uncertainly upon the damp pavement. On train and ferry, he had been leaping gloriously through pages of high romance with a gentleman adventurer and his "novel, brave men of the sea," and now, upon stepping out of the rose-tinted covers of his book, he was momentarily startled, as though he had strayed into another world.[5]

Similarly, this theme is re-echoed at the very end of *The Tattoed Man*, as Tod, like Howard Pease, his first voyage over, returns to port in San Francisco, "bringing home a cargo of knowledge safely imprisoned beneath the hatches of his memory. That would be with him always."[6]

On this last night on the old tramp steamer, *Araby,* Tod looks up at the stars, contemplating their vast distances and trying to gain a sense of perspective in the face of almost incomprehensible reality. It was a reality that Howard Pease insisted that his readers know and understand:

> . . . Night after night at the helm had brought him the realization of what they were, and the little place that his own world held with them. He had unloosed all those misconceptions which he had brought with him aboard ship. Here, before his very eyes, lay reality, a reality more magnificent, more glorious, than any childhood fairy tale.[7]

As he continues, one senses the zest for life, the openness to experiences of whatever kind that characterizes this children's author:

. . . Civilizations with their customs, their morals, and religions, were born, lived for their pitiful moment, and died even as those stars above him would flicker out some day. And what lay ahead? . . . Surely in that direction lay work for a god: to harness those half-known powers that might perhaps hold back the day when his own little universe would cool in frozen space. Or would it meet some wanderer of the heavens and in a fiery cataclysm hurl itself into dissolution? Ah, that would be living! That would be reality shorn of all illusion.[8]

Perhaps herein lies the secret of Tod Moran's universal appeal. He, like his creator, Howard Pease, dared to do those things that many sober, black-gowned, learned men only dream of doing, and thus, through the miracle of print, brought with him so many land-locked boys the world over.

NOTES

1. Tape-recorded interview with Howard Pease, by Shirley Jennings, Livermore, California, November 14, 1967.
2. Ibid.
3. Howard Pease's personal diary, 1926.
4. Tape-recorded interview with Howard Pease, 1967.
5. Howard Pease, *The Tattoed Man*, (New York: Doubleday, 1926) p. 1.
6. Ibid., p. 331.
7. Ibid., p. 326–27.
8. Ibid.

Lionni's Artichokes: An Interview

Rose Agree

A gifted artist, committed to the young and to life itself, Leo Lionni communicates with children in wonderfully inventive ways. Reactions to his books are as varied as the readers themselves. Each book, as with the leaves of an artichoke, is savored individually; the remarkable thing is the variety of flavors the books evoke in each child. What he suggests, or even omits, seems to intrigue the young and uninhibited. Astonishingly varied, original and delightful in concept, highly imaginative in execution, Lionni's books constitute rich veins for creative thinking.

My own preoccupation with Lionni stems from children's (and my own) reactions to *Little Blue and Little Yellow* as well as *Inch by Inch*. Unusual in depth as well as scope, the books evoke ideas, feelings, and questions that come pouring out—as readily with later titles as with the first two.

The Lionni Odyssey came to life for me in 1961 when I first heard him speak at the Freeport Public Library, started up again a few years later in Cranbrook at an ALA Pre-Conference on Art in Children's Books held in Detroit and came to rest for a few hours last summer in Fabio Coen's office at Pantheon. En route from Italy, where he spends several months each year in a house of his own design overlooking the Bay of Genoa, Lionni stopped long enough to discuss some of his current thinking about children and books in general, and his own books, in particular.

Have your ideas changed in any way since you spoke to us at Freeport?

I think not. I don't remember really, but I know that my ideas have not changed that much. What you wrote then, would certainly still be true today. Only after you've done five or six books can you begin to understand who you are with regard to your books. Unfortunately, it takes a long time, but when you paint, you put down your paintings and then, after a few months, look at them

Reprinted from *Wilson Library Bulletin* 44, no. 9 (May 1970) : 947–50.

all together. You can then say, "This is really me and this is not so much me." I am beginning to realize more and more who I am now. The more books I make the more I have come to realize which are the ones that really satisfy me.

I once made a little exercise—I figured out that my books really make an autobiography—*Inch by Inch* was my life in advertising. When I had to make a living, I had to survive and I really made a living telling people things that they didn't need to know. That's what the inchworm did and he managed, very cleverly, to survive.

Then came *Swimmy* . . . which was a period when I became very involved in politics and the role of the artist in politics. I didn't think it was enough to be an artist—I had to be a protest painter—I felt I had to act politically too . . . that the artist is a man like other men . . . with the same responsibilities. But when the time comes, the artist must realize that he has a specific function to perform—he is the eye—not the body.

Then came a period when, I must admit, I had had it. I became more introspective and began to feel that, after all, as an artist, you're really justified enough; maybe you should, for a while, concentrate on that. You perform a function in society even if it does not actually involve running about in the streets with a flag in your hand. That was the period of *Frederick*.

Alexander found me tremendously involved. . . . I intended to do a group of books with mice as characters around the same theme. I feel that the great problem now is really personal choice. This is the choice that the world is troubled with in this age of change. Are we going to be real minds or mechanical minds? I also realize that I, who come from a certain upbringing, will react in a certain way, even if I understand it is a lost cause. I will have to fight my own battle against the mechanical minds and this is what *Alexander* is about. It's true, too, that I try to get the things which worry me most, and make a book out of them. While it isn't really *that* conscious, it's pretty reasonable. It's no accident that exactly those books which pose basic problems of choice are my favorite books—*Inch by Inch, Swimmy, Frederick,* and *Alexander.* They are the ones which, I find, say the most to me.

And yet, Little Blue and Little Yellow *is still an enormous favorite, particularly with the younger children. Reactions are always original, often complex. Many children love* Little Blue *as a family story in which they find strong resemblances to their own families and their own situations.*

With Italian children, wherever you go, when you ask "Who is the mother and who is the father," you always get the same answer—it's fantastic. Overwhelmingly, the round one is the mother and the long one is the father. I always ask that of every group of children.

I am very much concerned about the relationship between the mother and the child. It has always been important that grownups like my books—I have always said that I do not write for children specifically but for the child in myself as well as in other adults. When the mother or teacher reads the book, it is they who will act out the story; they will do a much better communication job if they like what they are communicating. It is for this reason, that the children's rooms in the public libraries are such an important part of America. Some people foolishly assume these collections exist for children—of course they do—but how wonderful when it happens mother and child go together—here is where our readers are made and then it is for always. So the rooms are just as important for the grownup, too.

I'd like to change the subject and ask about your views as to the function of art and illustration in children's books.

I see illustrations almost as stage sets, in which the story takes place, and somehow, I think it comes off in my books a little—the book really can do little more than provide the most beautiful and convincing sets for the action which takes place in words—and which can be verified and relived when the child looks at the pictures alone.

Do you think that librarians and teachers should know more about the technical processes involved in the art?

Generally, and I say this in the context of the general feeling I have, which I'm sure is not very popular, I think art is considered much more important that it actually is. I think an artist should do the best he can—give his all. But then, whether people know the secrets, I don't know. Is it necessary to take the magic out of it? I like to do my own tricks; what I hope that children will, and do, realize more than the quality of the art is the amount of care it takes. This may sound mystical and I'm really not that way—but I have the feeling that if you are very thorough and put love and care into a thing, it will come out well somehow. I have tried to do this—I really do take great care.

Looking at your books last night, I was again taken with On My Beach There are Many Pebbles—*I've noticed how frequently pebbles form part of your background in other books as well—can you explain this preoccupation?*

I've collected pebbles all my life—there really *are* pebbles on my beach and I always look for them when I go to the beach. I once did an ad for a printer and I could do anything I wanted—so I set type in the shape of pebbles and I wrote a continuing line—a line where the tail becomes the head and goes on endlessly. I don't remember exactly but it was something like "God shapes the pebbles on the beach but only man has succeeded in making a billiard ball."

I have never thought of it, but perhaps the pebble is a sort of symbol to me. I'm always fascinated by man's position in nature . . . perhaps the pebble symbolizes something nature tries to do which only man can really do . . . to make the perfect round stone. There may be another reason—partially unconscious perhaps. If you look in nature for portable things there are really very few. What have you? Berries, pebbles, feathers, nuts—a friend of mine claims that man became man when first he picked up a pebble and decided to keep and carry it around with him. But I use all these portable things. We have endless objects but nature has only a few and I try to keep things as close as possible to a very elementary situation.

Do you consider your books elementary?

No . . . but the things I work with are.

Certainly your style and manner of illustration have been quite varied.

Well, I feel that content and style must flow together—the style flows out of the content and is never predetermined in advance. My constant preoccupation is with content rather than form. I do not have intellectual fun being flamboyant or recognizable. Every problem of content requires me to do certain things which cannot always be solved by red, white, and blue triangles. Subject is uppermost. From it results the style which must be apropos. Nothing irritates me more than to have to look back on work I no longer consider satisfactory. I feel that the idea of the story must dictate the style. Most of all I try to give children doubt . . . more than anything else, it is doubt which will keep us free.

BOOKS BY LEO LIONNI

Little Blue and Little Yellow. New York: Macdowell, Obolensky, **1959**.
Inch by Inch. New York: Macdowell, Obolensky, **1960**.
On My Beach There are Many Pebbles. New York: Macdowell, Obolensky, **1961**.
Swimmy. New York: Pantheon, **1963**.
Tico and the Golden Wings. New York: Pantheon, **1964**.
Frederick. New York: Pantheon, **1967**.
Alphabet Tree. New York: Pantheon, **1968**.
The Biggest House in the World. New York: Pantheon, **1968**.
Alexander and the Wind Up Mouse. New York: Pantheon, **1969**.

Articles

Agree, Rose. "We Meet Leo Lionni," *Top of the News,* October 1962.
Lionni, Leo. "My Books for Children," *Wilson Library Bulletin,* October 1964.

Films

Lionni, Leo. "Little Blue and Little Yellow," McGraw-Hill, 1961.
Lionni, Leo and Giulio Gianini. "Swimmy," Connecticut Films, 1969.

Prizes

Prizes awarded to Mr. Lionni include the *New York Times Best Illustrated Books of the Year Award* (3 times), the *Lewis Carroll Shelf Award* and the German award for best children's book (*Deutscher Jugendbuchpreis für das beste Bilderbuch*). He has been a runner-up three times for the Caldecott Medal, and his books have also been selected by the American Institute of Graphic Arts and the Children's Book Show for excellence in design and artistic merit.

Ferdinand the Bull: Psychoanalytical Remarks about a Modern Totem Animal

Martin Grotjahn

I. Ferdinand, the individual

The case history of Ferdinand the bull, so far as he may be considered to be an individual and not an animal or social event, can be told in a few words:

"Once upon a time in Spain there was a little bull and his name was Ferdinand." All the other bulls would run and jump and fight, "but not Ferdinand." He liked to sit quietly under his favorite cork tree and smell the flowers. His mother was worried about him but she understood him and let him sit there and be happy.

Ferdinand grew and grew, became big and strong, but still he liked to sit under the cork tree and to smell the flowers while the other bulls fought each other and nursed their ambitions to be picked for the bull fight. One day five men came to select the roughest bull to fight in the bull fight in Madrid. Ferdinand didn't care. Quietly he sat down—on a bumble bee which, in return, stung him. Ferdinand jumped up, puffing and snorting, behaving as if he were crazy. The five men were deeply impressed and took him away to the bull fight. The matador was scared stiff. When Ferdinand got in the middle of the ring he smelled the flowers in all the lovely ladies' hair and he sat down, quietly, and smelled. He would not fight and be fierce "no matter what they did." And so they had to take him home. "He is sitting there still under his favorite cork tree, smelling the flowers just quietly—he is very happy."

The illustrations show Ferdinand in his Spanish environment, a powerful towerlike castle in the back ground;—the small Ferdinand and the cork tree; Ferdinand and the bumble bee, his sit-down strike in the bull ring, his homecoming and his happy reunion with his cork tree.

There are two factors in the phenomenon Ferdinand which may interest the psychoanalyst. 1. What the artist expressed by the creation of a bull who refused to fight; 2. why this creation struck a response in the unconscious of so large a

Reprinted from *American Imago* 1, no. 3 (June 1940): 33–41.

portion of the public, hitting apparently upon deep emotional needs; the answer to these two questions may reveal a contribution to the psychoanalysis of the comic and the humor.

The story of Ferdinand is the story of a little innocent calf born in a paradisiac landscape of green pastures and beautiful trees, flowers and butterflies. Ferdinand gets older and stronger but he refuses to grow up. He remains an eternal child, knowing neither the obligations and conflicts, nor the challenge which is connected with the fate of being a bull. He does not regress; he simply remains locked in his happy innocence, nursing himself with the abundance of infantile pleasure. He gives up even his mother who acknowledged the perfect solution of his narcissism. The only friends, whom Ferdinand accepts, are the flowers around him and the cork tree behind him. There is a suspicious absence of any father figure.

The cork tree belongs to Ferdinand just as a shell belongs to a snail, they are inseparable. The tree appears in all pictures except that at the bull fight episode. Ferdinand's tree is unlike little Washington's cherry tree and also unlike Adam and Eve's tree with the sinful apples of knowledge. It is a cork tree and of a special kind, because the corks grow on it like fruits. They are drawn with special care, so plastic in detail that the onlooker gets the bodily feeling of touching them. This feeling is unique for cork feels like nothing else—if not, somebody may compare it with a thumb without a bone or with a limp penis. The feeling of uniqueness for the *substance* cork is connected with a comical quality of cork as an *idea*. Nobody can take it seriously, it is not heavy enough for that. It is wood and it is not wood; it falls down but it does not seem to have any weight; it floats on water which drowns everything else after a short or long time. In the illustrations of Ferdinand, the cork-stoppers, hundreds of them, hang down from the cork tree. Aimless but distinct, they look as if they were ready to be used as stoppers for bottles—suggesting in this way their symbolic meaning once more.

The physical qualities and the useful function of cork force the reader of Ferdinand to recognize its symbolic meaning as phallus. But it is a special phallus, a limp, a light, a useless and impotent one. This impotence is put into a comical contrast by the large and impressive number of corks and their union with an old, majestic, very protecting and erect, powerful tree which gives Ferdinand the background of serenity and power. It is as if Ferdinand possesses the silly (cork) but still impressive penis (tree) of his father.

Ferdinand, however, prefers not to use it. After having depreciated it by calling it a cork, he could not use it very well anyhow, but its possession makes it possible for him to resign in happy pacifism.

The tree is not only related to Ferdinand and his father. It is an old tree with large, deep, and dark holes, with its roots in mother earth, with its loving and shade-spending branches protecting little Ferdinand—it is, in other words, father and mother together protecting their only child in a very one-sided—and that means preambivalent way—a way in which only mothers love their sons. This tree is altruistic in its love for Ferdinand, giving but not taking, spending but not demanding, expecting no return which would be hard for Ferdinand to deliver. In a happy union with his family tree and with the landscape he lives in,

Ferdinand grows strong. He is busy smelling flowers, indulging in this without guilty feelings, without fear, which is essentially unknown to him even in the situation of the bull fight. With all the pleasure of the suckling he drinks the smell of the flowers, his nostrils get wide, his eyes closed or even worse, half-closed, like the eyes of a woman in ecstasy. He is not bothered by this appearance because he does not know the difference between men and women. He only knows that this tree is *his* tree and his parents are unchangeably on his side. If someone should doubt that it is just the union of father and mother which makes the cork tree so important and gives Ferdinand his inner harmony and security, he may turn back once more to the first picture in the book "Ferdinand" and look at the castle, so very high, so very erect, so powerful with its high roof and towers, so continued into the sky by a high pile of clouds and so deeply cut by a dark canyon. Here we have again the symbolic expression of father's powerful phallus with mother's gigantic womb, forming the background of this picture. From here the onlooker's eye is drawn into the foreground, into the center of the picture to the repetition of the same motif: little Ferdinand under the cork tree.

Ferdinand would not be a comical person but only an idyllic one if his happiness, innocence, and resignation would be achieved and kept without any conflict. The bumble bee stings him, of course, without malice, but in self defence because Ferdinand tried to sit on her. The sensible and tender-nerved Ferdinand reacts as if in danger of death (or mortal danger) with a terrific anxiety attack. To put it mildly, he overreacts.

The fear of insects, especially stinging insects, is wide spread among many persons. After getting stung, the affected place gets painfully swollen, red and hot. We know from dreams how terribly frightening insects may become and that the unconscious sees in the sting of a bee something like a poisonous dagger. Ferdinand jumps into the air like a girl who sees a mouse, and the artist does not forget to show that he even destroys flowers and a little branch off the cork tree. For a moment Ferdinand loses the symbols of his security.

The experts from Madrid take the shocked Ferdinand as a man in fighting mood and off he goes to the sacred ordeal of the bull fight. Mistaken for that which he wanted to avoid, he is to be killed in ritual forms. He gets all the fame and reputation of a primitive totem animal when he is thought to be ferocious and wild, dangerous and heroic, ready to fight and die like a guilty Oedipus.

"But not Ferdinand." He refuses to be made the dying king Oedipus, ready to die for his dreadful desires and deeds. The smell of the flowers in the ladies' hair is enough for him. He is not out for forceful defloration. He quiets down and does not confess intentions which he never had. He refuses to die and is taken home in disgrace. No one can be allowed to kill the totem who apparently refuses to be one. Back home, "he is happy" again.

II. Ferdinand as a totem animal

The book "Ferdinand" may or may not have been written for children but its interest is surely not limited to them. As a matter of fact it is one of these books which the *adult* accepts because it is not directed to him but to children. Children like Ferdinand as an animal and as a bull but not as Ferdinand. They like it best just in all these situations in which Ferdinand is not behaving like Ferdinand but

in which Ferdinand behaves like El Toro Ferocio. Ferdinand may be bought for
50¢ as a toy. In utter neglect of his true character, children play with him in the
way in which Ferdinand does not behave and perform. They let him fight with
everything. Because Ferdinand is made of iron and rubber he can stand it and
belongs to the few indestructible children's toys.

Adults like to read this book to children telling them in this way that Ferdinand enjoys everlasting love, peace and happiness so long as he behaves like a
nice little calf who does not grow up. In this case the book is used as a clear-cut
castration threat, like most famous books for children (*Struwwelpeter, Alice in
Wonderland*).

Ferdinand found his way into the unconscious of the masses, the book became
a perennial best-seller, he volunteered successfully as a movie star. He enriched
the English language with a new word with the meaning "conscientious objector"
and fell short of being a national hero. He is not heroic in the common sense of
the word because he is not the superman but a victim, he is not great but small,
he has not the features of the sublime but of the tragi-comic and of the humorous.
He cannot be called a hero nor can he be called a totem animal; in the usual sense
of the word he is not a sacred symbol of the father and he has not the sacred
fate and the ceremonial death of a totem animal but he had some of these features
in disguised form, maybe in a form which is typical for our present time. Ferdinand is not only the son who successfully avoids the fate of Oedipus; he is also
the depreciated father about whom the son laughs before he identifies himself
with him. After all, little Ferdinand is not as harmless as he succeeds in making
us believe. Helene Deutsch pointed out similar features in the figure of Don
Quixote, and Jaeckels is of the opinion that depreciation of the father and giving
him the features of a son is the main motive in the creation of every comedy.

The heroic and beautiful beast of the bull fight is a totem animal symbolizing
masculine power, fighting spirit, and preparedness even to die. These features
of the father totem are destroyed by Ferdinand who simply smiles at everything
that father might have done in a similar situation. After depreciation of the
powerful father and after laughing at him and his defeat, we can like and love
him again. After the death of the totem animal we may incorporate him, identify
ourselves with him and we are then ready to accept him as some form of an ideal.
In the case of Ferdinand, it is the ideal of the sociable citizen. "You must be like
Ferdinand in order to live in these days of bull fights."

Ferdinand is not a pitiful figure. Our super ego would not permit us to laugh
if he was. According to Freud, laughter is aroused where energy is saved. In the
form of wit, aggression is freed; in a form of the comic, thought; in a form of
humor, emotion. We save the emotion of pity because Ferdinand is not unhappy.
We laugh it off with tears in our eyes, so typical of true humor. After all,
Ferdinand is the victor-like Charlie Chaplin, who also wins out through his
innocence and naivete. He simply refuses to accept defeat by reality. Ferdinand
and Chaplin, they do not believe in castration, always asking in moments of
danger, "So what?" with disarming results. This is an overcoming of reality by
the denial of its existence.

This denial must be made possible by certain reality conditions, otherwise the
reader of the book or the spectator at the movie could not follow. The denial must
be accepted as credible, it must be described convincingly. The special condition

which enables Ferdinand to live as he lives and the reader to identify himself with him, is the inner security and harmony which he gains from the knowledge of possessing father and mother.

The collective unconscious accepts Ferdinand not only because of this but even more because of the unconscious recognition of a little Ferdinand in every one of us. We have all considered for a period of time, more or less seriously, with more or less successful and lasting results, avoiding the curse of being an Oedipus. During the psychoanalytic treatment a similar feeling may often be observed. When the patient is freed from his most disturbing symptoms he often is puzzled: freed to do what? On the couch with the psychoanalyst behind him, he feels like Ferdinand backed by the cork tree, quite satisfied and most certainly not going to move.

Ferdinand is by no means altogether castrated even though he does not enjoy manifest genital activity. He enjoys the sense of smelling with all the signs of real excitement. The childish paradise of Ferdinand is beautified by childish pleasures. Freud knew the importance of the suppression of the sense of smell in humans and he even states that man's turning away from the earth and his repression of the smell pleasures are "largely responsible for his predisposition for nervous diseases." Ferdinand does not make this repression, he enjoys smell and he does not even need to fight for it—partially because he does not take away anything from anybody by smelling and partly because his understanding mother does not mind it.

III. *Ferdinand and the psychoanalysis of the comic and the humor*

Sigmund Freud recognized humor as a regressive phenomenon: as a triumph of the narcissism, a denial of reality, a victory of the pleasure principles. In humoristic attitude, the super ego acts toward the ego like an adult toward a child. The super ego speaks a kind word of comfort to the desperately depressed and bewildered ego. The contrast to such benevolent attitude is the "Spartan attitude" (Franz Alexander) with which the sadistic ego demands sternly the fulfillment of unpleasant duties. Because of this relation between ego and super ego the humoristic attitude is possible within one and the same person, no listening third is needed (Kris). In the case of Ferdinand, the super ego demands are satisfied without much conflict; the kindliness of the super ego is partially pictured in the tolerating mother who does not mind Ferdinand's strange behaviour and his smell perversion, and partially in the matador who does not kill Ferdinand when he refuses to fight back.

From the economic point of view the humoristic phenomenon is a saving of energy, a saving of emotion—again following Freud. Wit has a close relation to sadism, as Dooley pointed out, and humor has a close relation to masochism. Humor may be found where the Oedipus complex is going down under the weight of disappointment, fear, and guilt. The typical Oedipus complex, the tragic guilt about the Oedipus desires, are denied and displaced by Ferdinand; and this may give some more information about how the ego manages to be treated in such an unusually kind way by the super ego, as Freud suggested. The super ego is so kind because it is put aside by the desperate and aggressive ego. The ego relapses into primary narcissism. In the case of Ferdinand, it regresses into narcissistic resignation. Ferdinand behaves as if the world were not real but, as he wishes it to be: peaceful. In this way, as Bergler describes it, the ego assumes the child's behaviour of inner freedom about logic, thought, and emotion: a repetition of life before logic and before the Oedipus complex, a life in happiness and in pleasurable mastery of word and thought. The opposite of laughing is not weeping. In the instance of humor, the laughter occurs with tears. As a matter of fact we seldom laugh about Ferdinand. Usually, we only smile, using in this way a sublimated form of laughter. The contrast of laughter is the shock. In psychoanalytic literature it is never pointed out that the harmless shock is the only form of comic about which the child in pre-oedipal age is able to laugh. Children are comical only from the viewpoint of the adults, they have very little sense for humor or wit. The pleasure in this phenomenon is originated later; the small child laughs only if it is shocked by the kidding adult. The child is all set to react with fear or even with panic, then suddeny realizes that there is no true reason to be afraid and finally discharges the activated energy in the form of laughter. The same procedure is repeated in the grown-up who listens to a witticism. At the beginning aggression is stimulated, the tension is increased; this aggression is felt as a shock or threat to the super ego. Then the primary process, a process of disguise similar to that of dream work is started. After the disguise the aggression, now dressed in the form of the witticism, becomes acceptable and is presented as a surprise to the conscious, the super ego may relax and may assume a kind attitude because it faces a harmless joke and is now able to discharge the energy no longer needed for a suppression in the form of laughter. The form of this disguise is of outstanding importance for the judgment which we pass upon the quality of the joke. We never judge the tendency of the witticism; we always judge the form of it. If the disguise is incomplete, then and only then the joke is called a bad one and the shock does not change into laughter; instead of that disgust or shame occurs.

The disguise of what really is meant in the story of Ferdinand seems to be successful. In the disguise of the little Ferdinand, a totem animal and a father figure is depreciated, humiliated, is killed and revived in a form which is now acceptable even for a very strict Super Ego. This acceptance is not based upon special kindness of the Super Ego but is based on a desperate effort by the ego by means of regression, denial, negative hallucinations, and masochistic resignation. The aggression stimulated by all associations contained in the idea of being a bull is suppressed and the emotional pity for the castrated father is saved by the happiness of Ferdinand who succeeds in gaining a happy reunion between father and son, not even losing the mother's love. Smilingly we enjoy the mastery of the infantile past by infantile means. Then again after the reassurance of such an experience it is easier for us to subdue ourselves under the government of logic, rational behaviour, reality principle, and the super ego.

BIBLIOGRAPHY

1. Alexander, Franz. "Strafbeduerfnis und Todestrieb." *Int. Zschrft. f. Psa.* 15 (1929): 237.

2. Bornstein, J. "The Fairy Tale of the Sleeping Beauty." *Imago* 19, no. 4.

3. Brill, A. A. "The Sense of Smell in the Neurosis and Psychoses." *Psa. Quart.* 1.

4. Bergler, Edmund. "A Clinical Contribution to the Psychogenesis of Humor." *Psa. Rev.* 24, (Jan. 1937): 34.

5. Deutsch, Helene. "Don Quixote and Quixotism." *Imago* 20, no. 4: 444–49.

6. Dooley, Lucilie. "A Note on Humor." *Psa. Rev.* 21, no. 1, (Jan. 1934): 49.

7. Duff, Grant. "Snow White: A Psychoanalytic Interpretation." *Imago* 20, no. 1: 95–103.

8. Freud, Sigm. "Der Humor. Ges. Schriften. *Int. Psa. Verlag.* 11: 402.

9. Groddeck, Georg. "Der Symbolisierungszwang." *Imago* 8, (1922): 67.

10. Jones, K. "Zur Symbolik der Baeume." *Int. Zschrft. f. Psa.* 9: 79.

11. Jekels, Ludwig. "Zur Psychologie Der Komoedie." *Imago* 12, (1926): 328–35.

12. Kris, Ernst. "Ego Development and the Comic." *Int. J. of Psa.* 19, (1938): 1.

13. Kris, Ernst. "Das Lachen als mimischer Vorgang. Beitraege zur Psychoanalyse det Mimik." *Int. Zschrft. f. Psa. und Imago* 24 (1939).

14. Leaf, Munro. *The Story of Ferdinand.* Illus. R. Lawson. New York: The Viking Press, 1938.

15. Reik, Theodor. "Lust und Leid im Witz." *Sechs Psychoanalytische Studien.* Wien: *Int. Psychoanalytischer Verl*, 1929.

16. Reik, Theodor. "Die Zweifache Ueberraschung." *Die Psychoanal. Bewegung.* I. Jahrgang, 1929.

17. Sachs, Hanns. "Zur Psychology des Filmes." *Die psychoanal. Bewegung* 1 (1929).

18. Servadio. Emilio. "Psicoanalisi dei Tre Procellini" *Circolo* 4, no. 4, (1934).

19. Sterba, Richard. "Bemerkungen ueber drei Filmdarsteller." *Almanach der Psychoanalyse.* Int. P. A. Verlag.

Jack and the Beanstalk

William H. Desmonde

The following psychoanalytic interpretation of the English folk-tale is suggested by the fact that the terms "beans" and "stalk" are common symbols for the testicles and penis (2).

The story relates that Jack and his mother lived together in a small country cottage. Lazy, irresponsible, and pleasure-seeking, the boy was incapable of earning his living, since "his mother had almost never corrected him as he grew up." Jack's mother supported herself and her child by selling her property, until eventually all that remained between them and starvation was their last asset, the cow. However, instead of getting a fair price, Jack traded the cow for some magic beans. Upon his return, Jack's mother burst into tears at his folly, and in exasperation threw the beans out of the window.

Jack awakened the next morning to find a huge beanstalk growing up into the clouds. Climbing to the top, he stepped off into a strange country, where he met a "queer little old lady" with a wand, who told him that his father was imprisoned in a nearby castle by a cannibalistic ogre. Jack stole the giant's treasures, and was finally pursued down the beanstalk by the ogre. Taking a hatchet, he chopped at the root of the beanstalk. "No sooner had he done so, than of a sudden, the whole beanstalk shrivelled up and the giant burst like a monstrous bubble" (5).

We may interpret Jack psychoanalytically as an oral dependent. Incapable of competing successfully in the market, he returned home, the tale tells, feeling depressed and inferior, and went to bed without any supper. We may regard the remainder of the story as an incestuous masturbation fantasy or dream, of a regressive nature.

The miraculous stalk growing from the beans is the erect phallus, and the little old lady with the fairy wand is the phallic mother-image. The imprisoned father indicates Jack's Oedipal hostility, while the cannibalistic ogre is the same father

Reprinted from *American Imago* 8, no. 3 (September 1951): 287–88.

in a threatening aspect. Treasures are incestuous representations (3). Pursued by the menacing ogre for his thefts, Jack castrates himself: the beanstalk shrivels at the first touch of the hatchet, and the threatening father-image disappears.

It is instructive to note the parallel between "Jack and the Beanstalk" and the story of Aladdin and his wonderful lamp, which is also a masturbation fantasy, as Jung recognized (4). Aladdin is, like Jack, a scapegrace and good-for-nothing, who is supported by his mother. He invokes a *genii* by rubbing the magic lamp, who grants him all of his wishes, i.e., makes him omnipotent. There was only one of Aladdin's wishes which the *genii* refused—with great anger—to bring the egg of a giant female bird named the Rukh (1).

We will remember that, in classical antiquity, the word "genii" meant the ghost of the deified paternal ancestor. World-egg cosmogonies are frequent in primitive cultures, and result from a projection of the mother-image into the cosmos.

Both the *Aladdin* and the *Jack and the Beanstalk* stories contain the incest motive, it is apparent. The two tales may be connected by cultural diffusion, or may merely have sprung independently from similar psychic tendencies.

REFERENCES

1. Burton, Richard F. *The Arabian Nights*. New York: Blue Ribbon Books, 1932.
2. Ellis, Havelock. *Studies in the Psychology of Sex*, Vol. II, Part I. New York: Random House, 1936. p. 5.
3. Jung, C. G. *Psychology of the Unconscious*. New York: Dodd, Mead, 1942, p. 409.
4. Jung, op. cit., p. 187.
5. Miller, Olive Beaupre. *"Jack and the Beanstalk."* In *My Bookhouse*, Vol. II. Chicago. The Bookhouse for Children Publishers, 1920, pp. 371–85.

Old and New Sexual Messages in Fairy Tales

Diane Wolkstein

When I ask children at a storytelling session which story they would like to hear, the responses are often: "Hansel and Gretel," Cinderella," "Sleeping Beauty," "Five Chinese Brothers," "Jack and the Beanstalk," and "The Twelve Dancing Princesses." For five years now children have been writing to me at the radio station, asking for much the same stories.

What is the appeal of these stories to children? Excellent books and essays have been written on the fairy tale. *Once Upon a Time: On the Nature of Fairy Tales* by Max Lüthi, *A Psychiatric Study of Fairy Tales* by Julius Heuscher, and "On Fairy Tales" by J. R. R. Tolkien, to name a few. Lüthi discusses how the fairy tale helps man cope with all elements of his existence; how the fairy tale form simplifies and abstracts life. Heuscher interprets certain fairy tales as relating to specific sexual and spiritual stages in a child's development. Tolkien emphasizes the realm of the faerie, the movement from the material world into the magic, spiritual, and religious kingdoms.

The fairy tales are surely filled with all these worlds. They mirror life more fully than any other fare permitted and created by the adult for the child. As such, they are very potent.

Take "Hansel and Gretel" for instance. How much about life the story shares with the child! What a father and mother may talk about at night alone; how a mother may secretly feel about a child; how a father will choose between children and spouse. It also treats of whom children can count on for help: how to differentiate between those who intend you harm (the mother, the witch) and those who do you harm without such intentions (the birds who eat the bread-crumbs, the father). It even tells how to survive in the open wilderness as well as in the confines of a jail.

If we open ourselves to the fairy tales, we will find that they are so subtle; that with every hearing another intricacy of life's relationships will be revealed. And the more we, as adults, can see in the stories, the greater will be our understanding and appreciation of why children ask for these stories.

Reprinted from *Wilson Library Bulletin* 46, no. 2 (October 1971): 163–66.

Cinderella's Sensual Reward

I began to see some of the strength of Cinderella when I recently read a Zuñi Indian myth called "The Poor Turkey Girl," which is a variant of the familiar story. In this version, the turkeys act as the fairy godmother, arraying the poor girl in splendid robes and jewels. But when the girl fails to return to them by dawn, they leave her and she loses everything. It was then I realized the success of the girl, Cinderella. Here was a girl, who was being transformed from an unappealing, passive child to a sparkling and alluring woman, and who was yet capable and strong enough to leave her state of excitement and grandeur to return to her old self, when it was necessary. She was brought to the very peak of enjoyment and yet was able to stop and wait until the moment was ripe to enter into her new life and state.

In the fairy tale, the necessity of self-control and obedience to man and nature's laws is often taught. But not without reward, and a joyful, *sensual* reward —for the end is the perfect fit. In Cinderella, the shoe is right for the foot; the woman is right for the man; and all the joys that go with that are implicit.

What are those joys? Mothers and fathers today rarely broach that question of joy—sensual, sexual enjoyment. Parents and educators will spend any amount of time to increase a child's cognitive knowledge, or even his artistic skills, and a good proportion of parents concern themselves with a child's religious and moral growth. But what about a child's understanding of sexuality? His own sexuality? And yet few of us would deny the importance of accepting one's sexuality as a requisite to enjoying life. And we all wish our children to grow and live in joy.

The old tales, folk and fairy, as they mirrored all of life did not exclude sex. In all six stories cited above, the listener is given, along with life's other secrets, information concerning both female and male sexuality. But not the information in terms of the "plumbing" diagrams offered to children by sex education classes in school. A mother of a very sensitive, sophisticated, 13-year-old boy recently found out that her son had approached one of their older friends and had asked him about sexual intercourse. What the son wanted to know was not the technical answers but, "How *great* is it?

Most old fairy tales do not deal with the actual moment of intercourse. Those that do tend to treat it simplistically as the beautiful glorious marriage ceremony with the promise of its perpetuation throughout the lives of the couple. No wonder the boy wanted to know "how great is it" *really?* for the subtleties are not explored. What is portrayed by some of the old fairy tales is the atmosphere and feelings of the female and male prior *to* and *after* the state of consummation.

In "Sleeping Beauty" and "The Twelve Dancing Princesses," for instance, both heroines fall into trances before they attain womanhood. The trance may permit the adolescent to play through and prepare (as dreams allow us) for the sexual event itself. And yet at a certain time, the period of insulation and preparation must end. The one hundred years are over, and the heroine must meet the hero, and so Sleeping Beauty does. The first words she says upon being awoken are: "Is it you, dear prince? You have been long in coming!" (She is ready and lets him know.)

The youngest princess in one version of "The Twelve Dancing Princesses" plays a more decisive part when she ends the nocturnal fantasies of her sisters and their partners by insisting that Michel maintain his daytime identity of gardener's boy. By accepting the man, in his day and nighttime identities, she is then able to turn the nocturnal dreams and reveries into reality and soon becomes Michel's bride. Time and nature help Sleeping Beauty into womanhood. But the youngest princess takes the leap by herself because of her own realization of her love.

In Perrault's original version, Cinderella is also involved in problems related to her own sexual productivity. It is not that she does not know how to produce but rather that she (and the prince) hide their state of marriage as well as their sexual creations (their children) for fear of the cannibal nature of the prince's mother. In fact, when Cinderella at last is left with her two children at the palace of the prince's mother, the Ogress Queen, the queen attempts to kill and eat the three of them. The queen is foiled in the end by the fortuitous arrival of the prince and perishes in her own pot of boiling serpents and vipers.

This earlier version of Perrault's is rarely told now. Instead, the story ends with Cinderella's marriage, or Cinderella, after her marriage, inviting her stepmother and stepsisters to live at court with her. Does the modern child prefer a more independent, self-willed Cinderella than the one who let her children be stolen from her and survived only by the fortuitous arrival of the Prince? It is an interesting example of a change in a fairy tale. One wonders if other of the old fairy tales tending towards extreme sexist roles will be similarly adapted to reflect the changing concepts of sexism in contemporary society.

The Ogress Queen's nature of eating children is similar to that of the witch in "Hansel and Gretel." In the old fairy tales, witches and ogres always represent symbols of those who would rob life from others. Whether their evil natures are the result of unsatisfactory love relations, unsatisfied motherhood cravings (which take the metaphoric form of eating children in order to fill the stomach with child), or other disorders, if Cinderella and her children and Hansel and Gretel do not acknowledge these forces as their enemies (even if they are projections of their own destructive instincts) they will perish. When they do confront these monsters, they survive.

Are There Still Witches?

When I have told a story dealing with a witch, I am often asked afterward by the children, "Are there still witches?" And I answer something like, "Yes. Most of the people around you are kind and loving, but you may meet one person who will be very mean. Fortunately there are enough people who love you that you do not need to worry." As the stories offer children hope and joy, they also inform them of dangers; and if we would care for their joys, we would also prepare them to protect themselves and their pleasures and creations.

Sexual pleasure and creation is often as much coveted as gold. Similarly, the quest for the riches of manhood. In "Jack and the Beanstalk" we see that only one try up the beanstalk is not enough for Jack to maintain a relationship for his mother and himself; the money supply is soon exhausted. The second effort brings Jack a viable relationship with his mother (the hen supplies a continuous income) but Jack wants more. It is the third try that brings him the harp, and the greater world, for he shows it around and soon marries a princess.

The five Chinese brothers never attain manhood in a sexual way, for they return in the end to their mother. The story, in fact, is a modern folk tale authored by Claire Huchet Bishop in 1938. With the exploit of each brother, we learn of the male child's latent physical super-powers which enable the brothers to escape death. But there is no transformation to a fuller life as in the old fairy and folk tales. It has its fun and purpose as does much of the modern literature written by adults specifically for children, but until recently adults writing for children have preferred to edit out all notions of sexual responsibility, realization, and consummation—as if they were nonexistent.

Sensuality and Sendak

Maurice Sendak has brought the sexual experience back into young children's stories with his recent book, *In the Night Kitchen*. But he gives out different sexual messages than the ones in the past fairy tales. In his book, there is no female/male consummation, but there is a rich description of the state of consummation, and there is great pleasure and enjoyment for the individual, as opposed to the couple. The hero's (Mickey's) curiosity and impetuosity land him temporarily in a very hot oven, but he escapes and by his own imagination transforms himself and the material universe around him. He thus achieves what is needed and is rewarded by a joyful, sensual plunge into a full bottle of milk. The sequel to Mickey's sensual experience is that he brings forth the new dawn and the morning cake. He then returns to our world and his own bed.

Perhaps Sendak's exploration of an individual's sensual/sexual pleasures with the message being: "Child, you have great imagination and power and it's fun to use and enjoy your mind *and body*" is based on the fact that Sendak is writing for the young child who is more involved in himself than in the near possibilities of manhood, whereas the old folk and fairy tales were a part of an oral tradition that was originally intended for the entertainment of adults.

Or perhaps Sendak's message belongs to a new sexuality? One that wants and dares to explore not only what precedes and follows, but the act itself. Sexual roles are presently undergoing radical change. Are our views of sexuality also changing? Are the sexual messages in the old fairy tales relevant and sufficient?

Human sexuality is so complex and infinite that we need all the clues we can get. The old folk and fairy tales explore certain aspects and leave others untouched. They tend to stress patience, ripeness, persistence, and courage, all of which are pertinent to the enjoyment of the sexual experience. But there are other aspects of sexuality to investigate, and hopefully there will, with time, be new protagonists to walk the paths.

I look forward to new tales for children, not dealing simply with Sex—capital S—but lifting the mirror to all of life and showing sexuality/sensuality as an implicit part, thus offering all of us new approaches to life's possibilities.

Responding to Psychological Criticism

1. Author's Intent/Reader's Perception

CRITICAL COMMENT

Grotjahn suggested that children enjoy the hero of *The Story of Ferdinand* in a way not intended by the author. Children want Ferdinand to be a brave ferocious bull—the complete reversal of the actual Ferdinand who was shy and didn't want to fight.

WAYS OF RESPONDING

A. A classroom teacher's attempt to encourage group discussion of Lionni's *Swimmy* is described in an article by Frazier and Schatz.[7] Read the article and discuss the appropriateness of trying to have primary grade children state in their own terms the theme of the story. Is it a goal that is likely to be met by most of the children without undue probing and confusion? Why or why not?

B. Like *The Story of Ferdinand,* many books encouraged for children's perusal today are written on different levels of meaning. Some examples of these books are *The Cat Who Wished to Be a Man* by Alexander, *In Search of a Sandhill Crane* by Robertson and *The Mousewife* by Godden. Make a judgment about whether most children will go beyond more than the simplest story line. Do they understand the author's intent or, as Grotjahn suggested with Ferdinand, do they enjoy the hero—and other elements of the story—as *they* perceive them?

2. Symbols and Their Interpretations

CRITICAL COMMENT

Symbolic meanings of certain elements of stories were pointed out by Grotjahn in his analysis of *The Story of Ferdinand* and Desmonde in his discussion of "Jack and the Beanstalk." The use of the symbols aided the two psychologist-critics in psychoanalytically interpreting the two stories. Most of the symbols were interpreted with sexual allusions.

WAYS OF RESPONDING

A. Analyze some picture story books for the symbols used in the content and illustrations. You may want to use such books as *Henry the Explorer* by Taylor, *Obadiah the Bold* by Turkle, and *The White Marble* by Zolotow. Does the increased awareness of these symbols heighten your adult understanding or enjoyment of the story? Discuss with your colleagues whether you think such an exercise would be of value for children.

---

7. Alexander Frazier and Esther E. Schatz, "Teaching a Picture Book as Literature," *Elementary English* 43 (January 1966): 45–49, 59.

B. Recall some of the objects repeatedly mentioned in folk tales. For example, the following items have been used to the point of becoming symbolic in meaning:

a magic mirror	a magic sleep
a glass coffin	a white bird
a poison apple	a rose
a pricked finger	a high tower

As you attach interpretations to these objects, does the significance of the story change for you? Are you able to develop fuller meanings from the story? If you have a basic undergraduate education in psychology, do you feel that your interpretation of these symbols is profound or amatuerish? Do you believe that you are better able to understand the characters with this knowledge? How would you judge the value of your symbolic interpretation of folk tales?

C. Is it possible for children to enjoy and even to learn from books that contain numerous adult symbolic allusions? Investigate the symbols found in several children's classics such as Swift's *Gulliver's Travels* and Melville's *Moby Dick* as well as more modern tales such as Tolkien's *The Hobbit*. Seek children's initial responses to these books after they have read or heard portions of them. Does the factor of enjoyment come through as a primary response?

3. The Hero-Author Resemblance

CRITICAL COMMENT

Book heroes sometimes are in-print reincarnations of their authors. Such is the case for Tod Moran, the fictional hero created by Howard Pease. Moran is the "All-American-type"—an imaginary character to be idolized; Pease wove his character from his own life and personality.

Another case of hero-author resemblance is described by Barker who asserted that Edward Lear's nonsense characters were prototypes of Lear's distorted body image and confusion over his self-identity. For example, Lear, a parrot, and a cat were torn apart and then put together incorrectly—Lear's head on the parrot, etc. Barker suggested that Lear used his nonsense writing as a way of working through tension, noting, "What was good for Lear was also good for the world."

WAYS OF RESPONDING

A. Study the influence that authors' lives have on their book heroes. Many of the Newbery Award acceptance speeches and biographical sketches contain information relevant to the characters created in the authors' books. The speeches are published each year in the August issue of the *Horn Book* and many of these articles have been compiled in book form.[8] Make a survey of

8. Bertha Mahoney Miller and Elinor Whitney Field eds., *Newbery Medal Books: 1922–1955* (Boston: The Horn Book, 1957) and Lee Kingman ed., *Newbery and Caldecott Medal Books: 1956–1965* (Boston: The Horn Book, 1965).

this information and compile a list of books in which the heroes reflect the lives of the authors.

B. Read biographical sketches of authors of children's books to collect anecdotes that seem likely to be of interest to children. For example, children might enjoy Robert Lawson's account of seeing a certain large rabbit cross his yard preceding every major step in the writing and publication of *Rabbit Hill,* including seeing it just before he received the announcement of winning the Newbery Award. Or they might find humor in the fact that *The Duchess Bakes a Cake* was based on a true incident. A friend of Virginia Kahl put a cup of baking powder rather than flour in the biscuits she was baking and this spurred the author's imaginative story. Make a 5 x 8 file card collection of these anecdotes so that they can be put in an accessible place for children's use in the classroom. Sources of biographical sketches include *Language Arts* (formerly *Elementary English*), *Horn Book,* and book jackets as well as numerous book publications.[9]

C. Discuss the *necessity* of a book hero being reflective of the life of the author. Is it valid, for example, for an author to develop a character in a year-round Maine setting when the author himself has only vacationed there in summers and has not experienced the length of a Maine winter or the sense of calm that prevails when the summerfolk have gone? Is it as incongruous, as author Julius Lester suggests, for a white author to write of the black experience as it is for an Arab to depict the Jewish life style?

D. Should children be encouraged to read about the lives of authors, even if the data include uncomplimentary facts? If so, does such knowledge influence children's enjoyment of the author's works? Some cases in point might be the gruff attitude of Robert Frost toward his children and the alleged Communist activities of Frank Baum, author of the Oz stories. Set up a mini-experiment in an elementary classroom to determine the extent of such influences.

E. Is it possible to discover whether there is any value in children learning about authors through nonprint media? Prepare a survey procedure to note whether children select more of an author's book (by choice, not assignment) after experiencing biographical media. Examples of biographical materials are the Weston Woods films of James Daugherty and Ezra Jack Keats; the University of Michigan AV Center's audio tapes of recorded interviews with children's authors such as Rebecca Caudill and Phyllis Whitney; filmstrip and recording packages, such as those produced by Miller-Brody productions of the Newbery Award winning authors; or the video-tapes of authors produced at Temple University.

F. If you are in an area where librarians and teachers have provided authors as children's speakers during Children's Book Week and National Library Week, note the influence of the authors on children's remembered readings. For example, high school students might be surveyed to note their favorite

9. Martha E. Ward and Dorothy A. Marquardt, *Authors of Books for Young People* (New York: The Scarecrow Press, 1964). Also First Supplement, 1967; Lee Bennett Hopkins, *Books Are by People* (New York: Citation Press), 1969 and *More Books by More People* (New York: Citation Press), 1974; Anne Commire, *Something about the Author,* Volumes 1–7 (Detroit: Gale Research, 1971–1975).

children's books. The booklists might then be checked by librarians and teachers to note whether the books of author-speakers from preceding years appear with any significant degree of frequency.

4. Morals and Themes

CRITICAL COMMENT

Moral issues are often reflected in children's books. Lionni told of his intentional use of value-laden issues in *Swimmy*, *Frederick*, and *Inch by Inch*. Some critics, as well as authors, strongly favor the use of moral themes in literature.

WAYS OF RESPONDING

A. Is it likely that two or more readers will agree on one moral or theme for a story? Listen to a story such as *Rain Makes Applesauce* by Sheer, *Peter Rabbit* by Potter, *One Monday Morning* by Schulevitz, *The Jazz Man* by Weik, or *A Pair of Red Clogs* by Matsuno. Have each person in the group of listeners write a brief statement of the story's moral. Compare the statements.

B. Compare the morals appended to the following fables when interpreted by different authors: "The Fox and the Ox" in *Aesop's Fables* by White and *The Fables of Aesop* by Jacobs; "The Wolf in Sheep's Clothing" in *Jack Kent's Fables of Aesop* by Kent and *The Fables of Aesop* by Jacobs; and "The Grasshopper and the Ant" in *Aesop's Fables* by White and *John J. Plenty and Fiddler Dan* by Ciardi. Find other examples of differing morals. What generalizations can you draw about the use of explicit morals with children's stories?

C. Some books seem to have more obvious moral themes than others. As cases in point, read: *The Alphabet Tree* by Lionni, *The Country Bunny and the Little Gold Shoes* by Heyward, *Manners Can Be Fun* by Leaf, and *The Little Engine That Could* by Piper. Would the explicit statement of morals as is the case in most of these books preclude children's ability to *discover* a moral? Discuss your adult response to these books with your colleagues.

5. Sexuality/Sensuality

CRITICAL COMMENT

Wolkstein wrote of the inclusion in fairy tales of traits of sexual behavior such as self-control, obedience to the laws of man and nature, patience, and persistence. She encouraged a new attitude toward sexuality/sensuality in literature—an attitude which would enable the child reader to feel the joy of his own body and to appreciate the aspects of sexuality/sensuality which have previously been unspoken and unwritten.

WAYS OF RESPONDING

A. What is the feeling in your community toward current children's writings that deal with sexuality? Survey a group of parents concerning their opinions of sexually controversial books such as *In the Night Kitchen* by Sendak, *Before You Were a Baby* by the Showers and *About the B'nai Bagels* by Konigsburg.

You might prepare your survey instrument in the form of an annotated list of books with a rating form to be completed by the parents, or you might give an oral summary of the books at a PTA meeting and record the spoken comments following your presentation.

B. Reread some familiar versions of the old fairy tales with a concern for their sexual messages. What sexual behavior traits do you find in such tales as Perrault's *Puss-in-Boots*, Grimm's *Rapunzel* and *Hansel and Gretel?* How obvious do you think these traits would be for children? Are they traits you consider to be appropriate and worthy of discussion by children?

C. Read some of the folk tales included in Minard's *Womenfolk and Fairy Tales.* Discuss the attitude concerning sexuality in these tales that were especially selected to portray the importance of the women as main forces in the stories.

D. Encourage a selected group of children to read some of the following books that contain explicit discussions of sexual/sensual acts and emotions: *The Long Secret* by Fitzhugh, *Mom, The Wolf Man and Me* by Klein, *Up a Road Slowly* by Hunt, *Then Again, Maybe I Won't* by Blume. Be sure that the children are all good readers, but choose those who have varying personality traits—shy, extrovert, sophisticated, naive, immature, mature, etc. Record their individual reactions to the books. From these data, draw some generalizations about children's reactions to books of this type.

6. Sexist Views of Fairy Tales

CRITICAL COMMENT

Perrault's original version of *Cinderella* was compared with a more modern adaptation in order for Wolkstein to point out the change that takes place in fairy tale retellings. The older version showed a weak-kneed heroine dependent upon her husband's protection, while the later version depicted an independent, self-directed Cinderella. Wolkstein queried whether the old tales will soon be altered to reflect today's changing views of sexism.

WAYS OF RESPONDING

A. Select an old tale such as "Snow-White and Rose Red" by the Brothers Grimm and rewrite it in terms of modern day sexual mores and liberal sexist views.

B. Compare original and later versions of the same fairy tale to note changes that might have been made in accordance with sexist views of the time in which they were retold. A good bibliographic source for locating various versions of fairy tales is Cook's *The Ordinary and the Fabulous.*[10] Cook's book also includes specific examples of versions of "Cinderella" such as those noted by Wolkstein.

---

10. Elizabeth Cook, *The Ordinary and the Fabulous* (Cambridge: Cambridge University Press, 1969).

FURTHER READING

Braun, Saul. "Sendak Raises the Shade on Childhood." *The New York Times Magazine* (June 7, 1970): 34–54 (not inclusive). An interview with Maurice Sendak reveals much about his childhood and adult values that appear in his illustrations.

Burns, Lee. "Red Riding Hood." *Children's Literature* 1 (1972): 30–36. Several versions of this tale are described from Perrault to Anne Sexton's 1971 poem. Sexual symbolism abounds.

Helson, Ravenna. "Through the Pages of Children's Books." *Psychology Today* 7, no. 6 (November 1973): 107–12. A study of Victorian, turn-of-the-century, and contemporary fantasies shows significant changes in relations between characters between the older and more recent writings.

Haugaard, Erik. *Portrait of a Poet: Hans Christian Andersen and His Fairytales.* Washington, D.C.: Library of Congress, 1973. After translating Andersen's works, Haugaard delivered these remarks concerning the effect of Andersen's life on his original fairy tales.

Marcus, Donald M. "The Cinderella Motif: Fairy Tale and Defense." *American Imago* 20, no. 1 (Spring 1963): 81–92. A psychiatrist relates the case history of a patient who had a Cinderella fantasy and longed for her dead mother to return in the form of her fairy godmother and grant all her wishes.

Mintz, Thomas. "The Meaning of the Rose in 'Beauty and the Beast.' " *The Psychoanalytic Review* 56, no. 4 (1969): 615–20. The folk tale is analyzed for its sexual message and the rose's symbolism is discussed thoroughly.

Peller, Lili. "Daydreams and Children's Favorite Books: Psychoanalytic Comments." *The Psychoanalytic Study of the Child* 14 (1959): 414–33. Several fantasies typical of childhood are discussed along with children's stories that relate to them. Books contemporary to the time of the article are noted, as well as classics. This is an example of analyzing book characters.

Petty, Thomas A. "The Tragedy of Humpty Dumpty." *The Psychoanalytic Study of the Child* 8 (1953): 404–12. Psychiatric case histories are used to contend that "Humpty Dumpty" symbolizes a major trauma in the life of a child: the birth of a sibling.

Róheim, Géza. "Tom, Tit, Tot." *The Psychoanalytic Review* 36, no. 4 (October 1949): 365–69. Rumpelstiltskin tales are described and certain story elements are characterized as sexual symbols.

Southall, Ivan. "Call It a Wheel." *Horn Book* 50, no. 5 (October 1974): 43–49. The noted Australian author of children's books writes a self-study of how his book, *Josh*, began.

Wolfenstein, Martha. " 'Jack and the Beanstalk': An American Version." In *Childhood in Contemporary Cultures,* edited by Margaret Mead and Martha Wolfenstein. Chicago: University of Chicago Press, 1955, pp. 243–45. In this comparison of the English and American Appalachian versions of "Jack and the Beanstalk," many symbols of masculine sexual prowess are noted.

REFERENCES

Alexander, Lloyd. *The Cat Who Wished to be a Man*. New York: E. P. Dutton, 1973.

Blume, Judy. *Then Again, Maybe I Won't*. Scarsdale, New York: The Bradbury Press, 1971.

Ciardi, John. *John J. Plenty and Fiddler Dan*. Illus. Madeleine Gekiere. Philadelphia: J. B. Lippincott, 1963.

Fitzhugh, Louise. *The Long Secret*. New York: Harper & Row,, 1965.

Godden, Rumer. *The Mousewife*. Illus. William Pène Du Bois. New York: The Viking Press, 1951.

Grimm, Jacob and Wilhelm. *Hansel and Gretel*. Illus. Arnold Lobel. New York: Delacorte Press, 1971.

————. *Rapunzel*. Illus. Felix Hoffman. New York: Harcourt, Brace, 1960.

————. *Snow White and Rose Red*. Trans. Wayne Andrews. Illus. Adrienne Adams. New York: Charles Scribner's Sons, 1964.

Heyward, Debose. *The Country Bunny and the Little Gold Shoes*. Illus. Marjorie Flack. Boston: Houghton Mifflin, 1939.

Hunt, Irene. *Up a Road Slowly*. New York: Follett Publishing, 1966.

Jacobs, Joseph, reteller. *The Fables of Aesop*. Illus. Kurt Wiese. New York: The Macmillan Company, 1950.

Kahl, Virginia. *The Duchess Bakes a Cake*. New York: Charles Scribner's Sons, 1955.

Kent, Jack. *Jack Kent's Fables of Aesop*. New York: Parents' Magazine Press, 1972.

Klein, Norma. *Mom, the Wolf Man and Me*. New York: Pantheon, 1972.

Konigsburg, E. L. *About the B'Nai Bagels*. New York: Atheneum, 1969.

Lawson, Robert. *Rabbit Hill*. New York: The Viking Press, 1944.

Leaf, Munro. *Manners Can Be Fun*. Rev. ed. Philadelphia: J. B. Lippincott, 1958.

————. *The Story of Ferdinand*. Illus. Robert Lawson. New York: The Viking Press, 1936.

Lionni, Leo. *The Alphabet Tree*. New York: Pantheon, 1968.

————. *Frederick*. New York: Pantheon, 1967.

————. *Inch by Inch*. New York: Ivan Obolensky, 1960.

————. *Swimmy*. New York: Pantheon, 1963.

Matsuno, Masako. *A Pair of Red Clogs*. Illus. Kazue Mizamura. Cleveland: World Publishing, 1960.

Melville, Herman. *Moby Dick*. Illus. Mead Schaeffer. New York: Dodd, Mead, 1942.

Minard, Rosemary, ed. *Womenfolk and Fairy Tales*. Illus. Suzanna Klein. Boston: Houghton Mifflin, 1975.

Perrault, Charles. *Puss-in-Boots*. Adaptor, Hans Fischer. Illus. Hans Fischer. New York: Harcourt Brace Jovanovich, 1959.

Piper, Watty, reteller. *The Little Engine That Could*. Illus. George and Doris Hauman. New York: Platt & Munk, 1961.

Potter, Beatrix. *The Tale of Peter Rabbit*. New York: Warne, 1903.

Robertson, Keith. *In Search of a Sandhill Crane.* Illus. Richard Cuffari. New York: The Viking Press, 1973.

Scheer, Julian. *Rain Makes Applesauce.* Illus. Marvin Bileck. New York: Holiday House, 1964.

Sendak, Maurice. *In the Night Kitchen.* New York: Harper & Row, 1970.

Showers, Paul and Kay. *Before You Were A Baby.* Illus. Ingrid Fetz. New York: Thomas Y. Crowell, 1968.

Shulevitz, Uri. *One Monday Morning.* New York: Charles Scribner's Sons, 1967.

Swift, Jonathan. *Gulliver's Travels.* Illus. Arthur Rackham. New York: E. P. Dutton, 1909.

Taylor, Mark. *Henry, the Explorer.* Illus. Graham Booth. New York: Atheneum, 1966.

Tolkien, J. R. R. *The Hobbit.* Boston: Houghton Mifflin, 1938.

Turkle, Brinton. *Obadiah the Bold.* New York: The Viking Press, 1965.

Weik, Mary. *The Jazz Man.* Illus. Ann Grifalconi. New York: Atheneum, 1966.

White, Anne Terry, reteller. *Aesop's Fables.* New York: Random House, 1964.

Zolotow, Charlotte. *The White Marble.* Illus. Lilian Obligado. New York: Abelard-Schuman, 1963.

chapter two

Sociological Criticism

Sociological criticism is concerned with the view of society that is expressed in literature. The critic tries to interpret literature in light of the social, economic, and political milieu of its time.

Sociological criticism draws heavily on the principles of Marxist criticism. The *dialectic method* is one example. In this technique, one point is juxtaposed with a counterpoint so that an argument develops and is built step by step with all opposing ideas exposed. The philosophical belief is that ultimately reality will be determined through this technique. Pragmatically, however, the point of view espoused by the critic can, and usually does, emerge.

Another central issue of Marxist criticism is *realism*. The sociological critic ostensibly tries to show reality by being objective in commentaries.

Several other principles of Marxist doctrine concerning literature became elements fundamental to sociological criticism: the use of literature to spread the party line; the depiction of the ideal character—a heroic model for the masses to follow; the ability of authors to dissociate personal philosophies from the philosophy about which they wrote—a technique that enabled the reader to accept the character, not the author, as the one who spoke the truths of life; the use of class distinctions based primarily on economic circumstances; a concern with temporalism to the extent that literature should be judged in terms of the time of its writing as well as in the time of its reading.

Pros and Cons of Sociological Criticism

Sociological criticism offers the reader an opportunity to deepen the understanding of the literary work by bringing to light the social, economic, and political implications of the work of art. This is the basic value of this type of criticism for it enables the reader to view the literary work in the context within which it was written.

Of central importance in sociological criticism is the seriousness given to literature wherein the artist could lose his life, his freedom, or his citizenship if he did not adhere to the party line in his writings.[1] This has been demonstrated conclusively in recent years.

A number of problems plagued sociological criticism. Few techniques were established for criticism. Coinciding with this problem was the seemingly total emphasis on the social environment to the ignorance of artistry. The critics Edmund Wilson and James Farrell were both concerned with the lack of attention given to aesthetic values in Marxist criticism, Wilson believed that the critic had to bring imagination and taste to the work of art as well as an understanding of its place in society.[2]

The use of literature for propaganda was a major issue of controversy. The literary form summarized the philosophy of the party from the perspective of different economic categories. Thus, the artist was in a position to bring about change by supporting the idea of the goodness and value of the party beliefs. Many arguments ensued over this issue. Upton Sinclair contended that all works of art were basically propagandistic,[3] whereas Newton Arvin believed that there was no compunction for literature to support the beliefs of any party.[4]

Sociological Criticism of Children's Literature

Sociological criticisms of children's literature reflect the political, social, and economic trends within the adult world. Causes and movements are written into children's books that find themselves in changing states of favor and disfavor due to the refocusing of issues with the times. Cases in point are several of the Newbery Award winning books, such as Fox's *Slave Dancer*, de Trevino's *I, Juan de Pareja*, and Armstrong's *Sounder* which have received much criticism because of their negative images and stereotypes of blacks. The readings offer an assortment of sociological criticisms that have appeared over a period of years.

Political Criticism

Historically, the criticism of children's books shows a flourish of socialist writings. In historical retrospect, it is often easier to see the blatant use of propaganda techniques and the deliberate use of fiction to indoctrinate children into the political views of a country.

The depiction of the ideal hero is discussed by Mayne in his criticism of the strong piece of Fascist propaganda developed as a sequel to *Pinocchio*. The classes in this book are Fascists and non-Fascists, or Italians vs. foreigners.

Winters' survey of children's books published in the 1930s in the Soviet Union gives examples of the propagandistic nature of those books. The themes are based on the socialist ideology that was being hailed in that country at the

---

1. George Steiner, *Language and Silence.* (New York: Atheneum, 1967), p. 322–23.
2. Walter Sutton, *Modern American Criticism* (Englewood Cliffs, New Jersey: Prentice-Hall, 1963), p. 77.
3. William Van O'Connor, *An Age of Criticism: 1900–1950* (Chicago: Henry Regnery, 1952, Gateway Edition, 1966), p. 111.
4. Sutton, *Modern American Criticism.* p. 79.

time. The books are highly moralistic, showing the idealized Lenin and depicting the virtuous gains of the masses in the socialist system. Reality is also very prominent; nonfiction books espouse the technological advances of the nation. Fairy tales are not the fare of the child of a revolution.

Krasilovsky's survey provides an interesting comparison to Winters' article. This survey of contemporary Chinese children's books suggests that these books use propaganda in the same manner as the Soviet children's books of the 30s. The ideal hero is again present, although this time often a heroine. Moralism abounds and the stories and poems tend to be highly political.

Political trends within the United States are noted in Moynihan's article. She offers ideological views that resulted from her analysis of several children's books written by United States' authors. The comparison of these books with Milne's British views depicted in *Winnie the Pooh* offers a rather startling mirror reflection of a national culture.

Social Criticism

The wave of social consciousness that grew out of the midcentury Civil Rights Movement and spread to all races, religions, ethnics, and sexes is reflected in children's books and their criticisms. The style of Marxist criticism is not as pointed, but certain elements of this style are retained.

The readings included in this section were not chosen as representative samplings of their particular causes because the intent of this book is to show examples of critical styles, not to promote sociological causes, no matter how just the causes might be. Thus, the articles do not offer middle-of-the-road positions that would be necessary if they were to be this book's standard bearers for racism, religious prejudice, and sexism.

Schwartz discusses elements of racism in *Mary Poppins* following an interview with the author. He uses the dialectic method of examining one point, then countering with another, to build his case. The author, P. L. Travers, adopts the attitude of dissociation; she refuses to be considered racist, claiming that her characters are simply an expression of her imagination, not extensions of a racist attitude. The point of temporalism is raised in that the book was a product of the 30s and therefore should be judged in terms of those times.

A strong criticism is made by Cohen of Speare's slanted use of selected particulars to give the essence of realism in *The Bronze Bow*. Cohen points out the author's fallacies in reporting historical trends and shows how the lack of adequate characterizations makes the novel propagandistic, historically disfavoring the Jew. An example of dissociation is suggested in that Cohen doubts that Speare was truly trying to be anti-Semitic in the novel although her characterizations make this the real case.

Propaganda is the charge leveled at numerous children's book authors in Fisher's criticism of the sexist nature of children's books. Like other critics, she doubts that authors, especially women, intentionally try to exploit women and girls in their novels, but that the characters exhibit this negative image and therefore present this reality to the reader.

Economic Criticism

Criticisms of books dealing with economic trends and technological advances are concerned with the effect of supposed progress on the value systems of the persons affected. The literary critics are not always supportive of the results of such movements. Economic values are one of the several types of values McClelland discusses as a result of an analysis of children's books from many nations. He suggests that children's books are very important in the development of children's values.

A view of the future is provided by Greenlaw who discusses the effect that technological advances have on science fiction. Her examples from children's books depict future classes of society and specific technological and environmental changes that make the setting seem very real. Greenlaw notes that the themes of science fiction focus on the questions of value that must accompany all technological change. Thus, rather than using temporalism as an aspect of judging a work of the past, she suggests that readers might gain a way of studying and finding answers to future questions through science fiction.

READINGS

Pinocchio turns Fascist

W. G. Mayne

Some fifty years ago, the Italian author Carlo Lorenzini, called "Il Collodi," wrote his *Pinocchio* which has delighted children and parents alike. It is full of adventure and has many an instructive moral not only for children but also for grown-ups. As it was doubtless the author's intention to amuse and educate children regardless of their nationality, there is no indication, except for the names of the characters, that the setting is Italian. *Pinocchio* is simply a children's book with a strong moral appeal. The author's political neutrality has made his book one of the favorite fairytales of the world. Walt Disney's cartoon-film revived its fame and contributed a great deal to Pinocchio's popularity in our days.

Contemporary Italy, where Pinocchio has always been a familiar figure, is using that widespread popularity for political ends. Pinocchio, in a sequel published some months ago under the title of *Pinocchio's Fiancée*, is no longer unconcerned with politics. He is presented to Italian children today as the model of a hundred percent Fascist.

The plot, in short, is as follows:

Pinocchio, now a grown-up young man, is far from Florence, dedicating himself to engineering studies. A girl, made of wood like himself and destined to be his wife, meets him on a sea trip after many adventures. They immediately fall in love, and the happy end of the story may easily be guessed.

Within the frame of that simple plot, the author has put a number of figures that can be divided into two classes, namely, Italians and foreigners. The Italians are all ardent patriots, and here the Fascist system, through the pen of the author, reveals the political credo which it seeks to impose upon youth. Love of country is not enough: it must be developed into a feeling of superiority. The Italians in the fantasy are without spot or blemish. They are all brave men and women who, on any occasion, stress their nationality and the preeminence of their people. They are incapable of evil, because all Italians are good.

Reprinted from *Living Age* 359, no. 4493 (February 1941): 569–71.

The intention of the author is clear. Young readers are to be gradually led toward super-patriotism. The system, in order to play a leading part in the world's affairs, must show that it is entitled to that dominance by proving the superiority of its nation, and that a people all of whom are honest, brave and virtuous has a divine right to leadership. This is the educational purpose of the book, and Italian youth, fed such doctrines, will as adult chauvinists be the most fervent adherents of fascism. (Or so it is planned.)

The author uses other methods to instill super-patriotism in his readers. So far, he has drawn his Italian figures as models endowing them with positive qualities worthy of imitation, thus demonstrating the superiority of his people. But there is still to be emphasized the inferiority of the others who, through excess of negative qualities, supposedly provide conclusive proof of Italian moral supremacy.

While all the Italian characters are angelic figures, the foreigners are "devilish conspirators." French, English, North and South Americans, Scandinavians, Russians and others (with the exception of the Germans and Spaniards, of course), are drawn as criminals and thieves. They are portrayed as those who have the money with which they try to exploit the genius of poor Italy—here we have the official Fascist theory of the "have" and "have-not" nations cleverly adapted to the understanding of children. The foreigners pursue their aim—unsuccessfully, in the end—by all unscrupulous means. Their manners are ridiculed, their mental capacities belittled. They play the roles of kidnappers and betray one another. Their mode of speaking is puerile and their only thoughts are on money-making. For although rich, they want to increase their riches by seizing the Italian secret of creating beings from wood, which they are unable to do themselves. But the brave Italians, however poor they may be, do not want foreign gold. They invent people from wood for its sake alone; their genius, unique in the world, is not for sale.

There can be no doubt that contempt for all races, with one or two exceptions, is thus implanted among young Italians. Children reared on such prejudices will later form the strongest pillars of the Fascist system. It is easy to mobilize them in street demonstrations against nations which they only know in such versions. For the system does not allow its people to travel abroad to any great extent, for there they might revise the opinions so carefully instilled in them by way of these "innocent" fairytales.

This, then, is the first aim of the new *Pinocchio*: education of children as super-patriots and future world-rulers. The second is to hold up Pinocchio as a model-hero. The author depicts his Fascist protagonist at the height of his heroism. For example, he has seen his future bride on the ship, but has not yet made her acquaintance. The girl is insulted by a wicked foreigner, this time an Arab of Algiers. (A French subject, it is true. But an Arab! The author seems to have forgotten the protective role Italy has assumed over the Arabs. Surely a blunder!) During a fête aboard the ship, Pinocchio, the girl's noble protector, addresses the Arab in the most offensive terms. The other challenges him, but Pinocchio—the brave, the valiant, the hero of Fascist youth—refuses to fight a duel.

And now comes the interesting juncture that reveals the Fascist conception of heroism. To the cheers of his countrymen, Pinocchio gives this reason for his refusal to fight:

"First, I have every right to refuse to fight a duel because you, a foreigner, have publicly offended an Italian girl on an Italian ship. Therefore, you are unworthy of crossing the sword with a gentleman."

Most gentlemen would, of course, not content themselves with mere talk in such circumstances. But the Italian "gentleman" prefers to use grandiose phrases. He is bound to tell off his opponent. His strength lies in his skill of argument. By talk, he intimidates his enemy. After a storm of applause from his compatriots, Pinocchio continues:

"Secondly, our swords and our lives are consecrated to the defense of our country."

It seems that the Italian girl (on Italian soil) is not part of the country, and so does not deserve to be defended except by words. But Pinocchio tops off his argument by a third reason, which demonstrates that he is just the type fascism wishes to train. He says:

"Finally, punishment has already been inflicted upon you by the verdict of our public!"

And now the onlookers, the actors, and the ship's crew join their hero in insulting and shouting down the Arab. Pinocchio ends the scene by replying modestly to the Captain's congratulations, as follows:

"I have done my duty. I was lucky in arriving before any other Italian who, however, certainly would have behaved quite the same way."

There we are. Fascism shows the way the Italian youth are to go: the basis is contempt and conceit, a profound sense of superiority; heroism consists in bullying and threatening.

This scheme has worked perfectly in the past. Italy's Fascist policy consisted of threats and big talk. Action was taken only against opponents who had no chance to resist aggression that followed the threats. Thus Abyssinia and Albania were subdued. France, so long as she appeared to be strong, was mildly threatened; when she was prostrate, her heroic neighbor stabbed her in the back.

But a weakness can be seen in this technique. England and little Greece and Albania have proved that garrulous "heroes" may be subdued by the less conceited and less talkative.

[Editor's Note: The United Press recently reported that Paolo Lorenzino, nephew of the author of *Pinocchio*, had asked the Italian Ministry of Popular Culture to sue Walt Disney for libel on the ground that Pinocchio as portrayed in the film "easily could be mistaken for an American."]

What the Soviet Child Reads

Ella Winter

A concerted attack has been made in the Soviet Union—to use modern Russian phraseology—on the Children's Book Front. What the subject matter of children's books should be, how they should be written, how to regard the child reader, are questions that have been discussed to an extent that would make pedagogues in other countries gasp. A catalogue of the Hundred Best Books for Children says: "Artistic literature should cease to be a means of recreation only. It should become a serious and attractive affair for the child, inspire him with creative desire. Just as a child brought up on cereals only will not grow up to be healthy, so one brought up on the pap of simple and meaningless stories will not develop a strong and creative imagination."

Children's books are taken most seriously as a branch of that education which is the cornerstone of the Russian revolution, of the building of socialism, of the achievement of all the Five-Year Plans. Social critics have been saying for years that education is the most important thing in our age. The Russians mean it. Writers of children's books occupy just as important a position in the Soviet scheme as the builders of factories or the Commissar of Railways. They have as many conferences as technical directors too. Every fortnight, for instance, writers and illustrators of children's books meet with pedagogues, librarians, artists, psychologists and literary critics in the Gosizdat (State Publishing House).

> The new books are discussed fully both from the point of view of ideology and the tastes and desires of the children (writes Jacob Meksin, for five years head of the Children's Book Section of the Gosizdat). These conferences not only discover individual errors, but decide also what subjects should be written about for the present-day child, and in what manner. For instance, should fantastic fairy tales be offered to children, should anthropomorphism be permitted to nature stories, should industrial themes and technical subjects occupy a central position? By these discussions editors and publishers of children's books can create a circle of active participants in their work. . . .

Reprinted from *New Republic* 73, no. 941 (December 14, 1932): 122–24.

Sometimes children themselves are brought to the conferences, as Russians believe strenuously in the right of self-determination. They listen to authors read their own works and are invited to comment. "Sometimes they take their role of expert with too much conceit," says Meksin wryly, "as for instance when one group of ten-year-olds sent in a book with the remark: 'We have read this and have decided that, on the whole, it may be printed.' "

Careful lists are kept in kindergartens, children's libraries and schools of the books read by children and of their notes and criticisms. One child's comment read: "This is too interesting, you can have a good cry over it." Another: "The most important thing he did not tell at all! Did the father buy the accordion for the child or not? For some daddies only make promises." A criticism of illustrations done in primitive or child-style ran: "Did children make those drawings? How badly they are done! I could have drawn them better myself."

The production of children's books in the Soviet Union vies in quantity with the proposed production under the Five Year Plans of coal, oil and tractors. Every week a new sheaf appears. They are sold not only in every shop of the Gosizdat but also at the many kiosks dotted about the streets that sell newspapers and magazines. Every few months the best are already out of print, although they are issued in editions of many thousands.

The best illustrators and artists are used both for illustrations and the musical settings of children's songs. I was taken to an artist's studio in Leningrad and found it large, clean and comfortably furnished, with still lifes and nudes on the walls; I could not imagine what this man lived on; one saw no evidences of any connection with the revolution, no posters or other commercial work. When finally I caught his name I recognized that of one of the most prolific illustrators of books for very small children.

Most children take their reading into their own hands and insist that their parents bring them home the new books. "My boys," a father of a six- and an eight-year-old told me, "ask for at least eight to ten new books every week, and nothing will put them off." Children take their new position of young adults, given them by the revolution, very seriously. Everything (except perhaps a tired or former bourgeois mother) conspires to have them know all about what is going on in the country. When a little girl of seven asked to have the political cartoon in Pravda explained and her mother told her she was too young to understand, she replied, "There is no too young. A child can understand everything if you will only explain it in terms that a child can understand."

The books for children foster such knowledge. Even for the tiny tots for whom pictures without words are printed, such picture books bear on the life of today— the Red Army parades, the new buildings of Moscow, the Park of Culture and Rest, life on a *kolhoz*. There are also, however, very charming picture books of animals, flowers, boats, circuses, which seem to have no visible connection with socialist reconstruction. But one cannot be sure. The book on Moscow buildings, which is of cardboard and opens out, has on one side only the new workers' blocks, attractively drawn in child-style by Chiffrine. Many picture books are serial stories, one called "Milk Factory" starting from the individual cow standing forlorn in a field and ending with great lorries bumping in every direction from the collective dairy to workers' homes.

As soon as a child can read there are books on every aspect of life today; historical, geographical, military, economic, social, political. World events appear reflected in children's picture books almost as soon as reported by Pravda. The story of Amundsen, with a shadowy portrait of the explorer on the cover, appeared in stacks everywhere while the icebreaker "Malygin" was in Arctic waters with Nobile on board looking for traces of the explorer. The headings in the catalogue of the Hundred Best Books for Children cover the field. Social and revolutionary books, science, production and socialist construction—among which appear such titles as "From Rubber to Galoshes," "Gigant," "Five Year Plan," "How a Tool Made a Tool." There are also funny and moralizing animal stories.

Many of the books contain morals about little boys or girls who wouldn't wash themselves; the dreadful tale "Moi Dadir," by Marshak, tells how all the household furniture turned against the culprit, food and forks and wash basin and soap. When he repented, they smiled benignly and returned, shoelaces, chimney pots, samovar, sponge. There are innumerable books about Lenin, his childhood, his youth, how he spent his leisure; these are adored by the children. They seem to have quite a special and personal love for their "little Lenin," not at all the dry and perfunctory homage paid by most children to their national heroes. And, indeed, in these books he does appear a very human and lovable person.

Most attractive are the international books with their brightly colored "brothers," little Negro babies, Chinese, Indian, Mexican peons, Europeans of all nations. They are shown at slave labor, Negroes hauling heavy loads on their backs, Indians picking cotton while a martinet with folded arms watches over them, little Chinese girls dully spinning. They end with the red star on their helmets or working side by side in the factories at last owned by themselves. One book of India is particularly attractively illustrated; it starts with men, women and children, backs bent at machines and in the fields, and ends with the Russian pioneers blowing trumpets, beating drums and waving their hands to a smiling army of Indian children advancing under the banner "We are ready."

Ideology and propaganda are very important. The many accusations of "propagandizing even the poor little children who cannot protect themselves" leveled against the Soviets are answered quite simply by Dr. Meksin. "After every great social and political upheaval the didactic nature of children's literature increases, and the new class which has just achieved power wishes to inculcate a new ideology in the consciousness of its children. This is why we pay special attention to technical books in Russia now, translating such stories as those by the American writer Lucy Sprague Mitchell, 'The Song of the Locomotive,' 'How Water Got to the Bathtub,' 'Skyscrapers' and others. Certain old classics and folk tales are being revived, freed, however, from undesirable elements, fantastic events, superstition and monarchical tendencies." Meksin himself has adapted a number of Russian folk songs and tales, "The Little Gray Duck," "The Cocks Have Crowed," "The Little Bird" and others.

One of the most exciting things happening in the field of children's literature is the new School of Children's Literature in Leningrad. This group consists of about twenty young men and women, all specialists in some field, who come together to discuss the methods of writing about their specialty for children. Not only for children, however. They want to describe their experiences and their knowledge so that grown-ups also will enjoy them.

The school in Leningrad is headed by C. Marshak, one of the most popular writers of children's verse in Russia and brother to the Ilin who wrote "New Russia's Primer." Marshak is a middle-aged, kindly-faced man, who lived some years in England before the war and translated Blake, Coleridge and Wordsworth into Russian. He is the only member of the Leningrad school whose "specialty" is writing; he was a poet for grown-ups before he took to writing children's verse. Ilin is a chemical engineer who lectures at the Technological Institute in Leningrad and has built a chemical factory; Potilov is a fireman, Bianki a naturalist who writes animal stories—a sort of Ernest Seton Thompson. His father was professor of Ornithology. Jitkov is a sailor and writes books popularizing technique. Tichailov writes on the new Soviet towns, Olenikov, on political and revolutionary books, Grigoriev, on books about the civil war and other historical events. There is one book on weights and measures by Merkuleva, a mathematician. She calls it "The Factory of Exactness' and it is as exciting as the "Primer."

There are also in the school a diver, a surveyor, a textile worker and two former *bezprizornie:* Kajevnikov, who writes so bitterly that some feel the books are hardly for children, and Panteliev, not yet twenty years old, who wrote at seventeen the famous "Schkid," the story of a homeless waif, which has been translated into German and has sold in large numbers both in Germany and Russia. Levin, a young Jew, lived as a child in southern Russia; he has written in "Diecet Wagonow," (Ten Cars) ghastly stories of the treatment of Jewish children in his district during the civil war—stories he knows well because he lived through them himself.

The school does not content itself with sitting in its editorial offices. It takes its office to the factory, reads the newest stories to the workers, invites criticism and comment, discusses the techniques of writing children's books. The engineer, the metal worker, the carpenter, the lathe operator, is to write his experiences for children, both that children may know about them and that the workers shall learn to write. Members of the school train and coach the worker-writers. "The art of the editor is something quite different in a collective society," says Marshak. "He is no longer a man with a blue pencil; he is a man who helps you find yourself."

Of course writers are not always successful in their attempts to write dynamically of the new life any more than illustrators always get the effect they want. But they are making the attack "in Bolshevik tempo" and mass formation. Shock brigades are taking up the matter of writing sufficient and sufficiently good books for children. The ideals of today did not attract writers and artists before the revolution. They wanted merely to "amuse the children," they thought children must not "be bothered" with grown-up concerns, must live "in a world of their own." Yet in Russia today Soviet children are more interested in great engineering projects like Dnieprostroy or the Volga Canal than in some Persian legend.

We want all writers of children's books to have had full experience of the subjects they write about (says Marshak), even textbooks must become dramatic. We cannot come to children with empty hands, we must not deceive them with false conversations. Science is a field of battle, not a peaceful dead thing, and every one who comes to our field must know something first hand. A child, you know, should come to us as to the third act of a play, knowing what came before, understanding what it sees and with a heightened sense of the beauty and drama it may get out of life by participating. Our children must carry the history of the problems of this period in their bones; they must never consider themselves as mere watchers. Each one of them is a little builder of socialism.

Children's writers who still persist in writing "meaningless" tales are considered "counter-revolutionary" and looked on with disfavor. The children themselves are not interested. "Bring me home something on Dnieprostroy, or the Turksib,"—the child will ask, "I want to know what is going on." My little girl friend of seven is honestly bored by fairy tales. "But what does he write those things for?" she asks. And fairy tales are not to be bought in the shops. At least not the fairy tales of the "good old days." Whether we like it or not, Tovarish Coal, Piatiletka and the adventures of airplane, Zeppelin, crane and tractor have replaced the knight, the princess on the pea and the broad bean that burst. The revolutionary child of today, though joyous and laughing, is really fully aware of the tasks that await him and the role he is going to play in building his country.

What Chinese Children Read: A Morality Tale

Phyllis Krasilovsky

When I was in Hong Kong last month, I bought a raft of 10- and 15-cent children's books at the Red China Department Store. A random sampling shows a general uniformity of price, quality and political message. Since these books were translated into English, one can only wonder what scores of other untranslated Chinese children's books are about and if they carry the same messages. I would guess that most of them do, since the subjects alone could be stretched unendingly to fill an up-to-date Chinese Communist children's library: and certainly they have a wide range of heroes and heroines to choose from for their idealized biographies.

Two 15-cent books which are for children about the ages of 8 through 12 are fairly strong stuff. "Stories From Liu Hu-lan's Childhood" dramatizes the good deeds of a revolutionary heroine from a peasant family who started her career at 13. When she was captured two years later, she stood up to torture which cost her her life.

According to the legend, she worked as a small child under miserable conditions to pick wheat. Her goal was a new dress, but her main concern was for her smaller sister whose perspiring face Liu Hu-lan constantly dried, and whose frailty constantly concerned her. When the reaping was finished, the small sister did not have enough grain so Liu Hu-lan sacrificed her own small fortune and, according to the illustration, enjoyed seeing her sibling decked out in the new finery she had provided.

Liu Hu-lan was also brave enough to stand up to two bullies, the sons of landlords, who refused her and her friends permission to dig wild herbs. She led a successful battle against them and when, a few days later, she caught them torturing other children, attacked them again. When she finally came up against the wrath of one boy's father, a landlord, she united the children into a band and defeated the enemies once and for all. In union there is strength, *sic veritas*.

Reprinted from *Publishers Weekly* 203 (February 26, 1973): 100–01.

Remarkable Hu-lan also helped to capture spies and sacrificed her gleaning money to buy eggs for a wounded soldier she nursed back to health. In all, the book is a thinly disguised manual on how to be a model child in a model commune in the model country of China.

The illustrations are 1930-ish, but with a wonderful flavor of China in its small landscapes and domestic backgrounds which, if always simple, are also cozy. Even a picture of Liu Hu-lan trudging through snow with her basket of hard-earned eggs reflects a feeling of tranquility and satisfaction. A child studying the illustrations couldn't miss the grateful expression on the soldier's face as he recovers, nor the fear on the faces of the spies Liu Hu-lan catches and, though there is no real depth to the heroine, a child in a similar commune would respond to the warmth of the illustrations and the wish-fulfillment heroic deeds.

The Chinese rate high on women's lib, at least from this sampling. Tasks aren't portrayed separately as boys' chores or girls' chores. Girls seem equal, if not superior, to every challenge, domestic or otherwise. Liu Hu-lan is a heroine, but instead of an idol to be in awe of, she serves as an example to be emulated.

On a slightly older level, we come to the least subtle book of the lot, "Huang Chi-kuang, A Hero to Remember," which carries a political message on almost every page. Our hero was born poor and orphaned early, thanks to a landlord who worked his father to death. The book illustrates through simple examples that the landlord and local officials were bad guys who made life terrible for good, simple people. Huang proved his bravery early by refusing to be publicly humiliated by them.

When the Communist Party liberates the village, life begins to get better. In 1950, the United States Imperialists attack North Korea, and Huang becomes angry enough to volunteer to fight for the Koreans. He is sent off in a blaze of glory, flowers, red banners and a band to spur his horse onwards. His mother advises him, "Just do what your commander says and give the American invaders a good beating."

Huang finds cities and villages destroyed and "thousands of old people, women and children killed by the U.S. imperialists" and vows they will "pay for their crimes in blood." The rest of the book describes with vivid illustrations battles he participates in until finally, in his last fight, he sacrifices himself for his battalion by throwing himself on a machine gun and blocking its muzzle. "His noble image shall always remain in the hearts of the Chinese people."

It comes as a shock to read of one's own country as the enemy in a children's book, but the strong underlying hatred is even more upsetting. It makes me eager to embark on a run-through of American children's books to compare the heat of propaganda.

American children's writers stretch and twist their imaginations, agonizing to create original stories marked with humor and fun. The mutual hope that authors and librarians share is that picture books will open the door to literature, that once joy is found in books, it will be sought again and again in deeper books, until one is finally hooked on reading. I wonder what happens to the little Chinese minds indoctrinated with such plebeian stories as "Hello! Hello! Are You There?," which is decorated like 10-cent birthday cards of the 1940s.

Little Fang Fang's family go to North China to work and little Sa Sa's family go to South China. Little Fang Fang and Sa Sa are such dull kids that they make Tom, Dick and Jane seem to light up the sky in comparison! The book is a recounting of the wonders in both the north and the south, and the two children are constantly on the telephone reporting mundane climatic differences, such as snow and palm trees. (Is it possible that telephone calls over distances comparable to that between Maine and Florida are subsidized by the State?)

Towards the end of the story there is this exchange. "Another time Fang Fang rang Sa Sa to say: 'The family is sitting around the stove. Father is sharpening his saw, and Mother is mending some clothes, brother is looking at a picture book, little sister and I have been singing and dancing. Outside the wind is howling, but our room is cozy and warm.' "

Sa Sa replies, "We have just had our baths, put on clean vests, and changed into our house-shoes. We are fanning ourselves and listening to father telling stories about his sufferings before liberation." Then Sa Sa seems to stamp her little foot as she says. "I am angry with those tyrants who used to bully him, and will not forget what they did."

Fang Fang ignores her passionate outburst and replies: "Sa Sa, isn't it wonderful how our fathers and uncles, from the north to the south, all doing different jobs, do not mind either the cold or the heat when they are working hard for socialist construction!"

Sa Sa, somewhat calmer now, concludes, "Fang Fang, how different our north is from our south! One so cold and the other so hot at the same time of the year. How beautiful and rich is our motherland! How vast it is!"

My favorite of the books is one called "I Am on Duty," illustrated with darling little children in pictures full of action and movement (sort of an advanced Golden Book.). True, they are all wearing uniform little red armbands with Chinese symbols, but otherwise they look like happy nursery-school children everywhere as they go about their average day's activities. Ah, but are the pictures deceptive? Here is a pretty little girl drawing above the following caption:

"Now it is time for drawing today. I do not draw flowers and birds or high mountains and streams but a little soldier hero."

In this book, several lessons come across: patriotic reverence, cleanliness, obedience, conformity, helpfulness. Even self-sacrifice gets a going-over:

"After our nap we have refreshments, tung-tung passes the sweets, I take round the biscuits. The large and good ones I give to other children, and keep the small ones for myself."

There is not a book among those I dipped into that does not stress usefulness. The messages of a couple of them keeps them from being like the cheap versions of Mother Goose nursery rhymes we buy to shut up our American children in supermarkets. I found myself sitting bolt upright reading silly little ditties about the flowers that grow or other everyday subjects because I knew there'd be a moral planted with those flowers.

From a poem called "Carrying the Goose:

I lay down my cane to carry the goose in my arms.
Goose, don't be angry with me!

I would never beat you.
I'm just afraid you may trample on our commune's grain.

Chinese version of "This is the way we wash our clothes," or, perhaps, Robert Louis Stevenson's "Gentle flows the river":

The breeze blows cool and gentle
    As we wash the clothes by the river.

    Clean clothes are healthy,
    We are skillful workers.

"Palm-leaf Fans" is illustrated by a beribboned black-eyed child holding two large fans:

    The big palm leaves
    Cut round in shape
    I make into fans to send to the frontier troops.
    You uncles steadfastly guard our frontiers:
    Let me make fans for you.
    It is only a small gift,
    But it is sent with deep feelings.

This poem is not the type one would expect children to be reading in peace time!

The illustrations—characterless little splashes of color of dogs, cats, little girls with hair ribbons, etc.—are of very poor quality, of the kind used to brighten cheap glassware. The art in most of the books is truly proletarian: yet, here and there even in the book about the young soldier, there is a wash of a cherry tree or a miniature bit of loveliness in the shape of a bush or a shadow of a house, as if the artist found such touches irresistible. Everyone in all the pictures looks very healthy, happy and well-clothed. Even the villainous boys are attractive: their frowns are temporary put-ons; the community will teach them how to be good.

I constantly found myself vacillating between pleasure at the realization that present-day Chinese children aren't starving as they were in "The Good Earth," but are healthily and happily learning little poems in kindergartens, and horror of the indoctrination that turned the poems to ashes before my eyes. But probably the messages, little Chinese fortune cookies of proletarian wisdom, will keep being inserted until full economic strength and stability are achieved in China.

Ideologies in Children's Literature: Some Preliminary Notes

Ruth B. Moynihan

Stories told or written for children are often indicators of the dominant values within a society. Various times and cultures reveal various attitudes, not only towards children but also toward life and society. As a Swedish specialist in children's literature recently said,

> Every age has felt the need to provide new instructions in its children's books on how life is to be lived. Thus children's books do not merely reflect the contemporary social scene and the problems of adult life; the simplified manner in which they treat their subjects also makes them something of magnifying glasses.[1]

The number of such magnifying glasses in our modern world is greater than ever before in history. An adequate discussion even of a particular era in one society could well be a major study. The purpose of this brief essay is merely to point out a few examples and to indicate some possibilities for further investigation.

The Wonderful Wizard of Oz, published in 1900 by Lyman Frank Baum, is one of the best known of American children's stories, but few have given much thought to the way in which its characters and plot reflect the political and social situation of the time. However, an article by Henry W. Littlefield recently described in detail the way the book serves as a populist parable. The Scarecrow, for example, represents Midwestern farmers, while the Tin Man represents the honest laborers bewitched by Eastern industrialists (personified in the Wicked Witch of the East). The Cowardly Lion is a parody of William Jennings Bryan. The Wizard, says Littlefield, "might be any President from Grant to McKinley. He comes straight from the fair grounds in Omaha, Nebraska, and he symbolizes the American criterion for leadership—he is able to be everything to every-

Reprinted from *Children's Literature: The Great Excluded* 2 (1973): 166–72.

body."[2] But Dorothy's innocence and her loving kindness, along with the brains, heart, and courage of her friends (which were within them all along though they didn't know it), are sufficient to unmask even the formidable Wizard and to achieve Dorothy's goals—the freedom of her friends and her own return to reality among her hard-working relatives in Kansas.

If we compare *The Wizard of Oz* to the English classic for children, *Winnie the Pooh*, the contrast is startling. A. A. Milne's story takes place in a sheltered circumscribed world, the easy-going world of the English upper classes, where one lone child might live on a huge green estate with a dozen stuffed animals for playmates, and in a fantasy world where he himself was in complete control. Baum's book, on the other hand, reveals a world full of conflict and danger where the heroine lives in a harsh grey world with only a little dog for a playmate (but a live dog, not a stuffed one) and can only escape into fantasy by being hit on the head in a tornado. Furthermore, even the fantasy world is full of dangers and harrowing experiences. Dorothy and her friends must deal with events as they occur, while Milne's characters generally frame or manipulate events according to their own expectations.

Winnie the Pooh, published in England in 1926, has been tremendously popular in America as well, though perhaps not as influential as *The Wizard of Oz*. It is better known to the intelligentsia, probably, while *Oz* is better known to the "common man." *Pooh* reflects a disillusionment with the pre-World War I world and its leadership. It is a sustained low-key spoof on official bureaucracies, the adult world in general, and the adventure and travel tales of nineteenth century imperial Britain. Where many earlier fairy tales were full of seriousness and took pretentiousness for granted as necessary and good, A. A. Milne's tales are all humor—especially in regard to pretensions. The ideology is that of a bumbling imperfect world, though a generally kind-hearted and not at all dangerous one.

Let us look at one chapter as an illustration. Chapter VIII, called "In Which Christopher Robin Leads an Expotition to the North Pole," reveals even through its title its deliberate parody of such earlier literature as *Robinson Crusoe* or the works of Robert Louis Stevenson.

This particular story concerns an expedition to the North Pole which Christopher Robin is planning. When asked by Pooh Bear what it is, Christopher says, "It's just a thing you discover," since he isn't quite sure himself, and then goes on to explain that all his friends can come because "that's what an Expedition means. A long line of everybody." Pooh goes off to gather the friends and they set off. After passing a "dangerous" part of the river where Christopher claims there might be an "ambush," they settle down in the first grassy area to eat their provisions—the best part of the "expotition" to most of the participants. After Christopher takes Rabbit aside to check wih him about just what the North Pole might look like, the crisis event occurs. Baby Roo falls in the water while washing his face. He thinks he's swimming, while everyone else tries desperately to rescue him. Finally Pooh rescues Roo with a long pole and is informed by Christopher Robin that he has also discovered the North Pole. They put a sign on the Pole to that effect and go home. Pooh, "feeling very proud of what he had done, had a little something to revive himself."

Within the story, each character carries a message, too. Eeyore, the donkey, is the complaining, old, self-centered, hypocritical relative wih whom society must be patient and forgiving. He doesn't ask things, he just tells people. He comes along only "to oblige" and everything is "all the same" to him, though when things start moving he says, "Don't Blame Me." He's a perennial wet blanket, full of self-pity, an eater of thistles who assumes that Pooh sits on them on purpose to keep them away from him. He preaches consideration, which he does not practice, and he "don't hold with all this washing" of Roo—"This modern Behind-the-ears nonsense." Finally, he's totally useless despite his painful efforts when it comes to rescuing Roo. The message is that the older generation is generally irrelevant, but well-meaning, and one must be nice to its members.

Owl is the intellectual who always knows about things, like the meaning of "ambush," and who tells "Interesting Anecdotes full of long words like Encyclopedia and Rhododendron" while his listeners fall asleep with boredom. In the emergency he explained that "in a case of Sudden and Temporary Immersion the Important Thing was to keep the Head Above Water," while the others hurried to the rescue. His knowledge is always either obvious or useless or both, but he is respected just for thinking and for his slightly mysterious potential usefulness.

Kanga is a spoof on motherhood. While she "explained to everybody proudly that this was the first time [Roo] had ever washed his face himself," he fell in the water and had a glorious time while she worried. The only female in the story, she represents a complacently sexist viewpoint—all women are mother figures and mothers are rather a nuisance most of the time. Piglet is a lovable coward in a world where there is nothing to be afraid of, while Rabbit has an unseemly number of relatives—message: fecundity is not really proper. Pooh is, of course, a "Bear of little brain"—the good and average person, and happily so. Presumably, the reader identifies with Christopher Robin, the paternalistic natural leader and protector simply by virtue of his superior birth, even though he is not much smarter or more capable.

It seems clear that this North Pole Expotition is intended to parody the great exploratory polar expeditions of the previous fifty years, especially those of Admiral Robert E. Peary. Peary had planned and provisioned several expeditions during the 1890's and even took his wife and new-born baby along. The Peary Arctic Club consisted of a few of his friends helping him towards his goal. Finally, on his sixth attempt in 1909, with much publicity, Peary succeeded in planting the American flag at the desolate site of the Pole. Milne's plot is debunking the imperial myth while preaching an easy-going, live-and-let-live myth. The leader doesn't know where he's going or what he's looking for, his friends and followers are mainly concerned with eating and enjoying themselves, the minor crisis as well as the major quest is resolved purely by accident by a bumbling good-natured hero, and everything is happy and okay because they all really love one another. The message is that goals don't matter so long as everyone enjoys himself and is kind to one another along the way. And in a way, the whole book suggests that reality itself, whatever that may be, doesn't matter much either if everyone is happy.

American books on the other hand, are usually firmly rooted in some aspect of reality and in the pursuit of specific goals. For example, *The Little Engine That*

Could by Watty Piper, published in 1930 (and regularly reprinted ever since), clearly reflects the official optimism with which most of the nation entered the depression. Even though the "happy little engine," carrying all sort of toys and good food to the children on the other side of the mountain, had broken down, apparently irreparably, and even though the shiny new Passenger Engine and the big strong Freight Engine and the Rusty Old Engine refused to help, the Little Blue Engine which had never been over the mountain at all was willing to try. And, of course, it succeeded. As Hoover told the nation at that time, it was the willingness of all the little people to make temporary sacrifices and work a little harder which would soon solve the problems of the depression. And Roosevelt too, after 1933, as most historians agree, set all the little engines to work without really changing the system for wealth and industry.

The American myth of innocence, goodness and determination which was so much a part of *The Wizard of Oz* is revealed again in this simple book. Furthermore, it implies that there is no need to be more than temporarily sad at the refusals of big business or wealth or the older generation (whose interest in toys and good food for children could not really be expected anyway), since there is bound to be a "little Blue Engine" who is equally capable and glad to help. The world of great passenger and freight engines is not really our concern. If we just keep hoping and trying, everything will be all right. There is nothing wrong with the system, only with small parts within it. "I think I can, I think I can" became the motto of a whole generation of depression parents and their children, while society's general structure remained unchanged.

A similar message shines out of *The Little House* by Virginia Lee Burton, winner of the Caldecott Award in 1942. An extremely simple, but endearing, story of the life history of a little house overwhelmed by urbanization and industrialization, the story is clearly a parable about the development of American society. This little house which had weathered the seasons for an untold number of years sees the beginning of the destruction of its country idyll with the coming of the first horseless carriage "down the winding country road." Inexorably, the car is followed by steam shovels, highways, houses, tenements, trolleys, subways, skyscrapers, and abandonment. "No one wanted to live in her and take care of her any more," but she remained because she was so well-built. Furthermore, her wise original builder had said, "This Little House shall never be sold for gold or silver and she will live to see our great-great-grandchildren's great-great-grandchildren living in her."

It is this stipulation which suggests that the house represents something more than just rural life. The house stands for a whole civilization and perhaps also for the American Constitution—the system of government which many conservatives felt was threatened by the New Deal as well as by increasing industrialization. The story preaches a nostalgia for the past and the rural innocence of snow and stars and apple trees and daisies. And when "the great-great-granddaughter of the man who built the Little House so well" recognized "the shabby Little House" in the midst of the hurly-burly city, there was an obvious solution— move it to the country. "Never again would she be curious about the city. . . . A new moon was coming up. . . . It was Spring . . . and all was quiet and peaceful in the country."

The flight to suburbia as a return to innocence and beauty is the message of *The Little House*. The world of the past was better, while the city and all of modern industrialization is evil and dirty. Nor is there any possible compromise or evolution, only escape. Even the class element is quite blatant, for it is only the well-to-do who can stop all the traffic to move a house out of the city. In this case it is also an "old" family, a fifth-generation family in 1942, which is thus representative of only a very small proportion of the population. (Interestingly enough, at approximately thirty years per generation, this also makes the house the same age as the Constitution.)

Horton Hears a Who! by Dr. Seuss, published in 1956, is a fantasy in form, but its ideology is very goal-oriented and socially concerned. While *Winnie the Pooh* centered on the on-going happiness of a group of mutually respectful but self-contained individuals, and *The Little House* on a nostalgic recreation of a lost rural past, *Horton* is, above all, concerned with the individual's crucial role as a member of society. And it is a society full of conflicts and antagonism, with constant crises and dangers, and social pressures of every sort.

The plot of *Horton* is very simple. A benevolent elephant hears a voice from a small speck of dust and immediately feels obligated to help and protect it "Because, after all,/A person's a person, no matter how small." This refrain is repeated again and again as the elephant faces one crisis after another. First some kangaroos mock him, then some monkeys steal the clover with the speck of dust on it. They give it to Vlad Vlad-i-koff the "black-bottomed eagle" who obligingly flies off with it and drops it in a 100-mile wide field of clover. Horton toils after it "with groans, over stones/That tattered his toenails and battered his bones" and then picks three million clovers before he discovers his speck of dust. The people on the speck are in real trouble (like the dolls and toys on the little train) because they had "landed so hard that our clocks have all stopped./ Our tea-pots are broken. Our rocking-chairs smashed./ And our bicycle tires all blew up when we crashed." Horton promises once again to "stick by you small folks through thin and through thick!" But the kangaroos have decided to rope and cage the elephant for "chatting with persons who've never existed" and for "Such carryings-on in our peaceable jungle!" Furthermore, they are going to boil the dust speck in Beezle-Nut oil. (How mild was the disdain of the big Engines for the toys in comparison!)

The action now shifts to the people of *Who*-ville on the speck, since Horton can no longer protect them. Their only hope, and his, lies in shouting enough to make even the kangaroos hear. As Horton puts it, "you very small persons will not have to die / If you make yourselves heard! *So come on, now, and TRY!*" They do try—desperately—but without success, until the Mayor "discovered one shirker," a very small one who "Was standing, just standing, and bouncing a Yo-Yo!" He lectured the lad that this was the "town's darkest hour! The time for all *Whos* who have blood that is red/ To come to the aid of their country!" Finally, "that one small, extra Yopp put it over" and the Whos "proved they ARE persons, no matter how small./ And their whole world was saved by the Smallest of ALL!"

The ideological message of this story is so blatant that one is tempted to interpret it almost too specifically. For example, it seems to reflect the Cold

War mentality of the Fifties—especially in the name of its arch-villain, the Eagle. It also teaches the general virtue of responsible paternalism—the big should take care of the little, the comfortable should protect the oppressed, no matter how great the cost. And then it further preaches that an individual's value is determined not by his own pleasure (playing with Yo-Yo's), but only by his contribution to the whole, his active participation in achieving the goals of his society.

Horton is not a "middle-of-the-road" story. The preservers of the status quo are the kangaroos, and they are clearly evil. They also represent the pressures for social conformity and against "hearing voices." The ideal which Horton represents is that of the sensitive, spiritual, artistic, dedicated lone defender of humanity with all the world against him. There is a similarity to the Little Engine of 1930, but Horton is far less humble and the stakes are much higher. This is a life-and-death struggle, not just a matter of toys and good food. Horton's non-conformism is shown as right because it is in a good cause benefiting others—just playing and minding one's own business like the *Who* with the Yo-Yo is clearly immoral. (*Winnie the Pooh* characters would certainly be frowned upon in *Horton* value system.)

One may suggest that Horton represents the messianic idealism which has been for so long a part of American tradition—with periodic eruptions on both the right and the left in internal affairs, and, in the twentieth century especially, on the international scene as well. Nixon, Johnson, and Kennedy could claim to be identified with Dr. Seuss's dedicated elephant just as well as Ellsberg, Dr. Spock, and Daniel Berrigan. Radical fighters for social justice come right out of the mainstream of American ideology, and violent confrontations are an accepted part of our world view.

In another way, *Horton* reveals the two main themes of a mass democratic society—the paradoxical importance of individual resistance to mass pressure for evil but cooperation with mass pressure for good. In such a society neither the large "elephant" nor the small "Who" is safe without the help of the other— and both are always in danger.

From the debunking of the Wizard in *Oz* and of the Empire in *Pooh*, America moved to an idealization of hopeful struggle in the face of difficulties in *The Little Engine* and of older rural values in the face of modernization in *The Little House*. And then in the Fifties we became newly aware of the irreconcilable conflicts of our mass modern society and also of the impossibility of escape. A study of our children's literature in its historical context might have forecast both a Viet Nam type encounter and the youthful upheaval of the Sixties. Both adults and students were acting out the values they had absorbed at an early age. And those values were taught by their own parents and in their own books. An analysis of the most popular children's literature indeed provides a magnifying glass for its society.

NOTES

1. Mary Orvig, "One World in Children's Books?" The May Hill Arbuthnot Honor Lecture, *Top of the News,* June 1972, p. 40.
2. "The Wizard of Oz: Parable on Populism," *American Quarterly* 16 (1964): 54.

Mary Poppins Revised: An Interview with P. L. Travers

Albert V. Schwartz

Did you know that there is a new version of *Mary Poppins*? This popular piece of children's literature, once described by the *Christian Science Monitor* as "whimsical, philosophic, and strong in the principles of good thinking," has been revised so as to mitigate its racism.

When I first made this discovery. I called the juvenile department of the publisher, Harcourt Brace Jovanovich, to find out how these changes had come about. I was told that certain portions of the original text had been revised in the 1972 paperback edition at the request of the author.

What had caused the author to make these changes? The editor said she did not know but she put me in touch with P. L. Travers herself, who is living in New York. I promptly called her and was delighted to hear that she was willing to grant me an interview.

I met Ms. Travers in her apartment on a rainy day. How appropriate to be arriving with an umbrella in my hand and rubbers on my feet! When we sat in her living room, I found I was face to face with the stern, bright, sharp "Mary" of my readings.

We talked for a long time before Ms. Travers would let me begin taping the discussion. She interviewed me almost as much as I her. I told her that the Council on Interracial Books for Children had been receiving more and more complaints about her stereotyped presentation of Africans, Chinese, Eskimos, and American Indians in *Mary Poppins*, most particularly in the chapter "Bad Tuesday."

Sitting tall and tense, Pamela Travers was aware of every word as she spoke: "Remember, *Mary Poppins* was written a long time ago [1934] when racism was not as important. About two years ago, a schoolteacher friend of mine, who is a devotee of *Mary Poppins* and reads it constantly to her class, told me that when she came to that part [i.e., the trip to Africa in "Bad Tuesday";] it always

Reprinted from *Interracial Books for Children* 5, no. 3 (1974): 1, 3–5.

made her shudder and squirm if she had Black children in her class. I decided that if that should happen, if even one Black child were troubled, or even if *she* were troubled, then I would have to alter it. And so I altered the conversation part of it. I didn't alter the plot of the story. When the next edition, which was the paperback, came out, I also altered one or two things which had nothing to do with 'picaninny' talk at all.

"Various friends of mine, artists and writers, said to me, 'No, no! What you have written you have written. Stand by it!' But, I thought, no, if the least of these little ones is going to be hurt, I am going to alter it!"

Picaninny Language

Ms. Travers told me that she didn't know where she had picked up the "picaninny" language since, she said, she had known no Black people at the time she wrote *Mary Poppins*. However, she had read *Uncle Remus* and still knows *Little Black Sambo* by heart.

I said that it was fortunate that she had also eliminated the references to watermelon and shoe polish. But when I asked why she herself still used the term "picaninny," she replied: "To me, even now the word 'picaninny' is very pretty. I've used it myself time and time again to children. Not to Black children because life hasn't brought me very much in contact with Black children, but I've used it time and again to small children."

When asked what language the Black characters used in the revised version, Ms. Travers said: "Formal English, grave and formal. Now that I've met Black people from time to time, they speak a formal English."

Many of my comments about other parts of *Mary Poppins* displeased Ms. Travers. "I refuse to be arraigned for what I wrote," she declared at one point. "You're overstressing from the point of view of racism, which is something I don't accept. I have no racism in me. I wasn't born with it. And it's never happened inside of me. And therefore I feel perfectly at ease and at home no matter what color anybody's skin is. I was brought up in a family and in a world where there was no hint of racism of any kind. And not because my family was liberal or because they had liberal friends. I was brought up by large-minded people who never had any sense of racism at all. I grew up in a rarefied atmosphere. I loved *Little Black Sambo* as a child . . . I only came across racism since I came to the United States."

Imagination vs. Sociology?

"If you grew up without racism, with parents who had no racism, then how do you explain that racism appears in your books?" I asked.

"Literature and imagination are my world. I don't like being pulled out of that world and being forced to live in a sociological world of which I am not a native inhabitant. Imagination is a pure thing. It is envisaging. Imagination does not depend upon the sociology of the time. More functional books do; imagination does not. Imagination goes whither it will. *Mary Poppins* is not a contemporary book. It is a timeless book, and probably it goes back a good deal to my own childhood."

"I am not really convinced that any harm is done," she continued. "I remember when I was first invited to New York by a group of schoolteachers and librarians, amongst whom were many Black teachers. We met at the New York Public Library. I had thought that they expected me to talk to them, but no, on the contrary, they wanted to thank me for writing *Mary Poppins* because it had been so popular with their classes. Not one of them took the opportunity—if indeed they noticed it—to talk to me about what you've mentioned in 'Bad Tuesday.' "

Another question I had for P. L. Travers regarded the insulting use of the term "street arab." Miss Lark, a character in *Mary Poppins*, calls to her dog to get away from the other dogs: "Andrew, Andrew, come in my darling! Come away from those dreadful street arabs."

Pamela Travers laughed at the question. "Is that a pejorative term? 'Street arab'? There are 'street arabs' in Morocco, aren't there? Little boys running around asking for hashshish? Are you trying to arraign me for that? Because I shan't be in any way arraigned or put in a witness box. I used it! Very well, then. That's what it meant to me at the time, and there it is. I never thought of changing it. If anybody said it made them squirm I would have changed that too. But I don't think that any normal person would squirm at that term."

Pamela Travers agreed that Mary Shepard's illustrations for the chapter, "Bad Tuesday" were stereotypes but said that she was not responsible for them. (The editors at Harcourt Brace Jovanovich later said that when revisions of the book were considered, at no time was any thought given to changing Mary Shepard's illustrations, which often show stereotyped Third World people.)

"Friend Monkey"

The subject changed to Ms. Travers' latest book, *Friend Monkey*, also published by Harcourt Brace and Jovanovich. She was annoyed that I had not yet read *Friend Monkey,* and she began to read to me from the book:

"Miss Brown-Potter was a female explorer, who now lived in retirement. Once on a trip to Africa, she had rescued a baby from a crocodile on the banks of the River Tooma. He belonged, she had learned, to the Fan tribe, and since his family seemed not to want him—perhaps because the child was deaf—she had brought him back to England with her and named him after two famous explorers."

I asked Ms. Travers if she didn't think that having a Black family reject a child and feed him to crocodiles because he is deaf would be offensive to Black parents, especially in a children's book? She avoided my question by stating that this was an actual practice of the Fan tribe in Africa. [To the Council's best knowledge, the only Tooma River is in New South Wales—it should be noted here that Ms. Travers, who is considered an English author, was born and reared in Australia. Records consulted by the Council indicate that Fan is a variant spelling for the Fang of Gabon, in West Africa. However, the Council could find no substantiation for the assertion that the Fang leave handicapped children on river banks.]

A New Look at Old Books: The Bronze Bow

Phyllis Cohen

The Bronze Bow is two books in one. One book is a short story of Jesus' ministry. The other is the story of the Jews' striving for liberation from the Roman oppressors. Daniel, the hero, is caught between these two stories and acts as a bridge between them. The author, unfortunately, vastly oversimplified the political, economic, and religious situations at the time. Briefly, the author seems to divide the people into Romans and Jews (with some foreigners in the cities), and the Jews themselves into the masses, the Pharisees, and the rebellious malcontents. The book implies that the Pharisees and rebels, though far apart in everything else, are alike in that they reject Jesus—the Pharisees for his loose interpretation of the Law, and the rebels for his preaching for nonviolence. The masses are Jesus' followers. There is a bit wrong with this picture. It implies that Jesus' teachings were completely revolutionary, too difficult for the scribes, rabbis, and elders of the synagogue to understand, that his followers took him on faith alone. The doctrine of love he taught was not so new; vengeance, to which Daniel had given his life, had always been reserved for the Lord in Judaism. Compassion for the poor and needy was specifically dictated by Jewish Law. Provision for orphans, widows, and others in need had been mandated for centuries. (Daniel's resentment of his treatment by the rabbis in the village merely sounds like that of a hot-tempered apprentice resisting his master's discipline.) Permanent slavery had never been permitted—all slaves were freed after seven years bondage. And the laws governing these bondservants were for the times, extremely liberal and unknown elsewhere. What was new, was Jesus' very free interpretation of the Laws and the strong emphasis on one aspect of the Laws—the humanitarian one. As the author rightly shows, Jesus was a practicing Jew, although not a Pharisee.

Many leaders were springing up at this time of oppression. It was a bewildering and confusing time. Some leaders were thieves, like Rosh; some were sincere, but misguided; some were wild-eyed revolutionaries; some preached

From *Young Readers' Review* 3, no. 2 (October 1966): 12.

cooperation with the Romans, etc. Authority, in general, took a dim view of all the new movements. There were two factions in Judaism already, and only unity and cohesiveness, backed by tradition, would hold the Jews together as a nation. The reader gets little inkling of the tremendously turbulent times. All he sees are Rosh and Jesus—one all evil who preys upon his own people under the guise of liberating them, and the other all good and self-sacrificing. This over-simplification extends also to the other characters.

Daniel himself is a very simple character; his are just the trappings of complexity. Can anyone but a simpleton spend so much time with Rosh and his men (all of whom are bandits) and not know that they are merely acting patriots? Can a real person, with real feelings learn about the death of the slave, Samson, and gain so little from it? Can anyone but a stupid oaf drive his sister back into the darkness of her madness so ruthlessly and carelessly? Oh yes, he supposedly was sorry about it all afterwards. Leah had withdrawn from the world, yet Malthace and Marcus and Daniel had slowly drawn her back into it. Assuming that her brother's accusations could drive her deeper into herself so suddenly, how could she come out so quickly, so completely healed? She did not want to be healed. (How she could ever have become friends with Marcus, a stranger in the uniform of those who crucified her father, is extremely difficult to understand).

Simon the Zealot appears, originally, as a kind, conscientious, intelligent young man. He is puzzled by the times he lives in. He is searching for freedom and truth. Finally, after months of listening carefully to Jesus he becomes one of his followers. Simon accepts a purely spiritual answer to his search for freedom on the basis of his feeling that Jesus is the Messiah. His explanations to Daniel of how man can be free even in chains, amounts to "To those who have faith, no explanation is necessary; to those who lack it, none is possible."

Both Simon's and Daniel's acceptance of Jesus are not vivid. Though the author describes Daniel's spiritual awakening, somehow it is not convincing. Both Simon and Daniel turn to Jesus only because there is no one else. There are no alternatives—Rosh or Jesus. Choose! (Had Daniel waited about thirty years, he could have been part of a glorious rebellion.) The author implies that all those who fought for freedom from Roman oppression were misguided, silly, or thieves.

We meet no Romans in the book except as passing persecutors. Only Marcus (who is a German) is shown in any depth. All the characters are Jews. Therefore, all the unpleasant characters are Jews. All deniers, all who reject Jesus are Jews. The author even implies that there is a conspiracy amongst some of the Temple authorities to kill Jesus. There are no pleasant, good, just, or wise non-converted Jews in the book.

I doubt that Miss Speare believes that. I feel that it is an unfortunate effect of her choice of characters. But it does have the effect of perpetuating the canard of deicide. For Jesus is more than a man, a teacher, a healer in this book. His presence alone is illuminating, healing, and inspiring. He is magnetic, and contact with him always has a startling effect.

Daniel is forced to choose between freedom and spirituality. Isn't this a false choice? Granted that his principal motive, revenge, is an awful one, does it then follow logically that freedom from Rome is not worth fighting for for any reason? Patriotism may be the last refuge of scoundrels, but oppression can lead to genocide. Rosh was a scoundrel, but others weren't. Though the might of Rome was formidable and left the bands of youths who rescued Joel shaken, it took Rome four years, their crack legions, and greatest generals to subdue the Jews when they finally revolted. And then Rome had to destroy the Temple and disperse the Jews to ensure that there would be no more plotting. Were all these early champions of religious and political liberty wrong because they did not accept conquest by love as a doctrine to live by?

The Bronze Bow is a pacifist novel. Fine. But the author's omission of admirable characters on the side of fighting for justice and freedom, makes this book a piece of special pleading, a piece of propaganda, rather than a historical novel. Christians may find this book inspiring. Non-Christians may find it rather insulting.

The Second Sex, Junior Division

Elizabeth Fisher

We live in a sexist society. Almost from birth we are indoctrinated with the notion of male superiority and female inferiority, male rights and female duties. It is in the earliest years that children form images of their worth, their future roles, the conscious and unconscious expectations placed upon them. Investigating books for young children in book stores and libraries I found an almost incredible conspiracy of conditioning. Boys' achievement drive is encouraged; girls' is cut off. Boys are brought up to express themselves; girls to please. The general image of the female ranges from dull to degrading to invisible.

Since females comprise 51 per cent of the population of the United States, one would expect them to be equally represented in the world of picture books. On the contrary they vary between 20 and 30 per cent. There were five times as many males in the titles as there were females, four times as many boys, men, or male animals pictured as there were females. In special displays the situation was even worse. The fantasy worlds of Maurice Sendak and Dr. Seuss are almost entirely male. The three major prizewinners for this year, displayed together on a table at Brentano's, were all about males: "Sounder" about a black boy by William Armstrong, "A Day of Pleasure" by I. B. Singer, and "Sylvester and the Magic Pebble" by William Steig. Where are all the missing females? Have they been exposed to the elements, as with primitive tribes? Or are they sequesterd behind walls, as in Southern Italy or the Near East?

This preponderance of males is not limited to humans. Animals in books are male for the most part. Elephants, bears, lions, tigers are males or, as in the Babar books, isolated females are shown in the company of a majority of males. In the veld it is the female lion who does all the work; in the picture-book world she doesn't exist. There are some books about female animals, and an occasional reference to the female of the species. Cows, obviously, are female. Hens, too. In "Rosie's Walk" by Pat Hutchins a hen walks unscathed and unnoticing through

Reprinted from *The New York Times Book Review*, Sec. 7, (May 24, 1970): 6, 44.

all kinds of dangers—reenforcing the stereotype that nothing ever happens to she's. Sylvia the Sloth is the heroine of a not unpleasing book. Somehow the female animals tend to be those whose names are synonyms of derogation. Petunia the Goose, Frances the Badger—I suspect the choice of these animals reflects the low esteem in which women are held. A rhinoceros is male, a hippopotamus female. Leo Lionni's snail in "The Biggest House in the World" is a he who has a father but no mother, in clear controversion of biology.

Only in Noah's Ark does Biblical authority enforce equal representation for males and females. Except for Random House's "Pop-up Noah," which has eliminated Mrs. Noah and does not show the animals in equal distribution on the cover—males have a slight edge of course. The wives of Ham, Shem and Japheth, present in the Old Testament, were missing from all three children's versions I examined. Things have come to a pretty pass when one has to go to the Old Testament for an upgrading of the female.

It should be mentioned that folk tales tend to treat women somewhat better than do books with contemporary settings. Possibly this is because the former are often based on themes of come-uppance and vindication of the underdog, spontaneous products of wish fulfillment and the unconscious, while the latter are written to please or to sell. After all, although Hansel comes up with the device of dropping pebbles so that he and Gretel can find their way home, it is Gretel who disposes of the witch by pushing her into the oven. Wives are smarter than their husbands, and women make fools of the powerful. The folk tales reflect a preindustrial culture where, though women may not have had equality, they did play vital functioning roles. They were not consuming or sexual objects, justified only by motherhood, as today's world all too often defines them. They were producers who functioned in agriculture and home industries such as spinning and weaving, who worked side by side with their men. Evidently the folk tales survive because they have certain psychological validities.

In the more modern downgrading of the female, not only are animals generally male, but personifications of the inanimate—machines, boats, engines, tractors, trains, automobiles—are almost invariably so. In life, ships are she's; in picture books—Little Toot, Max's boat Max in "Where the Wild Things Are"—I have yet to come across one that was not a he. Automobiles, at least in France where the Citroen D. S. 19 (déesse—goddess) is highly admired, are often thought of as feminine, but not by picture-book authors and illustrators. One exception to the masculinity of machines was written back in 1939 when Virginia Lee Burton created Mike Mulligan and his steam shovel Mary Anne.

This marked absence of the female applies even more strongly to books about blacks. Analogies between racism and sexism date back before the 19th century: both Mary Wollstonecraft and Thomas Paine compare black slavery to female slavery. In this country the woman's rights movement of the 19th century grew out of the Abolitionist movement, as today's Women's Liberation Movement relates to the Civil Rights Movement. History repeats itself. Just as black men achieved enfranchisement long before black or white women, so in the picture-book world have blacks achieved integration with whites and representation for themselves without a corresponding integration for the female, black or white.

One of the earliest efforts in this direction was Jerrold Beim's "Swimming Hole" about black and white boys swimming together, and since then there have been a spate of books about blacks and whites and about blacks alone. But the only picture book I found about a black girl was Jacob Lawrence's "Harriet and the Promised Land" based on Harriet Tubman's life. Ezra Jack Keats has done several picture books about small boys, and a recent one of his, "A Letter to Amy," does bring in a girl, but in a token and not altogether flattering way. Peter is bringing Amy a letter to invite her, the only girl, to his birthday party, when he bumps into her accidentally. Amy runs away in tears. Later, the other boys say, "Ugh! A girl at the party!" but she comes anyway. One little girl can make it in a group of boys, from Robin Hood's Maid Marian on down through the centuries, but she'd better know her place.

Virginia Woolf pointed out that throughout literature women were generally shown only in relation to men, and this is still true in the picture-book world. Friendship between boys is much touted; friendship between boys and girls is frequent; but friendship between girls gets less attention, though surely this is a norm in life. The frequent depiction of one girl in a group of boys would seem to represent wish fulfillment for girls as well as boys. A boy is considered unmanly in a group of females, but a girl who achieves acceptance in a group of boys has evidently raised herself, the exception that proves the rule of general female inferiority.

Since there are so few females in the picture-book world, one would think they'd be very busy, but such is not the case. What they do is highly limited; more to the point is the sheer unreality of what they do not do. They do not drive cars. Though children see their mothers driving all the time, not a single description or picture of a woman driver could I find. In the world today women are executives, jockeys, stockbrokers, taxidrivers, steelworkers, in picture books these are nonexistent.

Little girls in picture books tend to be passive, though sometimes manipulative. They walk, read, or dream. They seldom ride bicycles; if they do, it is seated behind a boy as in Dr. Seuss's "One Fish, Two Fish, Red Fish, Blue Fish." When I came across a little girl sailing paper boats in a book by Uri Shulevitz, I was overwhelmed with gratefulness. And the same might be said for my responses to Suzuki Beane and Eloise, both of whom are presented as highly exceptional.

Though there have been women doctors in this country for over a hundred years, and pediatrics is one of their preferred specialties, there is not a single woman doctor to be found. Women are nurses, librarians, teachers—but the principal is always male. They have emotions; they get angry; they disagree; they smile; they approve or disapprove; they want to please. What they do not do is act. Boys do; girls are—a highly artificial and unsatisfactory dichotomy.

In a country where over 40 per cent of the women work, I know of only one picture book about working mothers, Eve Merriam's "Mommies at Work." But it wasn't in stock in any of the book stores I visited. However, while commendable—there are Mommies who split atoms, build bridges, direct TV shows, who are dancers, teachers, writers and doctors—it is also highly apologetic. The end, "all Mommies loving *the best of all* to be your very own Mommy and coming home to you," (my italics) gives it away. We don't feel the need to say about Daddy that he loves his children more than his work. Couldn't Mommy matter-of-factly like working and baby, too, as I'm sure many do?

No boys and girls must get the message—it's all right to work, but only if your work is subordinated to your role as mother. What does it matter that that will last twenty years and the rest of your life may well be spent as supernumerary, doing some kind of busy work? Or semitrained and at the bottom of the labor heap? This is the kind of contradiction that produces guilt and neurotic conflicts in mothers, fathers, and children, instead of the simple sharing we could achieve if men and women were taught to expand their roles.

A few other books, selected not entirely at random, will show some of the methods by which children are indoctrinated at an early age with stereotypes about male activity and female passivity, male involvement with things, women's with emotions, male dominance and female subordination. "A Tree Is Nice" by Janice Udry, illustrated by Marc Simont, seemingly innocent, is actually devastating when analyzed with an aware eye: a boy is high up in a tree balancing while a girl is on the ground watching. Successive pages show a boy fishing, a boy rolling in leaves, and another holding a rake, while a big girl leading a small boy walks by. Then a double-page spread with a huge tree in the center pictures seven boys and three girls. One of the latter is on the ground, helping a little boy up into the tree; the other two are on low limbs close in to the main trunk. The boys are shown adventuring, one hanging from a rope, the other five climbing way out or high up. Other pictures show a boy drawing in the sand, a boy in a tree, and boys planting trees. Note that there are 19 boys pictured to eight girls.

Another seemingly innocent book is William Steig's "CDB," a clever pun-puzzle book with pictures captioned by dialogue in letters. This is a funny book but implicit attitudes about girls and women are revealed. There are twice as many pictures of boys as girls in the book, and the girls tend to be passive or helpers. When they do anything, they do it badly or are discomfitted. A boy is shown on skates; the girl has fallen down. A girl turns a somersault, but it doesn't agree with her, she is dizzy. A girl dancing in a field of flowers is an exception and, giddy from the unusual activity, she is in ecstacy. There are angry females, several of them, but no angry males. Male work is respected; a boy tells a man writing at a desk, "If you're busy, I'll run away." Women are never shown in this context; they are at everybody's service. A woman tells fortunes—the supernatural has offered one of the few exciting outlets for women down through the ages, and witches and still making it, in and out of the Women's Liberation Movement.

One of the worst offenders in this brainwashing about roles and expectations has, perhaps, the most influence—Richard Scarry. His "Best Word Book Ever" is a big illustrated dictionary with the Scarry trademark, humanized animals, demonstrating meanings and activities. Scarry's male-female divisions are scarifying: many more males, naturally, but they *really* do get to do everything. Toys, for example, are defined by showing 13 male animals playing with exciting toys— a tricycle, blocks, castle, scooter and rocking horse, as well as the traditional toy soldiers and electric trains. Two female animals play with a tea set and a doll! In the Scarry orchestra, out of 28 animals playing instruments, the two females were assigned those drawing-room clichés, the piano and the harp. The percentage in the New York Philharmonic is no better, but at least there the women play cello and bass viol. Many pages had only males as protagonists, but the one page which showed only women was . . . what else? "In the Kitchen." The most infuriating page was entitled "Things We Do." Males in Scarry's book world dig, build, break, push, pull and do 15 other active things, including eat. The only two things females do are watch and sit.

What kind of world will a little girl educated on Scarry expect to grow into? It's a meager, thankless, and unrewarding prospect. No wonder both boys and girls identify with the boy's role in life.

Particularly sad is the realization that these books are perpetrated by women as well as men—women authors, illustrators and children's book editors. There are very good reasons why women so often "fawn like the spaniel"—the phrase is Mary Wollstonecraft's—but isn't it about time we stopped? It's true that till now men have had all the power, and in a world steeped in patriarchy, women internalize the notion of female inferiority and transmit it to the next generation, perpetuating the cycle. But awareness is upon us. The task of bringing women up to full human status is not going to be easy. To start here, however, at the earliest years, should bring results.

Protests about the retrograde situation have already risen in the Women's Liberation Movement, including an article in the first issue of *Women: A Journal of Liberation*. Women active in the movement are writing new children's books. A conference is planned to educate children's book editors. Several groups have protested primary-school textbooks and "Sesame Street" to some effect. The quarterly *Aphra* dedicates part of each issue to feminist criticism of various aspects of our culture, with articles on child-care books and children's television in prospect. As the movement grows, so will the protests. Editors and authors take note. Better meet change now, head on, than be forced into it or bypassed later on.

Values in Popular Literature for Children

David C. McClelland

As part of a research project in social psychology, I read hundreds of stories for children in the third and fourth-grade readers of some forty different countries all over the world. It was a fascinating and enlightening experience— fascinating just to read what millions of Russian, Indian, Japanese, Turkish or Australian children are reading today when they go to school; and enlightening to discover that the stories, while similar in many respects, differ markedly from country to country in the values they express.

Stories from the Middle Eastern and North African countries like Turkey, Lebanon, and Tunisia, quite often are built around a theme of cleverness or ability to outwit somebody else. A typical Turkish story presents an idea in arithmetic in the following way: a young man hired as a clerk by a business firm when asked what monthly pay he expects, replies that he would be glad to be paid one cent for the first day, two cents for the second day, four cents for the third day, eight cents for the fourth day, and so on through the month. The owner agrees, thinking he is getting a bargain. When at the end of the month the clerk presents a bill for wages of over ten million dollars the owner suddenly realizes that through his carelessness he has agreed to pay in one month's wages more than his whole business is worth. Now the idea of what happens when you double numbers is one that teachers everywhere are interested in getting across but in Turkey it is presented in a form which stresses the triumph of cleverness and the dangers of being outwitted.

Many other stories from the Middle East stress the same theme. A farmer is worried that his sons will be lazy and not till the soil after he is dead. So in his will he states that he has left a treasure buried somewhere in the fields; and the sons spend the rest of their lives trying to dig it up, tilling the soil in the process.

Or a cobbler is very much annoyed by a pet monkey that gets into his shop when he is out, plays with his tools, makes holes in the leather, tears things apart,

Reprinted from *Childhood Education* 40 (November 1963): 135–38.

and generally destroys his day's work. The cobbler appeals to the monkey's owner and to the town authorities, but they are only amused and say they can do nothing to control the monkey. Finally the cobbler sees how he can outwit the monkey; he has noticed that the monkey watches him at work and then tries to imitate everything he does. So he takes a knife and passes it back and forth across his throat; the monkey does likewise and cuts his own throat! Needless to say, such a story contains ideas that would not appear in American readers used in the public schools.

Stories Reflect Country's Values

Other countries, of course, stress values in their stories which, unlike cleverness, would be more highly approved by American parents and teachers. In Chilean and Japanese stories great emphasis is placed on the importance of kindness and obligation to others and in German stories on the value of loyalty. Practically any theme will appear in at least one or two stories from a given country, but some appear much more frequently in some countries than others.

The conclusion is inescapable that popular stories for children reflect what the people in the country value most, what they think is important. And children learn from reading the stories what adults regard as important. As David Russell puts it, "In literature children and adolescents can find many of man's most important social-ethical ideas."[1] He goes on to discuss the importance of stimulating children to discover such ideas for themselves in the stories they read. He further notes that values described "in the lovely words of our language such as truth, justice, loyalty, and faith . . . are puzzling and difficult ideas for adults and even more for children, and yet they are the foundations of our society."

Nothing could sum up better the evidence of our research project, but I would add one footnote. I believe that children acquire the values or ethical ideas expressed in the stories, even without conscious and deliberate attempts to abstract them. It is the abstraction process which is difficult, not the ideas themselves. I believe that Middle Eastern children learn naturally and easily from what they read that cleverness is a good thing, just as American children learn that working together is usually the best way of doing things. Children come to take such ideas for granted because that's the way things "are" or "happen" in the stories they read.

Getting Across Values

To demonstrate the importance of popular literature in expressing and shaping such basic ideas, I once tried an interesting experiment with a class of primary school teachers. In discussing comic books, I discovered that without exception they were all opposed to them and that, also without exception, no one had ever read one. At least if they had, they wouldn't admit it in front of the class! So I gave out a number of copies of a popular Disney comic book dealing with Donald Duck and his three small nephews and gave the teachers as their next assignment the task of looking for the social-ethical ideas in it. They were a little surprised at the assignment, but even more surprised by what they discovered. The values expressed in the comic book stories were, at the very least, characteristic of the American way of life and at best what they, or any conscientious Sunday school teacher, would try to encourage in their pupils. Here are a few of the themes they decided were stressed:

Money may be the measure of success, but you should be generous with it as it means nothing in itself. (Uncle Scrooge in the comic is admired for his success, but his stinginess, as his name implies, is strongly disapproved.)

If everyone tries to do his best, competition is inevitable, but you must play fair. He who plays fair wins through in the end though he may seem to be losing for quite a long while. (The theme is constantly stressed in the relationship of Donald Duck and his "lucky" cousin Gladstone.)

It may appear that some people get lucky breaks, but in the long run it is the person who works hard who wins out. (Again the idea appears in the relationship of Donald Duck and his cousin Gladstone.)

Children should work together to accomplish their ends. (Donald's three little nephews, Huey, Louie and Dewey work constantly as a team to get Uncle Donald out of his scrapes.)

Evil contains the seeds of its own punishment. (Li'l Wolf's bad father is constantly being tripped up by his own schemes to do injury to others.) So here we find an emphasis on generosity, fair play, hard work, cooperation and the self-destructiveness of evil intent. Put in such big words, the children could hardly get the ideas at all, but in terms of concrete action and emotion, there is little chance that they will miss the "morals" of the stories.

A price is paid, of course, for such social-ethical teaching. The price is over-simplification, too much violence, limited vocabulary, and other comic-book vices so frequently stressed by parents and teachers.

What can we say of the child who reads nothing but comic books? We may take comfort in the fact that at least he is reading. Moreover, what he is reading is apt to be moral (except possibly for the horror comics, which figures show are read by a very small percentage of children).

I do not, by any means, mean to defend comics as an ideal form of popular literature. There is obviously better literature in basic readers and in the many excellent trade books that are increasing in number and more readily available to children through school and public libraries and through children's book clubs. There is no substitute for *good* books. They help develop skills and ideas which every child will need—in school and out—now and as an adult.

Shaping Children's Social-Ethical Ideas

For ten years, I have been a member of a selection board for a children's book club. I regard my job as important, because I believe that the books we select play a key role in shaping children's social-ethical ideas and values. Children's literature performs a great service in the moral education of the young.

For example, every young reader will be influenced to some extent by Robert E. Lee's integrity and compassion in *America's Robert E. Lee* by Henry Steele Commager (Houghton Mifflin); the love, hope, and courage demonstrated by the war-scarred children in Hilda Van Stockum's *The Winged Watchman* (Farrar); the self-knowledge and capacity for leadership discovered by the young hero of *The Boundary Riders* by Joan Phipson (Harcourt). Even the youngest beginning readers will respond to the point that considerate behavior is preferable to rudeness as shown in *Prince Bertram the Bad* by Arnold Lobel (Harper) or to the intriguing facts in a book such as *Birds Eat and Eat and Eat* by Roma Gans (Crowell).

In my work with the children's book club, I am constantly facing the problem of the sensitive or imaginative book that is excellent but a little "off-beat," one that cannot be chosen as a general selection because its appeal will be limited to a few. But for those few children it might mean everything in life. Fortunately that book can be put on the recommended list for parental purchase or library usage with a note as to the nature of its special appeal. There is a moral here, it seems to me, for all of us involved in choosing what children will read: we must be guided in the first instance by what will interest the most and by what best represents the values we cherish, but let us always be ready to recommend other books of an unusual or less popular sort.

One of the teachers in the class I referred to earlier brought me at the end of the course a clipping from the comic strip, "Peanuts," in which a little girl was explaining to a little boy reading Peter Rabbit that the story is really full of symbolism, that the farmer's hoe represents parental authority, etc. The little boy goes on reading and finally concludes, "I must be stupid . . . I thought it was just a story . . . !"

NOTES

1. David H. Russell, "Personal Values in Reading," *The Reading Teacher* 12, (October 1958): 3–9.

Science Fiction: Impossible! Improbable! or Prophetic?

M. Jean Greenlaw

Rockets, space ships, men traveling to the moon; all figments of a science fiction writer's imagination! These were general beliefs until modern technology made them realities. However, before they became realities, they were serious considerations for those writing in the field of science fiction.

Science fiction is the genre of literature that imaginatively depicts plausible events that are logical extrapolations of known facts and are descriptive of the social impacts of science and technology. Though the plots may seem impossible to man in his present condition, they do reflect the possibilities of the future.

Those writing in the field of science fiction for children are often scientists, technicians, or others with credentials enabling them to bring authenticity to their material. Great respect is accorded the best of these writers and David Riesman sees fiction as the illuminator of many societal issues.[1] Erich Fromm credits science fiction writers with more perspicacity than that shown by most professional sociologists and psychologists.[2]

A recent example will serve to illustrate the point. July 20, 1969 was a historic day for all mankind. On that day man set foot on the moon, fulfilling a long held dream of our society and a prophecy written in 1863 entitled *Journey from the Earth to the Moon*. Jules Verne, prognosticator of the future, foretold in his writing this and many other events that have become history and some which have yet to become reality. His imagination enabled him to predict the development of the submarine, helicopter, television, moving pictures, Sputnik, the diesel engine and other technological advances of our time. The imagination which allowed him to invent such miracles also caused him to realize that the advances of technology could actually threaten humanity with great danger.[3] Verne's writing was also a portent of the rise of Hitler, the creation of Buchenwald, and the development and use of the atomic bomb.

Jules Verne was an author of science fiction, yet much of what he wrote has become reality. He made a tremendous impression on the beliefs and technology

Reprinted from *Elementary English* 48, no. 4 (April 1971): 196–02.

of a society. Are other writers of this genre to wield similar power? Do they reflect the concerns of a culture in a period of great change?

Theme as a component of literature. An investigation of this question requires an understanding of theme and plot as components of literature. An author generally has a purpose for writing, a message he wants to present to his readers. This message is the theme of the book. The devices the author uses, the characters and action he employs to present the message comprise the plot of the story. The plot of the story is obvious but the underlying theme is not always apparent. Because books may influence the developing values of children, it is necessary to be aware that a purpose for the writing exists and to discover that purpose, or theme, as it is revealed in the action of the material.

Theme is the underlying component of literature and is generally related to broad questions of humanity. It is possible for books whose plots have no seeming relationship to be professing the same theme. Before examining the themes of science fiction being written for children today, let us consider the society which is influencing that literature.

A look at today's society. World War II marked the end of a way of living and the formation of a new society; one forged in the laboratories of science and powered by that same science. The forces of science have brought into existence a technology which influences the lives of everyone on earth. This technology seems to have three major directions of consequence: the possibilities of nuclear power, the development of automation and the formation of our society into corporate or mass structures.

The possession of nuclear power is an awesome responsibility. It has been used for destruction and we continue to produce and refine weapons systems which employ this power. Nuclear energy can be utilized in the production of peaceful industry, also, and already is used for peaceful purposes to some extent.

Cybernation, a new mathematical method of automatic control, has generated the possibilities of a new kind of economic and social organization. From every aspect, a look at the future indicates an ever increasing role for the computer. In almost every phase of our lives the computer will be present to make things happen more quickly, more easily and at less cost. The potential for the computer is unlimited.[4]

An effect of cybernation has been the reorganization of society into mass or corporate structures. The abilities of these machines and the expense of operation make it necessary for them to function in a system which is extensive and highly controlled.

Effect on man. These are realities of our existence. What effect have they had on man and his system of values? The themes of numerous science fiction books being written for children today reflect the concerns of scientists, philosophers, sociologists and other professionals for the continuation of man and the life he has known within this century. There has been a consuming interest in values in America since World War II. Science provides us with nuclear bombs, weapons of chemical and biological warfare, drugs to alter the human personality, and endless instruments for laborsaving, entertainment and the "happy life." But science has proven less satisfactory in its solutions for major human problems.[5]

A search of the literature concerning values, particularly as they relate to American society, reveals a tremendous interest in the related values of individualism and privacy. The impact of technology on these two values has been considerable; the interpretation of the impact has been varied.

The explosion of the atomic bomb as an act of war in 1945 caused man to reexamine his values. It was believed, prior to this, that scientific activity could be isolated from the realm of values. Science was a neutral entity. It is now believed, even by many scientists, that science represents a definite value position.[6] Research, however, fails to uncover what that value position is. Is it enough to merely state that it exists, or is it encumbent upon the promoters of science to make clear what that value position is within our society?

The system of control known as cybernation or automation and the resulting creation of corporate or mass institutions has altered our concepts of and our possibilities for individualism and privacy. Some see the control of society and the submission of the individual to the greater good of the group as being a more noble use of the abilities of each individual. Fitzpatrick states that:

> Life is so intimately intertwined and our interdependence is so clear, that industrial activity reveals itself more clearly as the cultural behavior of a whole people; as the expression of a state of mind that is shared by those outside the industry as well as in; as a form of activity which is more in the nature of a national effort than the achievement of a rugged individual. In this context individualism and freedom can lead to achievement more noble than that of the individual alone.[7]

Skinner concurs, with his belief that, "some kind of control of human behavior is inevitable. We cannot use good sense in human affairs unless someone engages in the design and construction of environmental conditions which effect the behavior of men.[8]

Others see this control as a negation of all that has made man what he is. They foresee, and some see now, a society of men controlled by the machines they have devised, not in the sense of machines consciously having subordinated man, but in the sense that man has subordinated himself and is now only the recorder of the effects and results obtained by various techniques. The proponents of instituting a halt to the massification of man and the return to individualism are numerous and eloquent. Bronowski, Ellul, Riesman and Fromm[9] are among those who cite the dangers of automation in causing man to be a consumer rather than a producer and the ensuing decline into a morass of boredom. These authors illustrate the growing lack of privacy which can be attested to by incidents of wiretapping, eavesdropping and the current government move to record all data concerning every individual in a central computer system. They lament, with Lewis Mumford that, "Many of us have now come to regard automation as the climax stage of human culture, thus wiping out richness and diversity, independent human selectivity and creativity."[10]

What relationship do these themes, prevalent in adult writing, have with children's literature?

Science fiction as a reflection of societal concerns. Much of the contemporary children's literature reflects what is occurring in the world today as accurately as does adult literature. Children are in and of the world and their increasing sophistication demands that authors present material which is pertinent to the lives these children lead.

The social aspects of science fiction are a reflection of the general advancement of modern technology. For example, the explosions of 1945 have wrought considerable changes in the science fiction of today. The social consequences of atomic fission and fusion are inescapable, for evil or good. The writing of science fiction must treat this matter in [sic] its prophecies whether the treatment entails the use of atomic energy for peace or for devastation.

A recent publication, *The Day of the Drones* by A. M. Lightner, reflects several of the themes discussed earlier as societal concerns. The story is a comment upon the effects of a controlled society upon individualism and the determination of some to become individuals even under great duress. It is also a statement of hope for a uniting of the white and black races in a common brotherhood. In the story, a closed society, caused by atomic destruction, has evolved in Africa. After five hundred years the survivors have designed a system in which, "Each of us must be fitted to his life and his way of life must be fitted to him."[11] Education is permitted only for those who are fit and that education is carefully controlled. The study of science is taboo as is the existence of argument, because these were the causes of the destruction. A reverse prejudice is also present. This society is a hierarchy of color, in which light-skinned are either killed or assigned to menial tasks and the very black are in the elite positions. The resistance of several members of the culture to the restrictions and the breaking of the law to educate a light-skinned boy results in an expedition into the outer world where a white culture is encountered. The white culture is patterned after the social order of bees and is also a very restricted society. The continuous struggle of the rebels to defeat conformity and the end of the story, which leaves us with a question as to whether they succeeded, truly reflects the problems man is facing today. The situation is exaggerated but the elements are all there.

The winner of the Newbery Award in 1962, *A Wrinkle in Time* by Madeleine L'Engle, is another piece of fiction which has as its theme the need to respect individual differences and the power of love to conquer evil. A powerful evil, described as a great shadow and referred to as "IT", is in control of certain planets and is beginning to overshadow the earth. As the plot unfolds one recognizes that this evil is that of conformity. IT believes that differences create problems, individuals must be done away with and that all must become *one* mind. IT assumes all responsibility, all burdens of thought and decision. IT is eventually defeated only by the ability of one individual to utilize her unique powers and by the ability of love to conquer hate. This fascinating story presents a powerful theme and enmeshes it in a fast-paced, gripping plot. It is a simple matter to correlate the theme of this book with the theme of adult literature which decries the formation of the "organization man." The growth of the corporate structure in which no one but the top makes decisions; in which all are to fit a pattern designed by a series of tests; and in which creativity and individualism are looked upon with distrust is evidenced in this writing.

The element of war and destruction is an integral part of much of the science fiction written for children. The plots revolve around communities formed as a result of a nuclear holocaust or the impending danger of war. This theme, that of the evil and devastation that war brings, is not always the predominent theme but it is present in most of the books. Andre Norton has written much science fiction for children. Two which consider the theme of the impact of war on individuals within a society are *Night of the Masks* and *Quest Crosstime*. In *Night of the Masks*, Nik, a disfigured refugee of a war in which he had no part, must decide whether he is to be a part of a future conflict. His actions as an individual force him to choose what he will be as a man and whether he will be an instrument for good or evil. His decision, that of one individual, plays an important part in the outcome of the impending war. *Quest Crosstime* employs a far different plot to promote the same theme. The incipient takeover of a universe by a group of "Limiters" who want power only for themselves is defeated by the forces of an individual, using his unique gifts to overcome the forces of evil with good.

The struggle to maintain individualism and free will is another recurrent theme of science fiction for children. This has been illustrated in several of the books discussed already and is the predominant theme in *The Pool of Fire* by John Christopher. He depicts the earth as a world controlled by a group of aliens who have taken over after the earth was devastated by war. War has been abolished, there is little disease and starvation but there are no freedoms for the people. They are "capped" at the age of fourteen and become utterly obedient to the wishes of the masters. A small band of free men has formed in an effort to defeat the aliens and return the people to individualism and freedom of will. In organizing the revolt there is dissent within the party as to whether they are really free or are being controlled by another power in the name of freedom. The answer promulgated is:

> Free men may govern themselves in different ways. Living and working together, they must surrender some part of their freedom. The difference between us and the capped is that we surrender it voluntarily, gladly, to the common cause, while their minds are enslaved to alien creatures who treat them as cattle. There is another difference, also. It is that, with free men, what is yielded is yielded for a time only. It is done by consent, not by force or trickery. And consent is something that can always be withdrawn.[12]

A question might be asked if this is possible? Once freedom has been relinquished can it be recovered? Is this not what we are being asked to do in our time for the good of all mankind? In *The Pool of Fire* the free men are victorious over the aliens and following the restoration of freedom to everyone a summit conference is convened to create a society in which man can be free but one in which the threat of war is abolished. A confrontation ensues and results in the disbanding of unity into national fragments and a foreshadowing of the whole cycle beginning again. Man has behaved as man usually does and the world continues in its path toward destruction with a few individuals vowing to work toward a system of peace again.

A final book, which incorporates all the themes discussed, is *The City Under Ground,* by Suzanne Martel. In this book we find a world where privacy, free will and individualism have been completely subordinated to the good of the society, which is situated underground because of nuclear destruction. The society is completely controlled because its living space is so confined. The members of the community dress alike, live in identical homes, have their meals planned for them and, because of the enforced diet, have even come to look somewhat alike. Exercise on a spiral walk and a daily swim are prescribed for everyone in Surreal since they must spend so much of their time in chairs. Decorum is the watchword: ". . . in a tight little world like Surreal, outbreaks could easily be thought antisocial."[13] Into this world come two disruptions—a break in the power source which sustains all life and the venturing of one individual out of the underground into the world. The discovery of nature, the world which has only been known through the books of ancient history, and the insistence of one individual to find out for himself what that world is, brings the revelation of a new life to the society of Surreal. A comparison of the world of Surreal to what could become, and is becoming, of our world today is easily made.

Uses of science fiction. In a recent study[14] this author analyzed one hundred and thirty-three (133) science fiction books for children and reached some conclusions concerning the nature and use of children's science fiction. The belief that children's science fiction is essentially escape literature associated with "Bug-Eyed Monsters" and space opera plots is fallacious. The genre includes significant themes and values which are commentaries on society in general and the impact of technology on human values in particular. This literature can be used to help create in children an awareness of social problems and a more perceptive understanding of the decisions one must make in the world.

Included in the developmental tasks of childhood are the development of scientific and social concepts necessary for everyday living and the development of values, attitudes, and conscience. Science fiction provides a body of literature that can aid children and youth in this process.

In addition, children's science fiction is a vehicle for social criticism and as such can be used to develop critical thinking and critical reading. Critical thinking and reading necessitate the process of judging and evaluation. Science fiction often presents a variety of choices, systems and values. It questions the validity of much in our society and predicts possible outcomes for the future. Science fiction depicts this in both theme and content and demands judgment and evaluation on the part of the reader.

Another valid use of science fiction is reading for pleasure. Because science fiction is usually fast-paced, exciting and fun, it makes attractive reading fare.

Conclusion. The development of technology has introduced a complex set of issues for individuals to encounter. Are the values which enabled us to become what we are—the values of individualism and privacy—to yield completely to the will of technology and all the ramifications of that technology? The question can only be answered by individuals. Science fiction for children reflects the implications of technology and the possibilities for the future. Through it can be provided a method of developing an awareness of some of the alternatives of the world's future.

Jules Verne was a man who invented the future. But his writings were only prophetic. It remains to be seen whether or not today's science fiction is only prophetic, or whether it will help to avert some of the awesome consequences of uncontrolled technology.

BIBLIOGRAPHY

Barrett, Donald M. "Value Problems and Present Conditions." *Values in America.* Edited by Donald M. Barrett. Notre Dame: University of Notre Dame Press, 1961.

Bolt, Richard H. "Man-Machine Partnership." *New Technology and Human Values.* Edited by John G. Burke. Belmont: Wadsworth Publishing, 1966.

Bronowski, J. *Science and Human Values.* New York: Julian Messner, 1956.

Dach, Sam. "Wiretapping and Eavesdropping." *New Technology and Human Values.* ed. John G. Burke. Belmont: Wadsworth Publishing, 1966.

Dubos, Rene. "Modern Horsemen of the Apocalypse." *New Technology and Human Values.* ed. John G. Burke. Belmont: Wadsworth Publishing, 1966.

Ellul, Jacques. *The Technological Society.* New York: Vintage Books, 1964.

Estrada, Jackie. "The Science Fiction Market." *Writer's Digest* (April 1969): 49–52+.

Fitzpatrick, Joseph P., S. J. "Individualism in American Industry." *Values in America.* ed. Donald M. Barrett. Notre Dame: University of Notre Dame Press, 1961.

Fromm, Erich. *The Revolution of Hope.* New York: Harper & Row, 1968.

Greenlaw, M. Jean, "A Study of the Impact of Technology on Human Values as Reflected in Modern Science Fiction for Children," Unpublished Ph. D. dissertation, Michigan State University, 1970.

Heinlein, Robert A. "Ray Guns and Rocket Ships." *Reading About Children's Literature.* ed. E. R. Robinson. New York: David McKay, 1966.

Huxley, Aldous. "Over-Organization." *New Technology and Human Values.* ed. John G. Burke. Belmont: Wadsworth Publishing, 1966.

Leinster, Murray. "Writing Science Fiction Today." *The Writer* (May 1968):16–18.

Michael, Donald N. "The Problems of Cybernation." *New Technology and Human Values.* ed. John G. Burke. Belmont: Wadsworth Publishing, 1966.

Mumford, Lewis. "Automation." *New Technology and Human Values.* ed. John G. Burke. Belmont: Wadsworth Publishing Co., 1966.

Reisman, David. "Leisure and Work in Post-Industrial Society." *New Technology and Human Values.* ed. John G. Burke. Belmont: Wadsworth Publishing, 1966.

Skinner, B. F. "Freedom and Control of Men.": *New Technology and Human Values.* ed. John G. Burke. Belmont: Wadsworth Publishing, 1966.

Williams, Robin M. "Values and Modern Education in the United States." *Values in America.* ed. Donald M. Barrett. Notre Dame: University of Notre Dame Press, 1961.

BIBLIOGRAPHY OF CHILDREN'S LITERATURE

Born, Franz. *Jules Verne: The Man Who Invented the Future.* Englewood Cliffs, U. J.: Prentice-Hall, 1964.

Christopher, John. *The Pool of Fire.* New York: The Macmillan Co., 1968.

L'Engle, Madeleine. *A Wrinkle in Time.* New York: Farrar, Strauss & Giroux, 1962.

Lightner, A. M. *The Day of the Drones.* New York: W. W. Norton & Co., 1969.

Martel, Suzanne. *The City Under Ground.* New York: The Viking Press, 1964.

Norton, Andre. *Night of the Masks.* New York: Harcourt, Brace & World, 1964.

————. *Quest Crosstime.* New York: The Viking Press, 1965.

Steinberg, Fred J. *Computers.* New York: Franklin Watts, 1969.

NOTES

1. David Reisman, "Leisure and Work in Post-Industrial Society," in *New Technology and Human Values,* ed. John G. Burke. Belmont: Wadsworth Publishing, 1966, p. 200.

2. Erich Fromm, *The Revolution of Hope.* New York: Harper & Row, 1968, p. 30.

3. Franz Born, *Jules Verne: The Man Who Invented the Future,* Englewood Cliffs, N. J.: Prentice-Hall, 1964, p. 87.

4. Fred G. Steinberg, *Computers.* New York: Franklin Watts, 1969, p. 87.

5. Donald M. Barrett, "Value Problems and Present Contributions," in *Values in America,* ed. Donald M. Barrett. Notre Dame: University of Notre Dame Press, 1961, p. 5.

6. Robin M. Williams, "Values and Modern Education in the United States," in *Values in America,* ed. Donald M. Barrett, Notre Dame: University of Notre Dame Press, 1961, p. 60.

7. Joseph P. Fitzpatrick, S. J., "Individualism in American Industry," in *Values in America,* ed. Donald M. Barrett. Notre Dame: University of Notre Dame Press, 1961, p. 104.

8. B. F. Skinner, "Freedom and the Control of Men," in *New Techniques and Human Values,* ed. John G. Burke. Belmont: Wadsworth Publishing, 1966, p. 289.

9. J. Bronowski, *Science and Human Values,* New York: Julian Messner, 1956. Jacques Ellul, *The Technological Society,* New York: Vintage Books, 1964. David Reisman, "Leisure and Work in Post-Industrial Society," in *New Technology and Human Values,* ed. John G. Burke, Belmont: Wadsworth Publishing, 1966. Erich Fromm, *The Revolution of Hope,* New York: Harper & Row, Publishers, 1968.

10. Lewis Mumford, "Automation," in *New Techniques and Human Values,* ed. John G. Burke, Belmont: Wadsworth Publishing, 1966, p. 129.

11. A. M. Lightner, *The Day of the Drones,* New York: W. W. Norton & Co., 1969, p. 31.

12. John Christopher, *The Pool of Fire,* New York: The Macmillan Co., 1968, p. 6.

13. Suzanne Martel, *The City Under Ground,* New York: The Viking Press, 1964, p. 31.

14. M. Jean Greenlaw, "A Study of the Impact of Technology on Human Values as Reflected in Modern Science Fiction for Children," unpublished Ph. D. dissertation, Michigan State University, 1970.

Responding to Sociological Criticism

1. Class Struggle

CRITICAL COMMENT

Class struggle was made apparent in a great deal of writing by sociological critics. The strife seems to have an economic basis as shown in the essays of the 1930s, which were concerned with capitalism, through those of the 1970s which were concerned with Civil Rights and women's liberation.

WAYS OF RESPONDING

A. Take a random sampling of a few years of the American Library Association's list of Notable Books. As you read through several of the books, do you find evidence of class struggle reflected in the books? What examples of capitalistic force are shown? Do the problems of racial, sexual, and ethnic groups show evidence of having been based in economic class struggle?

B. Read some of the books noted in the section on children from other countries in *Reading Ladders for Human Relations*.[5] What evidences of class struggle are apparent in these books? From your sampling, could you give a judgment about the reality portrayed in these books?

C. Compare translated books from other countries with contemporary stories from the United States. Are there marked differences in the class systems?

2. Propaganda

CRITICAL COMMENT

The essay by Mayne dealt with a book that was outright propaganda, done specifically with the purpose of indoctrinating. There was nothing subtle about the book. Some of the examples given by Krasilovsky were written in the same way. It appears that, no matter what the country or the time, political propaganda is a reality.

WAYS OF RESPONDING

A. Do a group composition of a morality tale about an imaginary new political system, such as a class system based on the color of the eyes. Set up rules for governing all group members and develop a fiction story that incorporates these rules.

B. If possible, find some children's books from a country whose political system strongly differs from that of the United States. Embassies and consulates sometimes have such collections, as do professors of comparative education. Examine these books for examples of blatant propaganda and indoctrination.

---

5. Virginia Reid, ed., *Reading Ladders for Human Relations*, 5th ed. (Washington, D.C.: American Council on Education, 1972).

C. Contrast the original and the Disney version of several books written outside the United States, such as Collodi's *Pinocchio*, Travers' *Mary Poppins*, and Fleming's *Chitty Chitty Bang Bang*. Are there evidences of Americanization in these adaptations? What is your feeling about the rightness or wrongness of this? What could you do about it?

D. Select six or eight inexpensive children's books at random from drug stores or supermarkets and analyze them in the style of Krasilovsky. What commentary do they give about the American way of life?

E. Cohen stated that *The Bronze Bow* was a pacifist novel—propagandistic rather than historical in concept. Read some other novels that deal with religious persecution, such as Ish-Kishor's *Boy of Old Prague*. Analyze these books for slanted characterizations, omissions of information, and for recurring elements of a theme that might not be the view of all persons involved.

3. Stereotypes

CRITICAL COMMENT

The use of stereotypes abounds in children's books to the extent that the reader's consciousness needs to be raised in order to become aware of many stereotypic features. Stereotyping is one form of propaganda and, as such, deserves to be studied as a style of criticism.

WAYS OF RESPONDING

A. Find the selection discussed by Schwartz in his interview with Pamela Travers. The chapter is "Bad Tuesday" from the hardcover edition of *Mary Poppins* copyrighted in 1934. Compare this with the revised edition published in paperback. Was Schwartz being overly picky in his comments? Does the revision in the paperback edition make the book free of derogatory stereotypes?

B. Read several essays from the quarterly journal, *Interracial Books for Children*, published by the Council on Interracial Books for Children, Inc. Discuss the accusations. Where do you stand on these issues?

C. Usually readers are unaware of stereotypes unless they are closely allied with the group that receives the bias. Read several books dealing with a racial, religious, ethnic, marital, professional, or sexual group with which you feel a strong relationship. Do you see examples of stereotyping? How do these portions of the books affect you emotionally?

D. In Fisher's essay on sexist books, a number of books are noted which, according to Fisher, give negative images of females. Select a few of these books and analyze them in a class-sized group. *Rosie's Walk* by Hutchins, *A Letter for Amy* by Keats, and *A Tree Is Nice* by Udry are examples of the types of books mentioned. Does the group consensus suggest that the books are totally sexist or are there mixed feelings? For example, in *A Letter for Amy*, does the theme of wanting Amy to attend the party give a more positive total image of women than the instance when a boy at the party says, "Ugh, a girl," gives a negative image?

4. Dissociation

CRITICAL COMMENT

One concept of sociological criticism is that the author does not need to be imbued with the idea about which he writes. He can dissociate himself and his personal views. The reality of what he says, however, comes through in the characterizations.

WAYS OF RESPONDING

A. Analyze several books for the image of women which is portrayed. Select books by men and women authors, being sure to include the work of some known feminists. After analyzing the books, find some information concerning the point of view of the authors on feminism. Do the characterizations suggest an image of women different from the view held by the authors? Is the image depicted through subtle or explicit means? Do you believe the authors would agree with your analysis?

B. Many critics of books about blacks contend that only black authors can write correctly about the black experience. Compare books about blacks written by black authors and by white authors. What differences in emotional tone, realistic description, and persuasive style can you observe? Some books that would be useful are *Sidewalk Story* by Mathis, *Whose Town?* by Graham, *The House of Dies Drear* by Hamilton, *Durango Street* by Bonham, *The Slave Dancer* by Fox, and *Sounder* by Armstrong.

5. Ideal Hero

CRITICAL COMMENT

Sociological criticism concerns itself with the emergence of an ideal hero, one that embodies the beliefs of the cause that is being furthered. The over-drawing of such a character is, of course, a problem with which the author must deal.

WAYS OF RESPONDING

A. In their zeal to champion a movement, some authors have created ideal heroes who are larger than life. At times reverse stereotypes are the result of attempts to right the wrongs and injustices that have existed in literature. Books of this nature appear when there is a rush to publish a certain type of book to fill a need. Read some books about blacks which appeared in the mid-sixties, for example, and some of the first books published by the feminist presses in the early 1970s. What instances of the ideal hero or heroine do you find in this literature? What are some suggestions that you would give the authors, if you were asked, for tempering the characterizations?

B. Select a racial, ethnic, religious, or sex group of interest to you and list elements of characterization that would embody the ideal hero of this group. Would any of the components you have selected conflict with others on your list if you were to use them all in developing a character? Which of these traits would it be possible to use and still create a believable character? It might be of interest to present this list of traits to a small group of people and have them check those which they consider to be the traits of the ideal hero/heroine of the group. Is there agreement? What does a comparison of the checklists indicate about the unity of feeling concerning the traits of any one group?

6. Temporalism

CRITICAL COMMENT

Books are generally good reflectors of the times in which they were written. They offer opportunities to understand the forces shaping decisions during certain periods of times.

WAYS OF RESPONDING

A. Do an analysis of children's books for selected decades to notice if trends of those times are reflected in the children's literature of those eras. For example, do children's books of the early 1930s reflect the Great Depression, with nonfiction books suggesting ways of coping with the money crisis? Do children's books of the late 1930s show a break from isolationism and an increased interest in international understanding? Do books of the 1940s reflect a preoccupation with World War II? Questions such as these directed to small periods of time could be the basis for some interesting analyses, resulting in information about the currency of books for children and whether or not United States children are shielded from reality.

B. Read some books such as Myers' *The Dragon Takes a Wife* or Williams' *Petronella*. In what ways could these books be considered modern cautionary tales, offering moralisms for the 1970s?

7. Realism

CRITICAL COMMENT

One style used in writing books of sociological impact is to use selected particulars in order to give the essence of reality. The total book is not developed with realistic events and items; only portions are actualities.

WAYS OF RESPONDING

A. Science fiction and other fantasy writing gains impact when the author uses certain elements of reality in the fiction. Study a book of science fiction and separate the true aspects from the fantasy. Make a judgment on how much reality must occur in order for the fantastic plot to be believable. Greenlaw writes that science fiction might be used as a means for decision-making concerning some of the values affected by technological advances. In your judgment, do you believe science fiction has enough reality for such decisions to be made?

B. Read a book of science fiction. The bibliography in Greenlaw's article lists a number of prolific authors whose works are usually quite good. Prepare some values clarification exercises based on the books, such as a forced choice questionnaire or literally taking a stand on a line designed to show variations in an issue from one extreme point to another.[6] Does the science fiction theme or plot lend itself to extending the discussion to currently relevant decision making issues?

8. Dialectic Methods

CRITICAL COMMENT

Sociological critics often build a case by stating one point and then juxtaposing that with a counter point. The argument proceeds point by point in this fashion.

WAYS OF RESPONDING

A. Select a group of books that are controversial, such as books about blacks: Taylor's *The Cay* or Lipsyte's *The Contender*, or books that deal with women and girls: Hunt's *Up a Road Slowly* or Darrow's *I'm Glad I'm a Boy! I'm Glad I'm a Girl!* Take one side of the controversy and try to build a case using the dialectic method. This would be particularly interesting if one of your colleagues chose the other side of the issue and built a similar case.

B. Study one of the issues discussed by Moynihan by making an in-depth analysis of several children's books dealing with that topic. As an example, Moynihan discusses Burton's *The Little House* as representative of the flight to suburbia and the high esteem given to rural life—the good life. Does this hold true in more recent books? Study the settings of twenty or thirty popular contemporary books. Do the settings reflect current views on choice locations? Use the dialectic method to make your point.

---

6. Some helpful sources for values clarification techniques are: Gene Stanford and Albert E. Roark, *Human Interaction in Education* (Boston: Allyn and Bacon, 1974) and Sidney B. Simon, Leland W. Howe, and Howard Kirschenbaum, *Values Clarification* (New York: Hart Publishing Company, 1972).

FURTHER READING

Berenberg, David P. "Rudyard Kipling: The Man Behind the Mask." *The Modern Monthly* 9, no. 8 (March 1936): 486–89. The critic gives Kipling just praise for his writing but speaks scathingly of his British imperialism beliefs.

Bird, Kathy. "The Value of Individualism." *Elementary English* 50, no. 5 (May 1973): 707–14. A discussion of several books suggests that American children's literature reinforces the value of individualism which is central to American ideology.

Clark, Susan. "Kids' Books." *The Second Wave* (Fall 1973): 36–39. An article in a feminist publication is by a feminist who discusses books with positive images of both males and females, emphasizing books of the early 1970s.

Hamilton, Virginia. "High John Is Risen Again." *The Horn Book* 51, no. 2 (April 1975): 113–21. The Newbery Award winning author describes her goal of writing about the essence of black life in America—the spirit as embodied in the folk hero, "High John de Conquer."

Harada, Violet. "Ginger Root and Ginseng Tea: The World of the Asian Novel." *Top of the News* 31, no. 2 (January 1975): 167–71. Four books, each dealing with a different Asian nation, are discussed for the universal themes.

Hawkins, Robert. "Nursery Rhymes: Mirrors of a Culture." *Elementary English* 48, no. 6 (October 1971): 617–21. A teacher suggests that much can be learned about various countries and times through nursery rhymes which reflect changing cultures.

Heylman, Katherine M. "No Bargain for Frances: Children's Trade Books and Consumer Education." *School Library Journal* 17, no. 2 (October 1971): 77–82. The relevance of fiction and nonfiction trade books for teaching consumerism is discussed by a school librarian.

Jones, Bartlett C. "A New Cache of Liberated Children's Literature—In Some Old Standbys!" *Wilson Library Bulletin* 49, no. 1 (September 1974: 52–56. Feminist criticisms of children's literature are attacked. The author cites numerous instances of positive female images in books that have stood the test of time.

Jones, James P. "Negro Stereotypes in Children's Literature: The Case of Nancy Drew." *Journal of Negro Education* 40 (Spring 1971): 121–25. An analysis of seventeen Nancy Drew books published between 1930–1941 suggests that Negro stereotypes may have been perpetuated through these stories.

Kimmel, Eric A. "Jewish Identity in Juvenile Fiction." *Horn Book* 49, no. 2 (April 1973): 171–79. Three contemporary books about Jews are criticized for their attention to ethnic trivia and their lack of concern for important issues of current American Judaism.

Latimer, Bettye I. "Children's Books and Racism." *The Black Scholar* 4, nos. 8–9 (May-June 1973): 21–27. A black educator describes various "syndromes" which are found in children's books. She asserts that many books fail because they are told from the white perspective.

Monjo, F. N. "Monjo's Manifest Destiny: Authors Can Claim Any Territory in Literature." *School Library Journal* 20, no. 9 (May 1974): 36–37. A children's book editor and author decries the revisionist trends in the writing of historical fiction.

Nilson, Alleen Pace. "Women in Children's Literature." *College English* 32, no. 8 (May 1971), 918–26. A survey of Caldecott Award winning books shows much sexism.

The author offers numerous suggestions for nonsexist books which would present models that show accurately the ways in which women and girls function.

Shutze, Marcia and M. Jean Greenlaw. "A Study of Children's Books with World War II Settings." *Top of the News* 31, no. 2 (January 1975): 199–209. Books written during and after WWII are different in their viewpoints; stronger statements are made in realistic books of the 70's.

Zarookien, Cherie. "Crikey, It's British, or, Can U.S. Kids Really Bear Paddington." *School Library Journal* 21, no. 7 (March 1975): 76–77. A librarian suggests that most British books, outside of fantasy and a few other types, are not understood by American children under ten years old because of the books' "Englishisms."

REFERENCES

Armstrong, William H. *Sounder*. Illus. James Barkley. New York: Harper & Row, 1969.

Bonham, Frank. *Durango Street*. New York: E. P. Dutton, 1965.

Colodi, C. *The Adventures of Pinocchio*. Illus. Attilio Mussino. New York: The Macmillan Company, 1961.

Darrow, Whitney, Jr. *I'm Glad I'm a Boy! I'm Glad I'm a Girl!* Illus. Robert Kraus. New York: Windmill Books, 1970.

DeTreviño, Elizabeth Borton. *I, Juan de Pareja*. New York: Farrar, Straus & Giroux, 1965.

Fleming, Ian. *Chitty Chitty Bang Bang*. Illus. John Burningham. New York: Random House, 1964.

Fox, Paula. *The Slave Dancer*. Illus. Eros Keith. Scarsdale, New York: Bradbury Press, 1973.

Graham, Lorenz. *Whose Town?* New York: T. Y. Crowell, 1969.

Hamilton, Virginia. *The House of Dies Drear*. Illus. Eros Keith. New York: The Macmillan Company, 1968.

Hunt, Irene. *Up a Road Slowly*. Chicago: Follett, 1966.

Hutchins, Pat. *Rosie's Walk*. New York: The Macmillan Company, 1968.

Ish-Kisher, S. *A Boy of Old Prague*. Illus. Ben Shahn. New York: Pantheon Books, 1963.

Keats, Ezra Jack. *A Letter to Amy*. New York: Harper & Row, 1968.

Lipsyte, Robert. *The Contender*. New York: Harper & Row, 1967.

Mathis, Sharon Bell. *Sidewalk Story*. New York: Viking Press, 1971.

Myers, Walter Dean. *The Dragon Takes a Wife*. Illus, Ann Grifalconi. Indianapolis: Bobbs-Merrill, 1972.

Taylor, Theodore. *The Cay*. Garden City, New York: Doubleday 1969.

Travers, P. L. *Mary Poppins*. Illus. Mary Shepard. New York: Harcourt, Brace, Jovanovich, 1934, 1962.

Udry, Janice May. *A Tree Is Nice*. Illus. Marc Simont. New York: Harper & Row, 1956.

Williams, Jay. *Petronella*. Illus. Friso Henstra. New York: Parents' Magazine Press, 1973.

chapter three

Archetypal Criticism

Archetypal criticism views the literary work from the standpoint of its theme. The themes or motifs studied have symbols that recur in all great literature over time and space. Myth criticism, a term sometimes used interchangeably with archetypal criticism, concerns myths that contain universal symbols of a person's most fundamental relationships with themselves, other people, and the universe, encompassing past, present, and future time. Certain themes in myths also have universal symbolism; these are called archetypes. Twentieth century archetypal criticism grew out of the increased development of the fields of anthropology, sociology, psychology, and religion. Many of the archetypes noted in this chapter, such as the divine child, rebirth from death to life and the quest, can be attributed to Jung and his followers.

Pros and Cons of Archetypal Criticism

Archetypal criticism, like the other forms of criticism, is embraced by some critics and rejected by others. One of its most significant values is the historical closeness it offers all humankind through its striving to relate the fundamental modes of thought from primitive cultures to the same basic beliefs held by modern persons. A second value of archetypal criticism is its necessity for a close relationship and drawing on other social sciences—anthropology, history, psychology, sociology, and religion.

The same aspect that was noted as a value in the preceding paragraph has also received negative criticism. Some scholars believe that the intermingling of so many types of criticism creates a hodgepodge and does not enable the critic to make verifiable statements of fact. Like psychological criticism, there is a tendency for some critics to go too far in seeking archetypes and symbols. There is also the tendency to consolidate all the themes of great literature to the point that only a few archetypes remain, thus reducing all of literature to a few basic myths.

Archetypal Criticism of Children's Literature

Essays concerning archetypes found within children's literature have often been written to make the point that children's literature is a part of the whole of world literature. When the motifs apparent in stories for children—such as the journey, the Earth Mother, and the three wishes—are related to adult literature and to timeless mythical tales, the argument of relatedness seems very logical. All of the essays collected here refer to certain motifs of the work under criticism that relate to the age-old myths. Each of the articles offers examples of varying elements pertinent to the methodology of archetypal criticism.

O'Dell refers to the importance of the classics in carrying important motifs that are meaningful throughout time to each new person who reads them. He describes how he was inspired by several readings of *Moby Dick* to write a story about one of its symbols, *The Dark Canoe*.

Carr explains the careful analysis of a character's actions, using Taran, the hero of Alexander's five-volume Chronicles of Prydain. She compares the motifs used in Taran's tale with the motifs characteristic of a hero detailed by an earlier literary critic.

Helson analyzes several books of fantasy, classifying them by types. Within each type she notes various archetypes such as the journey, a wizard, the divine child, the wise mother, and death. Her study is based on one particular aspect of Jung's psychological theory, the portion of the theory concerning the self and the changes it undergoes with maturity, especially the encounters which the self has with certain archetypes.

Religious rituals and symbols are the focus of Brady's essay. He relates the motifs of Lewis' Narnia tales to the themes inherent in Christianity.

Bruner's detailed discussion of *The Legend of Sleepy Hollow* shows the story as a parody of ancient Greek myths. Her discussion of the influence of the times and the environment on Washington Irving offers reasons why he might have chosen to write in this style.

Terry's comprehensive discussion of quest tales discusses the values inherent in the literature and suggests that children can have vicarious experiences and put themselves in difficult decision-making situations via literature. She gives examples of quest themes in several books.

READINGS

Acceptance Speech: Hans Christian Andersen Award

Scott O'Dell

Some years ago I wrote a story called *The Dark Canoe* (Houghton). These three provocative words, as you remember, were spoken by Captain Ahab on board the whaler *Pequod* as he pursued through Pacific seas the monstrous White Whale, his implacable enemy, Moby Dick.

The words *Dark Canoe*, as you will also recall, refer to the coffin which was built by the ship's carpenter for Queequeg, who felt that the time had come for him to die. The coffin was built from ship's lumber and placed on deck; and Queequeg stepped into it, made himself comfortable, and waited to die. After a few days, Queequeg, who was somewhat notional (as befits the son of a South Sea princess), decided that he did not wish to die. Whereupon he stepped out of the coffin and returned, smiling, to life.

The coffin, the dark canoe, was put away out of sight and forgotten. Until one day, as the *Pequod* closed in upon the White Whale, Queequeg remembered.

The dark canoe was dragged out on deck again, and the carpenter set to work to fashion it into a life buoy. He had already made a handsome ivory leg for Captain Ahab, and so he was able to make a handsome life buoy out of Queequeg's coffin. He caulked it with pitch, hung it round with thirty separate lines ending in Turk's-head knots, and tenderly fastened it to the *Pequod's* stern.

When at last the battle was joined and the *Pequod* sank and all the crew save one were drowned, then out of the spinning vortex of black waters the buoy shot from the sea and floated to Ishmael's side. Clinging to it, he was saved from death—saved to tell the story of Captain Ahab and the White Whale.

I liked Melville's *Moby Dick* when I first read it as a boy, for its story of a strange captain and crew and their adventurous fate. I liked it when I read it again as a young man, for the same reasons and for others as well—for one thing, the glimpse it gave me into the depths of the human heart. And later, reading it in maturity, these two readings of *Moby Dick* came to mind, but for

Reprinted from *The Horn Book Magazine* 48, no. 5 (October 1972): 441–43.

the first time I began to see Melville's masterpiece for what it is—a fleshed-out symbol, a myth. It is a myth in the tradition of Pygmalion and Galatea, of stone-burdened Sisyphus, of Tantalus, of the ill-starred lovers Orpheus and Eurydice, in which man's feelings of terror at the mysteries of life—its lurking demonisms and its delights, man's most fervent hopes and secret desires—are given substance.

Having read and thought about *Moby Dick* over many years, aware by returning to it from time to time with refreshed interest and new insights, which to me is the hallmark of a book's greatness, I was moved to write a story about Ahab's dark canoe.

I was convinced, thinking of the story I wished to write, of the canoe's immortality. It lived in my mind. It therefore must live in the minds of others. And living, having floated Ishmael to safety, not yet finished with its appointed mission, where was it now? On what shores or ocean seas would I find it?

I imagined it floating into Magdalena Bay in Baja California, still bearing the marks of the thirty life lines ending in thirty Turk's-head knots, put there by Ahab's carpenter.

The plot of my story is conventional, but suspenseful enough, I hope, to hold a child's attention, to hold it long enough for the young reader to see and above all to feel what the story attempts to say.

What I wished to say was both simple and many-leveled. It was this: The stories which have been written by great writers possess lives of their own. They live through the years and through the centuries. They are as substantial as mountains, more lasting than habitations. We know the odes of Sappho, for instance, but under what dust heap lies the place of her birth?

Hans Christian Andersen was a great writer. He filled a ship—ark is perhaps a better word, because it has a more youthful sound—with a cargo richer than all the wealth of the Indies. His ark has sailed around the world many times and will continue to sail. It is an honor that I deeply cherish and will always cherish—to be, for one voyage at least, a member of his phantom crew.

Classic Hero in a New Mythology

Marion Carr

Taran, Assistant Pig-Keeper hero of the Chronicles of Prydain,[1] at the outset merely dreams of heroic glory; but he is also, like all heroes, an opportunist. He knows precisely what kind of hero he wishes to be: one of noble birth and unquestioned valor; a comrade of kings and great knights; and one worthy of the love of a princess. Heroic glory seems a long way off, but by seizing every opportunity to perform valiantly, Taran begins to assume the proportions of the classic hero of Western literature.

Through the first three volumes of the story, Taran develops in keeping with the classic tradition. Then, in *Taran Wanderer,* he confronts his own myth; and by the end of *The High King* the form of the hero has undergone a change, one which has been brought about by the fact that Taran is not, in the later volumes, operating within the classic mythology. He cannot, therefore, perform in the classic manner.

Of the many attempts to codify the characteristics of the traditional hero, one of the most scholarly was that made by Jan de Vries in 1959. About the hero in general he said[2]:

> In considering the history of various heroes we are struck by the appearance of the same or at least similar motifs. A dragon-fight as well as the liberation of a maiden seem almost obligatory for a hero. A hero's youth is usually passed in secrecy and humiliation: he is hunted and so has to remain in hiding. His birth is not like that of an ordinary mortal, there is often difficulty in having it legitimatized.

One familiar with the Chronicles of Prydain recognizes several of its motifs within de Vries' paragraph. De Vries emphasized that not every hero exemplifies each of his ten motifs,[3] and yet Taran—a character of fiction rather than of folk myth—operates within eight of them:

Reprinted from *The Horn Book Magazine* 47, no. 5 (October 1971): 508–13.

I. *The begetting of the hero.* It is in his wishes rather than in discovered fact that Taran resembles a classic hero within this myth. Nevertheless his hopes and fears until late in the Chronicles are centered on his genealogy. He desperately hopes to learn that he is the offspring of nobility.

II. *The birth of a hero.* The only living person, a swaddled baby hidden among the trees in a forest by one unknown and unknowable, found in the vicinity of a corpse-strewn battlefield, Taran is born—figuratively speaking—from the corpse of his society.

III. *The youth of the hero is threatened.* The exposed child is discovered by Dallben, who hopes that the boy will be the fulfillment of an ancient prophecy. There are many similar tales of abandoned hero-children discovered by shepherds, taken in, and reared by them. Taran is reared by Coll, formerly a warrior, presently keeper of the magical pig Hen Wen for Dallben.

IV. *The way in which the hero is brought up.* (He early reveals unusual characteristics). Taran very early reveals courage and resourcefulness beyond the expectations of his station in life.

V. *The hero often acquires invulnerability.* Taran does not operate within this motif.

VI. *One of the most common heroic deeds is the fight with a dragon or another monster.* Taran encounters both gwythaints and the Cauldron-Born, monsters of marvelous invention.

VII. *The hero wins a maiden, usually after overcoming great dangers.* Surely one of the most remarkably satisfying declarations of love in all literature for children (and perhaps in an even broader range) is Eilonwy's decision: "If enchantments are what separates us, then I should be well rid of them."[4]

VIII. *The hero makes an expedition to the underworld.* The storming of Annuvin is in the classic mold, although often the hero made the journey for information only.

IX. *When the hero is banished in his youth he returns later and is victorious over his enemies.* Taran is not involved with this motif.

X. *The death of the hero.* This is the most fascinating of all of Taran's relationships to the classic motifs; for Taran does not die but the hero does. Presented with the opportunity to join the immortals (after all, that is what heroism is all about), Taran rejects it to assume the responsibilities of mortal life and human promises.

> "Once, I hoped for a glorious destiny," Taran went on, smiling at his own memory. "That dream has vanished with my childhood; and though a pleasant dream it was fit only for a child. I am well-content as an Assistant Pig-Keeper."[5]

Not a speech for a classic hero, nor a fitting choice for one. The classic death of a hero promised immortal glory in exchange for his fatal support of an aristocratic established order. Saving kings, princesses, and even Christendom itself at the cost of his life has been the role of the traditional hero; and the reward, of which he was usually cognizant, was to be the perpetuation of his name in song and story.

And Taran, what will he do? He proposes to build a seawall—as he had promised to the King of Mona—and to rebuild what has been destroyed in the battles: civilian work.

Has Lloyd Alexander then denigrated Taran? Certainly no heroic poet of the twelfth century would have turned his hero in the end to such plebeian tasks; but the poet of those times was placing his hero in the context of his own mythology. Scholars generally agree that the age of the epic hero ended sometime around the end of the thirteenth century. Since then the high hero has been in a predicament, showing up as a shadow in such tales as those of pirate-heroes, cowboys, or such mock heroes as Pecos Bill and Mike Fink. The high hero passed out of serious literature because his myth was dead.

Yet, Mr. Alexander has revived him successfully. As in all really good fantasy, the reader believes, believes in Taran and his friends, believes their cause is right, their hearts pure. He hopes that what Taran so desperately wants and so valiantly strives for will come to him. He knows it is fantasy and he wants it to come true. Then suddenly, or so it seems at first, the author catches him up by the heels: Taran may be baseborn.

With the introduction of Craddoc in *Taran Wanderer*, Mr. Alexander skillfully shifts Taran from tenth- to twentieth-century mythology. There had been earlier hints about life's permanent values, but Taran himself had been creating his own image as high hero in a like-minded age. He then officiates at his own rebirth, which is painful—as births necessarily seem to be. Having spent a lonely, despondent, and despairing winter thinking that he is Craddoc's son, and still tied to his dreams and never-to-be-forgotten hopes, Taran confronts his own myth when Gurgi brings word that Craddoc has fallen into what seems to be an unreachable gorge.

> "Even if we could make our way to him, how should we bear him up? And if we fail—not one life lost but three."
> His hands were shaking. It was not despair that filled him, but terror, black terror at the thoughts whispering in his mind. Was there the slimmest hope of saving the stricken herdsman? If not, even Prince Gwydion would not reproach Taran's decision. Nor would any man. Instead, they would grieve with him at his loss. Free of his burden, free of the valley, the door of his cage opened wide, and all his life awaited him; Eilonwy, Caer Dallben. He seemed to hear his own voice speak these words, and he listened in shame and horror.
> Then, as if his heart would burst with it, he cried out in terrible rage, "What man am I?"[6]

The transfer to the new mythology is complete with Taran's acceptance of manhood. The rest of the Chronicles is consistent with his discovery of himself. Although Lloyd Alexander holds out at the end of *The High King* a choice for Taran—to be a traditional hero and immortal or to accept a mortal life—the radical decision had already been made in *Taran Wanderer*. In many ways, this is the most remarkable of the volumes, disclosing how various and fascinating human life is, and how much too much there is for any one man to master. No one man can be all; he can only appreciate and at times approximate the possibilities of being. Life is fragile, beautiful, and irreplaceable.

The Chronicles of Prydain has not suffered from lack of praise. It has been called "the finest work of fantasy for children ever produced by an American author."[7] and "the strongest high fantasy written for children in our times."[8]

While it is true that the volumes may be read separately, the Chronicles of Prydain is thematically an entity. Separate reading will not convey the dramatic tension inherent to the series, and The High King, for instance, is essentially meaningless read alone. The dramatic movement of the total Chronicles involves not only the coming of age of Taran, but of his and his readers' coming to terms with true glory. This can be done only slowly.

What has been gained? The idealism, color, and tremendous challenge of the old heroism has been retained. The selfless, endless struggle against evil forces so ingenious as to demand recognition of an immortal evil (Arawn), the clash of arms, the high drama of supernatural creatures, grand titles, and the accouterments of court life; and on Taran's personal level, the flattering acceptance of the foundling boy by the greatest and best knights of the land—these have been carried over from the heroic literature of times past. What is lost is well gone: the credo of death in order to save an established order.

A further gain is the recognition of the richness, color, and excitement of the reader's own world: the depth and variety of human love (Adaon); the goodness inherent in human beings (Llonio); the glory of human handiwork (Hevydd, Dwyvach, Annlaw) and of human political skill (the Free Commots); but, above all, the soul-satisfying glory of man's acceptance of responsibility. With Craddoc helpless in the gorge, Taran chose once and for all to be a man. The hero and his myth were laid aside; responsibility (as the Little Prince was responsible for his rose) became Taran's hallmark.

Taran's leap into the gorge to save Craddoc carried him into our myth. Because we live in it, we cannot name it. Names for myths are very like tombstones, coming as they do only after death. We do recognize, however, that Taran's decision is the one which we all ought to make. In our best moments, we see what our work is: being responsible for his earth and the men and women upon it—building their seawalls for them when they no longer can. Our ideal is our myth. We do not always live up to it; but Lloyd Alexander has reminded us how much we treasure it. By utilizing a countermyth, he has shown us our own.

It may well be that Lloyd Alexander's greatest contribution in these stories is the revelation of a device for saving the best of two worlds for the freshened delight of children in his new world of high deeds and good men.

NOTES

1. The Chronicles of Prydain are composed of *The Book of Three, The Black Cauldron, The Castle of Llyr, Taran Wanderer,* and *The High King* (all originally published by Holt, Rinehart and Winston).

2. Jan deVries, *Heroic Song and Heroic Legend* (London: Oxford University Press, 1963), p. 210. Originally published in Holland by Uitgeverij Het Spectrum N.V., Utrecht/Antwerpen, 1959.

3. Ibid., pp. 211–16.

4. Lloyd Alexander, *The High King* (New York: Holt, Rinehart, and Winston, 1968), p. 283.

5. Ibid., pp. 274–75.

6. Lloyd Alexander, *Taran Wanderer* (New York: Holt, Rinehart and Winston, 1967), p. 181.

7. Helen W. Painter, "*The Marvelous Misadventures of Sebastian*—A Review," *Elementary English* 47 (December 1970): 1158.

8. Lillian N. Gerhardt, "*The High King*—A Review," *School Library Journal* (February 15, 1968): 876.

Fantasy and Self-Discovery

Ravenna Helson

Many people of all ages enjoy fantasy, and certainly it occupies a central position in children's literature. One sometimes feels, however, that comments about fantasy—that it is like poetry, that it expresses our primitive fears and awe of nature, gratifies our wishes, sounds the deeper meanings, enhances spiritual development, enables the author to engage in "subcreation"—seldom are sufficiently articulated to give more than a hint why fantasy is not only enjoyable but important.

I would like to present a special but comprehensive point of view about the significance of fantasy written for children. My ideas derive from Jungian writings, especially those of Erich Neumann, John Perry, Esther Harding, and—of course—from those of Jung himself. I have also been interested in what writers such as C. S. Lewis, J. R. R. Tolkien, Philippa Pearce, L. M. Boston, and Lloyd Alexander have had to say about fantasy, as well as in critical treatments of the subject by Paul Hazard, Annis Duff, Lillian Smith, and Margery Fisher. And I am deeply indebted to Mae Durham for her generous aid in launching a study of fantasy which will eventually be used to give body to my argument.

In Jungian personality theory, the important developments of the first part of life are that the individual becomes separated from his original state of unity with the mother and that the ego is strengthened against what becomes, after separation, the "unconscious." The individual develops the "ego-qualities" of independence, foresight, and endurance; he learns skills of various kinds and becomes able to take a useful role in society. So our toddlers become juveniles who form gangs or secret clubs, who learn to throw and catch and outdo one another, who then leave home, take the premed or liberal arts curriculum, and eventually perform surgery or take care of a household. The young adult dreams of what he will achieve next year, or of what he will do for his children.

In the second half of life, says Jung, this trend is reversed. The strong and socially directed ego turns inward to seek a new rapprochement with the un-

Reprinted from *The Horn Book Magazine* 46, no. 2 (April 1970): 121–34.

conscious. The middle-aged person begins to feel disenchanted with his social roles. He—or she—feels limited by them and tires of the effort to win the admiration of others, to take care of others—always to be doing as others expect him to do. If circumstances and his own standards permit (in many cases one or both do not), he considers himself. With the redistribution of energies that accompanies this shift in attention, there may be a weakening of defenses, perhaps a breakthrough from the unconscious. Anxiety may be so great that the process stops. However, if it continues, an awareness of the "self" begins to develop.

The term "self" is used by Jung to mean the ego and those parts of the unconscious to which it is related. The first stage in the new awareness of self may involve a reworking of childhood conflicts. Increasingly there are encounters with what Jung calls the archetypes of the collective unconscious—the Shadow, the Wise Old Man, the Earth Mother, and others. The process of becoming aware of these "personages," of working out a new integration of ego and unconscious, is called individuation.[1]

Whether such a process as this commonly takes place in the second half of life has apparently not aroused the curiosity of many psychologists, perhaps because of our unquestioned conviction that youth and adjustment to outer reality is best, perhaps because Jung's formulations have been regarded as too complex and mystical to test. However, findings from some of the studies of maturity and old age are quite consistent with these ideas, and Jungian analysts have reported much evidence from case histories of their patients.

Frank Eyre, in *Twentieth Century Children's Books*, remarks that when scholars or writers for adults have set aside their customary work to write something for children, what they write usually takes the form of fantasy. In fantasy, of course, can best be expressed the strange creatures and unfamiliar laws of the unconscious. I believe we may credit these works of middle age to the "individuation" process. It is necessary to add, however, that individuation may take place before middle age in individuals who have suffered an emotional crisis or who are particularly sensitive to the voice of the unconscious. Creative persons are among those who resent and resist the unhappy consequences of the alienation of ego from unconscious: As the child matures, colors fade, elves disappear; one can no longer talk with animals. Since creative individuals are particularly successful at working out patterns of communication with the unconscious, a bookshelf filled with their works of fantasy may be regarded as a gallery of "self" portraits, in which we may recognize poses and expressions relevant to our own increased awareness of the self.

From a good fantasy then, the child may receive context and expression for his feelings and emotional experiences, while the adult may rework his childhood, become more aware of archetypal relationships, and develop a new, less "ego-centered" self.

In a study being conducted at the Institute of Personality Assessment and Research at the University of California at Berkeley, a sample of seventy-two fantasies written since 1930 for children in the 8-12 age range were submitted to a panel of judges for evaluation.[2] I would like to describe several types of fantasy which we have identified among the books considered by the judges to be excellent. Since fantasies by men differ from those by women, we shall discuss the types separately for each sex. Within each sex, what differentiates the types is, as we interpret it, the nature of the relationship between ego and unconscious.

The first type of fantasy written by men is represented in our sample by six books: *The Twenty-One Balloons*, *Half Magic*, *The Phantom Tollbooth*, *Higglety Pigglety Pop!*, *Many Moons*, and *Time at the Top*. All have to do with wish fulfillment, with wonderful discoveries or strokes of luck which bring riches, success, good things to eat, excitement, adventure, or the heart's desire. To describe the style of these books, the raters in our study used adjectives such as charming, clever, interesting, fluent, humorous, ingenious, original, and rational. There is in the Type I fantasies a characteristic combination: the author's virtuosity and his creation of a central character—often female—whose wishes are gratified by magic or by luck or by means of a gesture of effort or of virtue.

In our view, such a story describes a state—oedipal, some would call it—in which the ego is separate from the unconscious but not independent. Youthful charm and prowess are used to woo the unconscious, not to master it. The humor and cleverness of these books may derive from characteristic underlying conflicts. The young ego feels drawn toward the unconscious but is also afraid of being overpowered by it. On the one hand, there is a yearning for pleasure, passivity, affection, good things to eat, but on the other a desire for attention, admiration, and honorable status. Sexual identity fluctuates. There may be a fear of, or distaste for, the aggressiveness, pomposity, or other features of the mature masculine role, or resentment over the discipline and restrictions which the father imposes. The story usually expresses aspects of these conflicts and suggests a real or fantasy resolution. For example, in *The Twenty-One Balloons*, the ambivalence toward the unconscious is symbolized by the volcano surrounded by diamond mines on the island of Krakatoa. The precarious relationship between conscious and unconscious is expressed in the elaboration of inventions and foresightful devices to insure a pleasant life on the island and to afford escape if the earth should begin to tremble. In the situation which frames the book, the central character, recuperating from his adventure, attains what are usually incompatible desires: An eager audience listens to his story as he lies in bed on the speaker's platform!

In *Half Magic*, the confrontation with Sir Launcelot during the trip back in time (referring, perhaps, to childhood) is probably the most memorable event. Launcelot is portrayed in an unusual way. He represents unpleasant, resistant masculine dignity, which it seems must nonetheless be tolerated, because to topple him off his horse produces an awkward social situation. It is surely a proper use of fantasy to express such impulses and see how they work out. There is also in *Half Magic* a sympathetic adult male character who gains the confidence and affection of the children, and, with the help of the magic coin, marries their mother.

The relevance of the Type I fantasies for the child is clear, and most adult males will rework these common conflicts in the course of individuation. Furthermore, the hedonistic relation of ego to unconscious is one of the final forms of integration. It can, of course, be carried out at a mature level. We are all indebted to the authors of this type of fantasy for the delights that they have given us.

Books which best represent the second type of fantasy are *The Hobbit, The Lion, the Witch and the Wardrobe, Elidor, The Book of Three,* and *The Mouse and His Child.* While all emphasize aggression, achievement, and order, at the same time they also emphasize humility and a sense of wonder and awe. Typically, the story involves the journey (development) of the ego, as portrayed by the central character or group of characters. They are allied with companions in an attempt to help a wizard or prince to regain a territory which has fallen to evil and demonic powers. The central characters learn courage, fortitude, and resourcefulness. In the end the enemy is overcome, and a treasure is won or a kingdom united, or a desolate land becomes green again.

The ego, we infer, aspires in this case to be independent and the dominant influence in the personality. It regards itself as different from and superior to the instinctive or passive. This attitude seems to constellate "enemies" in the unconscious, and thus is generated the battle between good and evil which is a characteristic feature of these books. The small ego is strengthened in its struggle by the band of friends who are united in loyalty to the archetypal figures of masculine spirit and courage. The purpose and strategy of the struggle is to master the undesirable aspects of personality and then to reclaim the riches which have been cut off since early childhood. So the boy grows to manhood and the treasure is the maiden whom he makes his wife; and it is also—especially during individuation—his own freer access to emotion, pleasure, and beauty, and to the vitality which comes from the lessening of divisions and suppression in his personality.

Each of the books of this type offers its own complex and particular elaboration of what we may call the heroic or patriarchal fantasy. In Tolkien's book, fifty-year-old Bilbo sets out on an individuation journey. Lewis's book is concerned with philosophical and religious questions; Alexander's with youthful personality development; and Garner's with dynamic interplay between conscious and unconscious in personality change. On another level, the symbolization of evil—to take one example—suggests different emphases. The dragon in *The Hobbit,* who guards a treasure under a mountain, is an old symbol for the negative side of the unconscious which, if overcome, releases its riches. The White Witch in Lewis's book lays emphasis on the barren state of separation from the maternal matrix, and at the same time suggests the threat to the young ego of the temptation to remain under the mother's influence. The evil powers in *Elidor* are projections of what is in one's own imagination. In the real world of the children they appear first as shadows, and of course the Shadow is the name Jung gave to the evil side of ourselves, which we find unacceptable and shut out of consciousness.

It may have been observed that the authors of Type II fantasies make considerable use of myth and legend. That this wealth of legend exists, of course, attests to the age and importance of the patriarchal pattern of personality integration in western civilization. However, the story may be told with other materials, as *The Mouse and His Child* illustrates.

If the first main type of fantasy was comic and the second type heroic (it is worth noting that the Aristotelian categories seem quite apt), then the third type is tender. Here some books from our sample are *Charlotte's Web, The Little*

Prince, The Animal Family, Tistou of the Green Thumbs, and *The Grass Rope.*
These fantasies emphasize tender feeling more than plot; they help us "realize"
how to give love or beauty or faith, how to accept and appreciate the patterns
and mysteries of life and death. We infer that the ego has achieved considerable
maturity but that it defines itself not in opposition to the unconscious but as a
loyal son or ally. The most characteristic "hero" of these books is the child—
sometimes the divine child. When there is an antagonist, it is social insensitivity
or hypertrophied ego activity, such as compulsive achieving, planning, or order-
ing, or unyielding rationality.

It is fitting that a Type III book—*Charlotte's Web*—should give us our most
direct and eloquent treatment of the archetype of the good and wise Mother, but
it is true that most contemporary "tender" fantasies do not have prominent
mother figures. Natural settings recur, however, and the ideal relationship of the
individual to nature has the quality of the primal mother-child relationship.
Perhaps as children the authors of the Type III books had cause to know the
value of tenderness, learned discipline and fighting with misgivings, and in the
course of individuation returned to, or came to, a philosophy different from both
the hedonistic and the patriarchal. The treasure, these books tell us, is not
guarded by any dragon but by our own ego turned against nature with contempt
and suppression. The ego has its place—to keep the Baobabs from one's planet
(*The Little Prince*), to heighten one's awareness and appreciation of life (*The
Animal Family*). But essentially the treasure is all around us, and we receive it
when we are "childlike"—open, spontaneous, loving, and obedient to our natures. Even death, which is a theme in all of these books, has its place and its
transfiguration.

Here then are three philosophies, all of them very old. I am suggesting that
they are related both to developmental stages in childhood and to relationships
between ego and unconscious—to visions of selfhood—in mature individuals.

None of us is all male or all female, and the developing or assertive ego tends
to have a masculine character whatever its housing. For these reasons and because women are well-versed in masculine values, most women can respond to
the various types of fantasy written by men. And yet, for whatever reasons, the
best fantasies by women do not fit the categories which have been described.

Certainly, there are fantasies by women which emphasize the independence,
courage, and resourcefulness of the ego—*The Gammage Cup, The Pushcart
War, The Borrowers, Pippi Longstocking.* But how different they are from the
heroic fantasies by men! They utilize no traditional legend material. They are
humorous, modest, sometimes downright diminutive. No Gandalf or Aslan
leads them, and there is no promise of treasure or kingship—only of one's own
small place in a community or one's own sphere of self-expression. The violence
in these books is mostly good fun, not to be taken seriously. The real enemy
comes not from the unconscious—not even in *The Gammage Cup*—but from
cultural restrictions in the way of individual expression or power used by the
big against the small. These themes appeal to the child who is being forced to
conform to the social ways of adults or beginning to develop independence. For
the woman undergoing individuation, the theme is her own struggle for self-
expression against the entrenched power and values of the patriarchal system.

The modest character of these books may reflect the inferiority feelings of women when they try to assert themselves along male lines and against convention, and the humor may be associated with sex-role conflict, just as it was in the Type I fantasies written by men. One may speculate that the girl or woman who is expressing her independence and resoluteness (ego-qualities, developed characteristically by separation from the unconscious) against the masculine and against society, is receiving little aid from any quarter. If she is to become a real individual, she must probably go into this stage of development, but in it she has a small space in which to operate and must be ingenious in her maneuvering. Pippi Longstocking inherits aggressive vigor from the author's resourcefulness in finding her a widowed "cannibal king" for a father. The pushcart peddlers band together and combine their talents. Nowhere is more clearly expressed the ingenious maneuvering of many small individual elements than in another book of this category, *The Return of the Twelves.*

A second group of fantasies by women also has characters (predominantly dolls or cats) who are independent, courageous, and resourceful, but there is an additional significant feature: the "transformation." In *The Cat Who Went to Heaven* and *The Dolls' House,* an act of sacrifice of egoistic interest in favor of feeling brings about a miraculous conclusion to the story. In *The Blue Cat of Castle Town* the transformation is more gradual, and its parts are perhaps more clearly laid out. The turning point is the fearful encounter between the blue cat and the villain. The blue cat almost dies, but unknowingly the villain has snatched out the blue cat's "three ordinary hairs" and afterward the blue cat shows the humility, unselfishness, and devotion which effect, or perhaps are themselves, the transformation. *Miss Hickory* was rated somewhat lower than the other books that have been mentioned, but here again is an instructive transformation. The apple-twig doll has learned to make her own way but also to accept help from males. She has become aware of how she limits herself by her "hardheadedness." When she gets her hickory-nut head bitten off by a hungry squirrel, she miraculously does not die, but finds a way to graft herself to an unproductive apple tree, and they both blossom.

These fantasies seem to be concerned with the right relationship between the ego and the life of feeling or aspects of the unconscious. They tell us that this right relationship is found in a dramatic, miraculous experience which follows the sacrifice or near-death of the ego. What is there, we may ask, in the experience of the girl and the woman which might help us to understand why there is a cluster of stories with this theme?

For the girl, the early experience of the archetypal father has the quality of an overwhelming of the ego simultaneously from above and below, a psychic event so threatening to her young ego that it is often repressed, or dimly symbolized as an encounter with a terrifying serpent or beast. (Fairy tales tell us that the beast may later be transformed into a prince, but this theme is not represented in our sample.) At any rate, the mature woman may undergo the archetypal encounter again in the course of individuation. Several Jungian analysts have described the phenomenon. If the "death" of the ego is suffered, the personality emerges with new vitality and, as this group of fantasies testifies, a new sense of being established in the lap of God, or of fitting into one's fruitful place.

The remaining high-rated fantasies in our sample by women authors may be assigned to a third type of fantasy, one which lays its stress on the exploration of inner life. In the relative prominence of setting and character over plot and intellectual analysis, these books are indistinguishable from Type III books by men. We infer that the ego is receptive to, and allied with, the unconscious, much as it is in the Type III fantasy by men, but that attention is directed inward, rather than outward, and that the prevailing mood is a sense of mystery and awe. Even the titles of many of these books suggest this mood—*The Children of Green Knowe, Tom's Midnight Garden, Fog Magic, An Edge of the Forest.* There is seldom a structured unreal world, but past is brought into present, senses are enhanced, or there are other "unrealities" which indicate that the laws of everyday life do not apply.

The Type II books by men were called patriarchal, and we observed the frequency of the figure of the wizard, prince or king. The Type III books by women may well be called matriarchal. The figure of a magical woman or grandmother appears in every one of them. To the child, the Type III fantasy offers access to these matriarchal archetypes; to the woman-author, it helps to bring a realization of the matriarchal self. If the goal of the patriarchal hero is to inherit the kingship, to become the father of himself, the goal of the matriarchal heroine is perhaps to feel the full presence of herself. Toward this goal the author of *Tom's Midnight Garden* brings the "tom"-boy aspect of herself into communication with the little girl, the young lady, and especially and finally, the grandmother. Perhaps one finds the complete or attained matriarchal self best expressed in Mrs. Oldknow's unobtrusive but central position in her ancient and richly mysterious Green Knowe, or in Mary Poppins—her vocation, her circle of wondrous friends, her tartness, vanity, and umbrella.

To me as a psychologist, one of the intriguing parts of our study has been the development of objective measures for the description of fantasy. We want to show objectively that these types exist and how they differ from one another. Those in the field of children's literature, however, can judge for themselves whether these categories set up on the basis of Jungian theory seem interesting, and whether most creative fantasies fit naturally into them. I do not mean, of course, that a book should be reduced to what it has in common with others in the category, but that its association with the others should clarify and enhance some of its important themes and symbols; and further that the set of categories as a whole should present us with an array of significant themes.

Perhaps to those with a technical interest in literature it is useful to classify fantasies according to "devices"—whether there are talking animals, changes in size or time, or other worlds. Certainly there are relationships between the nature of unreality in the story and what from a psychological point of view are more fundamental features of theme and style. The classification presented here is imperfect and there are important subjects which have gone unmentioned, but most creative fantasies do seem to yield wisdom—for adult and for child—when regarded as chronicles of the development of the "self."

TYPE CLASSIFICATION OF FANTASIES

FANTASIES BY MEN

Type I: Wish-Fulfillment and Humor

The Twenty-One Balloons by William Pène du Bois (Viking)

Half Magic by Edward Eager (Harcourt)

The Phantom Tollbooth by N. Juster (Random)

Time at the Top by Edward Ormondroyd (Parnassus)

Higglety Pigglety Pop! by Maurice Sendak (Harper)

Many Moons by James Thurber (Harcourt)

Type II: Heroism

The Book of Three by Lloyd Alexander (Holt)

Elidor by Alan Garner (Walck)

The Mouse and His Child by Russell Hoban (Harper)

The Lion, the Witch and the Wardrobe by C. S. Lewis (Macmillan)

The Hobbit by J. R. R. Tolkien (Houghton)

The Sword and the Stone by T. H. White (Putnam)

Type III: Tender Feeling

Tistou of the Green Thumbs by Maurice Druon (Scribner)

The Animal Family by Randall Jarrell (Phantheon)

The Grass Rope by William Mayne (Dutton)

The Little Prince by Antoine de St. Exupéry (Harcourt)

Charlotte's Web by E. B. White (Harper)

FANTASIES BY WOMEN

Type I: Independence and Self-Expression

The Return of the Twelves by Pauline Clarke (Coward)

The Gammage Cup by Carol Kendall (Harcourt)

Pippi Longstocking by Astrid Lindgren (Viking)

The Puschart War by Jean Merrill (William Scott)

The Borrowers by Mary Norton (Harcourt)

Type II: Transformation

The Cat Who Went to Heaven by Elizabeth Coatsworth (Macmillan)

The Blue Cat of Castle Town by Catherine Cate Coblentz (Longmans)

The Dolls' House by Rumer Godden (Viking)

Type III: Inner Mystery and Awe

The Children of Green Knowe by L. M. Boston (Harcourt)

Martin Pippin in the Daisy Field by Eleanor Farjeon (Lippincott)

The Magic Stone by Penelope Farmer (Harcourt)

Tom's Midnight Garden by Philippa Pearce (Lippincott)

Fog Magic by Julia Sauer (Viking)

An Edge of the Forest by Agnes Smith (Viking)

Mary Poppins by P. L. Travers (Harcourt)

NOTES

1. Individuation—the process of becoming an individual, an entity.
2. I would like to acknowledge my gratitude to Jerome Cushman, Barbara Dillon, Mae Durham, Quail Hawkins, Carolyn Horovitz, Helen C. Kidder, Winfred Ragsdale, and Robert Shogren, who served as judges, and to Laurel Robinson and Susan Stanton, who served as raters. The study is supported by the National Institute of Mental Health, and will be reported in detail elsewhere.

Finding God in Narnia

Charles A. Brady

> "In the juvescence of the year
> Came Christ the tiger."
> —T. S. ELIOT

The year was 1920 and the tiger was in *Gerontion*, a poem about an old man which marked a revolution in literary sensibility in its day. Now, thirty-six years later, marking another milestone along the road of literary sensibility—for children this time, though the older reader will be very foolish to overlook a masterpiece, however miniature—comes Aslan the Lion. He owes something to Eliot's tiger and something to Blake's, something, even, to Spenser's great dame, Nature, whose face "did like a Lion shew," but even more to the Lion of Judah and to the medieval bestiaries. It is the fall of the year, not the juvescence, in the seventh and final volume of C. S. Lewis' seven chronicles of Narnia, which mark, it seems to me, the greatest addition to the imperishable deposit of children's literature since the *Jungle Books*. Narnia takes its place forever now beside the jasper-lucent landscapes of Carroll, Andersen, Macdonald and Kipling.

Lewis' Aslan, like Eliot's tiger, is also Christ—a totem of the heraldic imagination, however, and not, as in *Gerontion*, a totem of the philosophic mind. It is probably not necessary for the secularized children who are lucky enough to get the Narnia books as presents to know this fact. For, among the many beauties of Dr. Lewis' achievement, are the other facts that the story is self-sufficient and that the echoes attract the mind's ear even when the mind's eye cannot tell for sure the source of the echoes. If the meaning is hidden, it is only because the world, outside of orthodoxy, has temporarily lost the key. Like the adults, the children, too, must be coaxed inside again. Many are, I suspect; and more will be. One of the most trodden, if least acknowledged, roads leading to Damascus is the old imperial high road of the sovereign imagination. Though Dr. Lewis'

Reprinted from *America* 96 (October 27, 1956): 103–05.

Anglican sympathies might prefer to say Canterbury, all roads lead to Rome in the end, including the enchanting one that opens out of the Narnian portal.

But if it is not absolutely necessary for the child-readers to know the explicit correlations of the major symbols, it is still better that they do; and some of them will travel farther down the road for finding out. It is also quite necessary to point out to the apprehensive Catholic that Dr. Lewis' imagination, while audacious, is audacious after the fashion of the eagle of Revelation, not after that of the heresiarchs. It flies high; it does not depart from orthodoxy.

In an age when lesser men are extrapolating power to achieve Apocalypse, if not Utopia, Dr. Lewis has extrapolated Apocalypse and Ragnarok—always on a child's scale—to achieve Paradise. He extrapolates the theological facts of Christianity and the historic facts of Christendom into a different dimension, a different idiom—not an altogether different one, though—and a different set of images. But the facts do not change. They still add up to Christianity as the medievals knew it in heraldry and as the child mind can treasure it in the context of primal wonder and perennial adventurousness.

The whirligig of time effects strange things. The 1950s may one day be remembered, by recorders of literary anniversaries, not as the decade which saw the death of Mann and the Nobel award to Faulkner, but as the span of time which saw the successive appearances, one each year for seven years, of the seven tales of Narnia. The tales, in order of publication, which is also the order of reading, are: *The Lion, the Witch and the Wardrobe; Prince Caspian; The Voyage of the Dawn Treader; The Silver Chair; The Horse and His Boy; The Magician's Nephew; The Last Battle.* Their literary value is, naturally enough, uneven. It seems to me that the first, the last and the second-last volumes are far and away the best. The installments in between are all good, though; and all should be read, even as one should read all the Cantos of the *Faerie Queene.* (Incidentally, the Narnia stories are like Spenser's masterpiece in more ways than one, even down to being similarly unsynopsizable. And here and now is as good a place as any to note another of their great merits. Besides being a nursery *Faerie Queene,* they are also a child's *Nibelungenlied* and *Divina Commedia,* too.)

All seven volumes deal with the adventures of several related sets of contemporary English children, girls as well as boys, in Narnia—the name seems to echo both Angria and the Norns; but this is not the place to play out any further that seductive adult game of literary derivation.

But Narnia is nothing so science-fiction-crude as another planet. It is another world, another mode of being, another *place.* The twin poles of the seven stories are the enchanted Narnian lands, where anything can and does happen, and the mellow light of that manmade flower, one of earth's old-fashioned iron lamp posts. Between these two immutable boundaries of all successful fantasy—the soaring unfamiliar and the earthbound familiar—stretch the far marches of world myth: Western, Northern, Arabian, classic, medieval.

Though Lewis' achievement is *sui generis,* it also stands somewhat in debt to the practice of such predecessors as E. Nesbit in the *Bastable* books; and to George Macdonald in both the *Curdie* books and in *At the Back of the North Wind.* It owes even more to the great Northern and Celtic hero tales and to the romances of chivalry. But if the matter is mainly medieval, the manner is opulently Renaissance. In fact, the effect is almost that of a great Masque for children, with music by Purcell and mottos from the Shakespeare of *Midsummer Night* and *Much Ado*. As Peter Quince enjoined his artisans of earth, these chronicles of Narnia bring "the moonlight into a chamber." As Don Pedro said to Hero at the masquerade: "My visor is Philemon's roof; within the house is Jove." Earth's lovely mask is everywhere apparent. The high festivity in this kingdom of the imagination is what the ritualists call *aspectus festivus*.

Childhood's Responsiveness

The child will not respond to these values at once, though they will awaken in his memory when the time comes for full realization. He will respond immediately, however, to the narrative sweep; to the evocation of the heroic mood; to the constant eliciting of the numinous. Very possibly this latter service is the most startling one Lewis renders contemporary childhood, contemporary Catholic childhood not least. He touches the nerve of religious awe on almost every page. He evangelizes through the imagination. It is no accident that in his recent autobiography, *Surprised by Joy*, Dr. Lewis should have paid due tribute to Squirrel Nutkin and Sigurd of the Volsungs as two of the couriers who brought him to the foot of the seven-storey mountain.

One can never afford to be supercilious about the imagination, even in the complicated matter of assent to an intellectual proposition. We know enough now about the unitary nature of the human personality to spare us that particular folly. There is a real sense in which one believes more deeply, and not necessarily less rationally, through the imagination than through the intellect—as students of both John Milton and Thomas Hardy can verify.

Now there can be a dangerous misapprehension here. There is some reason to think that Catholics are not altogether free—though Catholicism must be—from the Manicheism sweeping the contemporary imagination, slaying both Dante's unread vision in the higher dream and the equally unread vision in elfland's lower dream. In the face of this pragmatic attack against the disinterested imagination, it is well to remember Christianity's historic hospitality toward the lesser gods of tree and fountain. Christianity slew Baal and Moloch; but not the fairies. Christianity smote Thor; but not the Christmas Nisse. It was Puritanism, after all, not Catholicism, which bade farewell to rewards and fairies.

Far More than Fairies

The fairies lingered longest in the old Catholic places—in Yorkshire, in Ireland. The medieval tapestries had a way of picturing both the Virgin and the Unicorn. In Narnia one still rides the unicorn; and, such is the personality's odd alchemy, the memory of that heady ride may well help armor virginity in the less magical years to come.

Allegory is strong in Narnia, especially in the final chronicle, *The Last Battle*, as befits a tale dealing with Armageddon and the things after Armageddon. It has been our century's bad fashion—a fashion that is passing now, however—to cry down allegory. Dr. Johnson spoke the worst that can be spoken against allegory when he harrumphed: "I had rather see the portrait of a dog I know than all the allegories you can show me." But Dr. Johnson knew only the dreary 18th-century brand which Mrs. Malaprop justly called "headstrong as an allegory on the banks of the Nile."

Dr. Lewis' allegory is 17th-century like Bunyan's and Milton's, and 20th-century like G.K.C.'s *Man Who Was Thursday*. It is unabashed and perennial, according to the Chestertonian tenet that every "great literature has always been allegorical—allegorical of some view of the whole universe." The Narnian allegory encompasses Creation, Sin, Time, Eternity, Death, Incarnation and Resurrection.

I suggested a while back that the greatest service Lewis does childhood here is to elicit a sense of the numinous. At least as great a service is *The Last Battle's* confrontation, in terms the child can understand, of the ineluctable fact of death. In this volume the door which admits the earth children to Narnia's strange realm is at once a more usual and a more terrible portal than the ones we have encountered before in the earlier stories; and Dr. Lewis' use of it involves him in what is probably the most audacious gambit in children's literature since George Macdonald sent little Diamond to the back of the North Wind. In a word, this door through which one enters Narnia and, after Narnia, the "real Narnia," is a door children's books have chosen to avoid ever since the pool of funeral tears which used to inundate the Victorian nursery offerings.

The Victorians were wrong, of course, with their constant and morbid "intrusion of the death wish," as Sheila Kaye-Smith puts it in her recollections of her childhood reading. But we realize that our own total avoidance of the unavoidable is at least as bad when she asks and answers her own question: "How many of the children or humanized animals in fiction today are allowed to die? I venture to say none—not even the bad ones."

What Dr. Lewis has done, on this plane, has long needed doing. Death, as a psychological experience on the part of the child who undergoes the loss, is a trauma from which there is no surcease but one: the surcease of religious belief in the survival of the individual human personality. This is the path down which in symbol Dr. Lewis leads his child readers up to, through and gloriously after the miniature Armageddon of *The Last Battle*. The Victorian nursery tear-jerkers were Lilliputian soap-operas, even as their adult equivalents, in *Dombey and Son* and *The Old Curiosity Shop*, were soap-operas of gargantuan proportions. *The Last Battle's* contemporary children cross over to the other side with a flourish of trumpets.

Introduction to Nobility

I should not like to convey the impression that these stories are really difficult. They are profound but pellucid. Their themes are as high as Paradise; but the entrance thereto is as low as Alice's door. If we must stoop our adult heads and become as little children to get through, the children themselves experience no such difficulty. It would do Dr. Lewis no particular service, either, to suggest that his splendid, original fairy tales accomplish more than they actually do.

They make children magnificently free of the primal literary things: of epic and lyric. The subtler essences of novel and drama must come later.

But it is much, certainly, to introduce the child personality to such noble and, nowadays, such neglected things as heroism, truth, beauty, duty, the great mystery of our animal kindred, the greater mysteries of time and eternity; to the fact that the earth is the strangest of all the stars and to the reconciling fact of Incarnation; to the numinous, God, death, and the fairytale resolution, which is yet so much more than a mere fairy-tale resolution, of life everlasting after death. Even at that, Dr. Lewis is the last person to wish his inventions over-praised. They are, as he once said of William Morris' romances, nets to catch larger and quite other fish. Things are not quite what they seem. We have known all along that Aslan, the redemptive Lion, is more than a lion. At the end of *The Last Battle* Aslan tells us himself:

> "The term is over: the holidays have begun. The dream is ended: this is the morning."
>
> And as He spoke, He no longer looked to them like a lion; but the things that began to happen after that were so great and beautiful that I cannot write them. And for us this is the end of all the stories, and we can most truly say that they all lived happily ever after. But for them it was only the beginning of the real story. All their life in this world and all their adventures in Narnia had only been the cover and the title page: now at last they were beginning Chapter One of the Great Story, which no one on earth has read: which goes on for ever: in which every chapter is better than the one before.

There are many things one can say against the savage century we live in. But, in its own odd way, it has been peculiarly a century of literary delight. On this plane, where adult literature and literature for children become one, Dr. Lewis' Narnia cycle takes an honored place—this is a high claim, but it measures up— alongside the *Jungle Books, The Wind in the Willows, Sherlock Holmes, Father Brown*, the romances of Buchan, the short stories of Saki, the Tolkien trilogy, the delectable contrivances of Kai Lung, C. S. Léwis' own interplanetary trilogy, and that part of the spacious Wodehouse canon which has to do with the amaranthine Jeeves. What other century, one queries proudly, can offer a bede- roll like this one?

The Legend of Sleepy Hollow: A Mythological Parody

Marjorie W. Bruner

Studies of Washington Irving's *Legend of Sleepy Hollow* have already been made showing the borrowings from Romantic German literature and from native American life and folk humor.[1] This present study attempts to show it to be a rollicking parody of ancient Greek myths and rites of Greek fertility cults, a *comic* story of death and rebirth, fertility and immortality.

A clue to this interpretation is given by Irving himself when he speaks of Brom Bones as having a Herculean frame, and the messenger who invited Ichabod to the Van Tassel's party as wearing a cap of Mercury. From here on Irving parodies the gods and goddesses and the rites of their worship at Eleusis in Greece.

Brom Bones, so nicknamed because of his powers of limb, was a rustic Hercules, of whose feats of skill and strength the whole countryside well knew. He was arrogant, boastful, had the temper of a lion, enjoyed fighting in single combat, and played pranks on unsuspecting persons like his godly prototype. While Hercules wore a lion's skin, which he took as a trophy after one of his labors, Brom Bones "was distinguished by a fur cap, surmounted with a flaunting fox's tail," which was identified at a distance by the country people. Hercules wrestled with Acheloos, a river god, for the hand of Deianira; Brom Bones competed with Ichabod for the favor of Katrina Van Tassel, but how?—by playing pranks on Ichabod at the schoolhouse and by engaging in the frightening ride through the dark woods. In the end both Hercules and Brom won their girls whom they married and lived with for some time. Hercules made a visit to the underworld on a mission and made a successful return to his land. So did Brom; his trip to the underworld was his ride through the forest as the headless horseman, and his mission was to frighten Ichabod out of the neighborhood. On the completion of his mission, Brom, like Hercules, returned to his community, married Katrina, and became a respected landholder.

Katrina Van Tassel, as her name indicates, corresponds to the corn goddess, Demeter, for everything concerning her and surrounding her suggests ripeness

Reprinted from *College English* 25 (January 1964): 274–83.

and fertility.[2] Katrina was plump and rosy-cheeked and she wore much yellow (Demeter's color). The whole Van Tassel farm is a symbol of fertility, for the barn seemed to Ichabod to be bursting forth with farm treasures; in the barn-yard were "rows of pigeons," "troops of suckling pigs," "a squadron of snowy geese," "regiments of turkeys and guinea fowls." Around the barnyard were "fat meadow-lands," "rich fields of wheat, rye, buckwheat and Indian corn," all symbols of Demeter, and "orchards burthened with ruddy fruit." Inside the house were rows of resplendent pewter, treasure of old silver and china, strings of dried apples and peaches and ears of Indian corn. Even similes used in con-nection with Katrina are those of food: Ichabod looked on her as a tempting morsel, and his dream of achieving her hand looked to him as easy as "a man would carve his way to the center of a Christmas pie."

The messenger who brought to Ichabod the invitation to the Van Tassel party was "a negro in tow-cloth jacket and trowsers, a round-crowned fragment of a hat, like the cap of Mercury, and mounted on the back of a ragged, wild, half-broken colt which he managed with a rope by way of a halter." He is a comic figure of Mercury who was not only the messenger of the gods, but who also acted as guide for wayfarers to the underworld. Because of this latter association, Mercury's symbolic color was black. All of the Olympian gods are represented in mythology as white-skinned, but in this parody of the gods, Irving uses Mer-cury's association with black and death to make his messenger a Negro.

Is Ichabod too a parody of a god? He seems to hold two positions in this comedy of Greek mythology. He is a parody of the river god, Acheloos, who struggled with Hercules, and at the same time he is a burlesque of a worshipper of one of the Greek Mysteries.

As a parody of a river god, Ichabod is quite plainly connected with water by his last name of Crane and his personal description which is made in terms of water and bird images. His appearance is that of a water bird: tall, lanky, lean with narrow shoulders, long arms and legs, feet like shovels, loosely-knit frame, small head, large green, glassy eyes, a capacious swallow, and a long snipe (also a water bird) nose similar to a beak. His head turned like a weathercock; he looked like a scarecrow; and when he rode Gunpowder his arms "flapped like a pair of wings," and his elbows "stuck out like grasshoppers."

Ichabod's nature was that of a quiet river: "wonderfully gentle and ingratiat-ing," a happy mixture of pliability and perseverance." He made his advances to Katrina "in a quiet and gently insinuating manner."

As a river was a major means of communication in the early days, so Ichabod was "a traveling gazette," bringing gossip from house to house. Like some meandering rivers he had no permanent home; he lived successively a week at a time at the houses of his students. He is identified with water also when the reader is told that his schoolhouse stood by a brook, his hours of leisure were spent beside a brook or stream or swamp. He sauntered with girls along banks of an adjacent mill-pond, and he courted Katrina beside a spring. Even his school-house fastening "borrowed from the mystery of the eel-pot."

Ichabod is also compared to a river at flood tide which appears to eat up the land as it advances, when Irving says that Ichabod "was a huge feeder, and though lank, had the dilating powers of an anaconda." Katrina, "a tempting morsel," found favor with Ichabod, but his feelings for her were prompted more by desire for her possessions than for herself, for "the pedagogue's mouth watered as he looked upon this sumptuous promise of luxurious winter fare. . . . As the enraptured Ichabod fancied all this, and as he rolled his great green eyes over the fat meadow-lands . . . his heart yearned after the damsel who was to inherit these domains" and his imagination roved to how he would turn all this to cash and move to Kentucky or some other new region, just as a river at flood tide, having devoured the land before it, would cut new channels for its course.

Finally, Irving seems to point to Ichabod's stature as a comic god when he establishes the social importance of the schoolmaster in the community. "The schoolmaster is generally a man of some importance in the female circle of rural neighborhoods . . . an idle gentlemanlike personage, of vastly superior taste and accomplishments to the rough country swains." "The more bashful country bumpkins" envied "his superior elegance and address." In the schoolroom he was "enthroned" in his "literary realm," "in his hand swayed a ferule, a scepter of despotic power." His mastery of Cotton Mather's *History of New England Witchcraft*, his delight in listening to supernatural tales, and his whole-hearted belief generally in the supernatural points also to his own identification with a supernatural god. Ichabod existed on a social and intellectual plane above his roistering rival, Brom Bones, just as Acheloos, a lesser divinity, was on a spiritual plane above Hercules, the semimortal hero of brawn.

Many more details of comparison can be found between Ichabod and Acheloos, whose story of the struggle against Hercules is to be found in Ovid's *Metamorphoses* (Book IX). In addition to these parodies of the individual characters of the mythological gods, the theme of *The Legend of Sleepy Hollow* itself becomes a parody of the rituals of the Greek Mysteries at Eleusis and Dionysos and their accompanying symbolic trips to the underworld.

Like a musical composer who announces his theme in the opening of his symphony, Washington Irving announced his by quoting from the *Castle of Indolence*, and expanded this dreamlike otherworld theme by the use of *Tarry-town*, *Sleepy* Hollow, "drowsy, dreamy influence," "bewitched," "under sway of some witching power," "continual reverie," "trances and visions," "see strange sights," "hear music and voices in the air," and so on. These are, it is recognized, characteristic details often used in Romantic novels, but they are also a part of the story dealing basically with midnight worship of a mysterious, awful, supernatural god involving music, frenzied dancing, and the beholding of strange and frightful dramas through which the initiate would attain union with the god. The theme of fertility, so important in the Greek Mysteries, is expressed by Irving in the food images and in the long, glowing descriptions of the abundance of nature at the Van Tassel home and countryside around, until the story becomes itself a paean to the corn goddess, Demeter, whose worship centered at Eleusis. Ichabod's "only study was how to gain the affections of the peerless daughter of Van Tassel," which in a parody of Greek Mystery worship compares to the worshipper's desire to attain union with the goddess.

The action of the story begins while a buzzing stillness reigned in the school-room; a Negro appeared with an invitation to attend a frolic that evening at the

Van Tassel's. As the rites at Eleusis, held at night, were open only to initiates, Ichabod too needed an invitation to the Van Tassel evening party.

"Ichabod spent an extra half hour at his toilet, brushing and furbishing up his best and indeed only suit of rusty black and arranging his looks by a bit of broken looking-glass." Ichabod, of course, is going courting, but the initiates too underwent a purification ceremony, and then donned garments of black. On his way to Katrina's house he noticed nature's abundance. "His eye, ever open to every symptom of culinary abundance, beheld a vast store of apples" in "oppressive opulence on the trees," "great fields of Indian corn" with yellow pumpkins lying beneath, buckwheat fields "breathing the odor of the bee-hive." All these are symbols pertaining to the fertility gods, and were represented in abundance along the processional way to the worship and at the shrines of the gods.

He arrived at "the castle of the Heer Van Tassel" (the shrine) which he found "thronged with the pride and the flower of the adjacent country" (other worshippers). Brom Bones was present the whole evening, just as Hercules was present also as an initiate of the rites of Eleusis. Ichabod entered the state parlor of the mansion wherein the food was laid out: cakes of all kinds including honey cakes, ham among other dishes, and the "motherly teapot." It is known that the worshippers at Eleusis ate before the ceremony a feast of honey cakes and roast pork and drank *kykeon*, a kind of mint tea. Van Tassel, as befitted his name, was the officiating priest of this worship of a corn goddess, who "moved about among his guests with a face dilated with content and good humor, round and jolly as a harvest moon. His hospitable attentions were brief, but expressive, being confined to a shake of the hand, a slap on the shoulder, a loud laugh, and a pressing invitation to 'fall to and help themselves.' "

Music for dancing followed the feasting. Ichabod's comic dancing is described in terms of the mad, frenzied dancing of the devotees of Dionysos: "Not a limb, not a fiber about him was idle; and to have seen his loosely-hung frame in full motion and clattering about the room, you would have thought St. Vitus himself, that blessed patron of the dance, was figuring before you in person."

After the dance Ichabod joined "a knot of sager folk" on the piazza, gossiping over former times and drawing out long stories about the war, then going into tales of ghosts and apparitions. These tales had much to do with death, funeral trains, wailings, dark glens, shrieks, storms, and the headless horseman who tethered his horse among the graves in the churchyard. "All these tales, told in that drowsy undertone with which men talk in the dark . . . sank deep in the mind of Ichabod." This emotional build-up of poor Ichabod relates to the drama played before the Eleusinian initiates to build up their emotions for the final dramatic moment.

Then the revel broke up, the farmers went home, but Ichabod lingered with Katrina. "What passed at this interview I will not pretend to say, for in fact I do not know. Let it suffice to say, Ichabod stole forth with the air of one who had been sacking a hen-roost rather than a fair lady's heart." He left "heavy-hearted and crestfallen." At the end of the first part of the Eleusinian rites, the crowds dispersed and only the year-old initiates could stay to participate. These second rites were highly secret, but the revelation affected the initiate emotionally and probably involved a vision of death. Certainly Katrina's revelation to Ichabod had been death to his high hope of attaining union with her and being master of her lands.

Ichabod's journey through the dark woods at midnight is equivalent to the Eleusinian's symbolical journey to Hades, the climax of the rite which took place at midnight. Ichabod approached the tree on which Major Andre, a British spy, had been hanged by the Americans during the Revolutionary War. To the Greeks, Dionysos was known as a tree spirit and a festival was founded in one part of Greece in which little images hung by nooses from trees were carried by the celebrants. These images became a fairly common part of the worship of Dionysos, god of wine and the fruited tree.

Ichabod came to a haunted brook over which was a bridge. "To pass this bridge was the severest trial," for the brook represents the river Styx which separated the lands of the living and the dead and was heavily guarded. Here Ichabod met a black horse and black rider also apparently guarding the stream. Ichabod called out, "Who are you?" but he received no answer. Then he discovered the rider was headless. Egyptian mythology depicts Isis as a headless goddess who personifies the dead. It is her duty to introduce the dead to Osiris and she is present at Osiris' judgment of the dead. Like Ichabod's headless horseman who supposedly lost his head in battle, she lost her head during a battle between Seth and Horus. The Greek and Egyptian worlds borrowed much from each other by way of Crete and Alexandria, so that Isis was well-known to Greeks.

Then began Ichabod's wild ride which reminds one of the pursuit of the Furies of Greek tragedy driving their victim to his destiny. Finally Ichabod saw a brook. "If I can but reach that bridge," thought Ichabod, "I am safe. . . . He thundered over the resounding planks; he gained the opposite side." This brook is a minuscule representation of the river Lethe, the river of forgetfulness, in which the Greeks believed the new souls must wash themselves before leaving the land of the dead and being reborn. Ichabod saw the goblin rise to hurl the pumpkin head at him; but too late. "It encountered his cranium with a tremendous crash." If one considers the long snip nose as well as the long lean figure of Ichabod to be a male phallic symbol, and the pumpkin to be the female *mullos*, this crash could be considered the moment of conception in this tale of death and rebirth. Ichabod tumbled into the dust and was possibly unconscious for a short time from the shock (would this represent gestation?), after which he picked himself up and walked off to other parts leaving behind him all the paraphernalia of his earlier existence at Sleepy Hollow. An old farmer visiting New York brought back news that Ichabod was living in a distant part of the country; he had "kept school and studied law at the same time; had been admitted to the bar, turned politician, electioneered, written for the newspaper and finally had been made a justice of the Ten Pound Court." Ichabod had been reborn into a new life; he had sloughed off his old life completely, even to the point of changing professions.

Brom Bones, who participated in the party at the Van Tassels' in the same way that Hercules was initiated at Eleusis before going to the underworld and who as the headless horseman rode the death-like forest, did not undergo death or rebirth (nor did Hercules) but he returned safely to Tarrytown where he married Katrina and became master of her lands. Hercules, having accomplished his last labor safely, returned to the upper world, married Deianira, and eventually became a god.

How did Irving know of these rites at Eleusis and Dionysos which were open only to initiates and were rarely hinted at in classical writings? Some details are found in Livy (Fourth Decade, Book IX), an author whom we are told Irving read.[3] We know also that Irving was in Paris in 1805 when a book was published by Jacques-Antoine Dulaure[4] which created much criticism in the press because it purported to show that the Christian rituals and customs had their origins in the cults of primitive ages. Irving, being an avid newspaper reader, probably read the articles involved in this controversy which filled the Parisian newspapers, and may even have obtained a copy of the book, so that details of the cults welled up in his memory when he began to write *Sleepy Hollow* a few years later.

We must not forget too, that the figures of Hercules and other classical heroes were well known to Renaissance and Classical writers and artists in Europe.[5] and that this influence was on the wane in Irving's period. By parodying these heroes Irving was helping to bury a subject matter that had been popular too long.

It is possible that Irving's contemporaries recognized his classical borrowings, although none of them has pointed these out. A writer in *Blackwood's Magazine* (1825) wrote: "We have no patience with such a man as Washington Irving. We cannot keep our temper when we catch him pilfering the materials of other men; *working up old stories*." These italics are mine; the whole quotation was originally used to point out Irving's borrowing of the wild ride from Burger's *Leonore*. Irving's reply to his critics was that he considered popular traditions fair foundations for authors of fiction to build on, and his comic use of classic mythology in the *Legend of Sleepy Hollow*, as well as his parody of the *Iliad* in the battle between the Dutch and Swedes in *Knickerbocker's History of New York* would seem to indicate that he included the classics as fair foundations for stories too.

Whatever classical sources Irving used for his *Legend of Sleepy Hollow* Irving's comedy is intensified through his use of mythological and religious parallels. What was once serious and spiritually elevating to the Greeks has become by contrast and exaggeration through Irving's genius something of rollicking mirth to be enjoyed for all time.

NOTES

1. W. A. Reichart, *Washington Irving and Germany* (Ann Arbor, 1957) and D. G. Hoffman, *Form and Fable in American Literature* (New York, 1961).
2. Sir James George Frazer, *The New Golden Bough*, ed. T. H. Gaster (New York, 1961), pp. 199ff.
3. Pierre Irving, *Life and Letters of Washington Irving*, Vol. 1 (New York, 1883), p. 12.
4. Jacques-Antoine Dulaure, *The Gods of Generation*, trans. A.F.N. (New York, 1933), p. xxi.
5. E. M. Waith, *The Herculean Hero* (New York, 1962).

To Seek and to Find: Quest Literature for Children

June S. Terry

As children develop they find themselves facing complex problems both without and within themselves. As the child becomes aware of concrete social obligations he also becomes aware of conflict in his social environment and the necessity to deal with these problems. He needs to know that such problems are universal and that he is not the first to have to seek their solution. Through the quest story he can see how diverse men, yesterday and today, have sought solutions to the human situation. Through the quest story, both past and present, he is helped to see the variety of mankind, the complexity of its problems and from an imagined world, or a real world transformed through myth, will develop the capacity for dealing with his world.

The best quest stories describe both an external and internal search involving not only an exciting journey where the chief character is put to the test, where the overcoming of obstacles shows his worthiness to fulfill the quest, but an inner reality representing to the reader stages of human development in story form. In stories like "The Quest of the Golden Fleece" and Alan Garner's *Elidor* the quest is on the surface an external one—Jason seeks the fleece. Roland seeks his lost brothers and sister. Gerda in "The Snow Queen" is also searching for a lost person, while in *The Three Royal Monkeys* by Walter de la Mare the monkeys, Thumb, Thimble and Nod seek a lost country. All these attain their goals because of or through the development of their own characters, exposed or refined by the hardships of their quest. The story of Jason goes further, for it shows how a flawed personality brings about self-destruction. As C. S. Lewis says in *Of Other Worlds* (Bles, 1966): 'The story does what no theorem can quite do. It may not be "like real life" in the superficial sense: but it sets before us an image of what reality may well be like at some more central region.'

Man is unique in that he can transmute common experience into symbols representing this inner reality. He uses these symbols to transmit to others,

Reprinted from *The School Librarian* 18, no. 4 (December 1970): 399–404.

particularly his children, the impression of these common experiences and how he as an individual perceived them. He does this in many ways—through drama, art, music, poetry and narrative literature. The quest story in particular presents reality both symbolically and representationally through several levels of common and individual experience. The reader, whether child or adult, can fulfil conscious and unconscious needs at his own pace and stage of development. He sees actuality from his own experience, but also through the eyes of the writer and finally through the characters in the story. Hans Andersen saw reason as a destroyer of innocence in "The Snow Queen," the reader may just see that Kay is growing up, while Gerda, the character in the story, sees Kay as "lost." Thus the reading of quest stories enables the child, as well as the adult, to share in a universal experience but he will also find views of this experience (i.e. growing up) which enrich him as an individual at his own stage of development. This enrichment will normally be absorbed unconsciously by the child while he will consciously decide that certain stories fulfil his individual needs, James Britton confirms this in an article called "Odysseus and commuters" (*Didaskalos—The Journal of the Joint Association of Classical Teachers*, Vol. 2, No. 3, 1968):

> It is principally in this last sense that the world of myth stands over against the actual world: over against the actual world in its most trivial, humdrum, irritating and fatuous manifestations. If a sinkful of washing-up in the morning and an unmade bed in the evening: or a rush-hour bus-queue in a winter drizzle: or a garrulous neighbour on a shared telephone line: if this sort of thing, any or all of it comes home to you as 'real' then you will appreciate the fact that we have, on the other hand, myth to remind us that life might be lived on a much grander scale. Clock-watching commuters can read of Odysseus' journey home from Troy, men with a grievance that drives them to fill up forms, sign petitions, write to their MPS, can remember how Perseus swept the board with the deadly sight of the Gorgon's head. . . . A world is set over against our world . . . I think as adults we project our inner needs more readily into worlds as psychologically complicated as our own, worlds nearer to our own world than the world of myth. It is in childhood, therefore, that most of us take myth into the bloodstream.

The child takes quest tales, including myths 'into the bloodstream.' What does he gain from this 'transfusion'? First he unconsciously absorbs the values of society, not only his society, but also human society past and present. The values inherent in the quest tales have been shaped through generations of human experience and those that emerge consistently are those universally accepted. In all the stories goodness is represented as a greater and more desirable virtue than wickedness. This conclusion will be absorbed consciously by the child for he will know that good actions bring benefit to himself and to others, while unconsciously this knowledge will affect his behavior and his judgement of situations and people. Of course, the individual child will find some representations of goodness fulfil his needs more than others. The adolescent may find the struggles of Frodo and Samwise to reach Mount Doom in *The Lord of the Rings* of greater relevance to his development than Gerda's journey in search of Kay. The infant can share the perils of Peter Rabbit in Beatrix Potter's tale, whereas the temptations besetting Sir Launcelot in *King Arthur and his Knights of the Round Table* would be outside his experience or understanding. Usually there is a quest story which not only meets a child's needs at each stage of his development but is also timeless, adaptable both to the individual and the contemporary values of his society. The reader can compare George MacDonald's Victorian conception of retribution with that of the modern writer C. S. Lewis and then again with that of the medieval writer Sir Thomas Malory. Each has written a tale involving a quest for an ideal city or kingdom. In MacDonald's *The Princess and Curdie* Gwyntystorm is to be restored from corruption to the ideal city; in *The Last Battle*, the children reach Aslan's perfect kingdom; and Malory has created Camelot, the city where truth and justice are supreme. Retribution falls upon those who corrupt or reject the perfection offered to them. In *The Princess and Curdie* the wicked attorney-general, who has twisted the law to benefit himself, finds he is entwined by a gigantic spider:

> When he awoke he fancied himself paralysed; every limb, every finger even, was motionless, coils and coils of broad spider ribbon bandaged his members to his body and all to the chair.

In *The Last Battle* by C. S. Lewis, Rishda Tarkaan pretends that an idol, Tash, created by his people the Calormenes, is really Aslan, the real ruler of Narnia. At the climax of the story Rishda finds that the idol he has used has become an evil force which turns and destroys him:

> A terrible figure was coming towards them . . . It had a vulture's head and four arms. Its beak was open and its eyes blazed. A croaking noise came from its beak.
> "Thou hast called me into Narnia, Rishda Tarkaan. Here I am. What hast thou to say?"

Again, in Malory's *Le Morte D'Arthur*, King Arthur's nephew Mordred, born of evil between the king and his sister Morgawse, brings death to them both. In the final battle Sir Mordred is mortally wounded by King Arthur.

> And when Sir Mordred saw King Arthur he ran to him with his sword drawn in his hand, and there King Arthur smote Sir Mordred under the shield with a foin of his spear throughout the body more than a fathom. And when Sir Mordred felt he had his death's wound he thrust himself with the might that he had, up to the burre of King Arthur's spear, and right so he smote his father King Arthur, with his sword, holding in both his hands, upon the side of the head, that the sword pierced the helmet and the tay of the brain. And therewith Mordred dashed down stark dead to the ground.

The child can set these views of justice against contemporary ideas and see that the fifteenth-century writer, the Victorian clergyman and the twentieth-century writer treat the subject in surprisingly similar ways. They have made a moral judgment and the reader is invited to share in this judgment.

Modern technology tends to blind man to the reality of his moral and spiritual plight. Imaginative literature is one way of opening our eyes to this reality. We are still groping to understand the real nature of man and technological and scientific achievement has distorted rather than enlarged our view. Reality is enriched and truth and beauty discerned through the imagination, but the imagination must be fed, exercised and stretched. Quest tales are able to free the child's imagination from the cramping effect of his immediate physical, intellectual and social environment. Such freeing of the imagination paradoxically helps the child to see things as they really are—he realizes his physical, mental and social restrictions—with imagination comes self-knowledge. For as J. R. R. Tolkien writes in *Tree and Leaf* (Allan & Unwin, 1964):

> Creative fantasy is founded upon the hard recognition of fact, but not a slavery to it. So upon logic was founded the nonsense that displays itself in the tales and rhymes of Lewis Carroll. If men really could not distinguish between frogs and men, fairy stories about frog-kings would not have arisen.

Freeing the imagination also helps the child to experience vicariously things that do happen, but may not happen to him. Men do set off on perilous voyages, mice are found in ships' holds, ships are dashed to pieces on jagged rocks and strange exotic lands do exist. So in his imagination a child can sail the high seas in the *Dawn Treader*, can enjoy the companionship of Reepicheep the Mouse, can with the Argonauts narrowly escape the Clashers and see with Nod the mysterious valleys of Tishnar. Thus, reading imaginative literature prepares a child for future experiences and creates a deepening intellectual awareness.

Quest stories open a window not only on the imaginative world but also on the world of the intellect. Educational research into child development shows that abstract concepts such as justice, truth and tolerance are most difficult for children, but the story can put over complex and profound ideas perfectly naturally. A solution too complicated for a child to reach can be presented in a tale and leave the child with much food for thought, but as he is vicariously, not personally, involved, he can judge the problems posed, intellectually not emotionally. Children can learn much about the nature of unhappiness from Kay in "The Snow Queen'; the possessive instinct from Thorin Oakenshield in *The Hobbit*; where real joy lies from the hobbit Bilbo Baggins; the different faces of love from Medea in 'The Quest of the Golden Fleece', from Gerda, and from Aragorn, heir of Elendil in *The Lord of the Rings*. They can learn of spiritual splendour from Aslan and Sir Galahad. They can learn truths about human nature in general and deepen their knowledge of people as individuals. Sir Launcelot, standing before the Holy Grail, is ashamed that his love for Guinevere betrays his own vows of honour and his loyalty to his friend King Arthur. Away from the Grail his thoughts return to her and finally his obsession brings both Guinevere and himself to disaster and destroys the kingdom of Camelot. To the young reader Launcelot is a betrayed knight, but to the adolescent the knight's character can serve as an insight into some of the conflicts of the adult world. Each time a quest story is read, new facets of character appear. Children are naturally curious, but especially about people. The more subtly developed a character is, the more fascinating he will be to the child reader. That is why children say they 'grew out of' certain books, while others last. Children will always find a character such as Bilbo Baggins curious and interesting. He is subtly presented. As a hobbit, he is a mixture of adult and child. To the child reader he is in the position of the real child in an adult world. He is small, likes comfort (especially food) and security, yet also yearns for adventure; he makes mistakes, yet learns from them; he is often frightened yet doggedly continues the quest and although he feels isolated, as a hobbit among the dwarves, he is conspicuously friendly. To the adult, Bilbo represents the ordinary man involved in his dismay in untoward events. As the reader matures, his understanding of the character matures too. Characters like Bilbo on his journey to the Lonely Mountain and Sir Launcelot seeking the Holy Grail show to their disadvantage the shallow, senti-mental characters of many so-called children's books. The greater the knowledge of people, the greater the understanding of their behavior. Characters realistically presented in literature deepen our knowledge of people and this leads to a better understanding of them. In quest tales, the people come alive, their values can be assimilated into the contemporary world and their stories are told with truth and dignity. This means that their triumphs and disasters add an enrichment and depth both to the reading of literature and the child's environment. In quest stories children find a freedom of the spirit which extends beyond limitations of time, major disasters and petty irritations. John Bunyan, imprisoned physically, was never chained in mind and spirit, but accompanied by Christian was seeking the Celestial City. The child imprisoned by poor health can explore underground caverns with Curdie or reach the Island of Voices with the crew of the *Dawn Treader*. The child walled in by loneliness can share the company of Roland in Elidor or Eustace Scrubb in Narnia. The truly free person is one whose mind can soar above the limitations of the present and the restrictions about him.

Of the many kinds of stories loved by children of all ages, quest stories have a special place as they offer such a comprehensive range of experience because of their long history of evolution and survival. The story of the quest for the golden fleece is one of the world's most ancient stories. Homer, who lived about 1,000 BC, knew it and variations on its theme are still to be found in modern literature. For the quest story most nearly reflects the whole of life. Unrelated events can be seen to grow naturally out of each other when part of a quest where anything can happen. Reality and imagination are merged. Pain and pleasure, life and death in all human preoccupations—can be set against the same preoccupations in imaginary worlds; thus some of life's most terrible aspects can be accepted or experienced vicariously. Such imaginative experiences not only enrich the life of a child but also aid intellectual growth which deepens enjoyment of the whole of life. Above all, quest stories are enjoyable to read and from that enjoyment can come an appreciation of literature generally. From deeper literary compre-hension the child learns—learns not only about himself, but also about others and the nature of human aspirations. Quest stories fuse together the timeless-ness of the past and the truth of the present. They contain treasure worth the seeking.

REFERENCES

Andersen, Hans Christian. "The Snow Queen" from *Fairy Tales and Legends*. The Bodley Head.

Bunyan, John. *The Pilgrim's Progress*. Penguin.

De La Mare, Walter. *The Three Royal Monkeys*. Faber.

Garner, Alan. *Elidor*. Penguin.

Green, Roger Lancelyn. *King Arthur and His Knights of the Round Table*. Penguin.

Green, Roger Lancelyn. *Tales of the Greek Heroes*. Penguin.

Lewis, C. S. *The Voyage of the Dawn Treader*. Penguin.

Lewis, C. S. *The Last Battle*. Penguin.

Macdonald, George. *The Princess and Curdie*. Penguin.

Malory, Sir Thomas. *King Arthur and His Knights*; ed R. T. Davies. Faber.

Potter, Beatrix. *The Tale of Peter Rabbit*. Warne.

Tolkien, J. R. R. *The Hobbit*. Allen & Unwin.

Tolkien, J. R. R. *The Lord of the Rings*. Allen & Unwin.

Responding to Archetypal Criticism

1. Classics: A Link to the Past

CRITICAL COMMENT

O'Dell commented: "The stories which have been written by great writers possess lives of their own." He described how one object, the dark canoe, *Moby Dick* by Melville, grew and developed in his own imagination to the extent that he wrote a book about the canoe itself. His thesis was that the stories are immortal, living always in the minds of persons who read them.

WAYS OF RESPONDING

A. Select a classic of children's literature, such as *Treasure Island* by Stevenson, *Peter Rabbit* by Potter, or one of the Hans Christian Andersen tales such as *The Nightingale*. With some of your colleagues, discuss meaningful remembrances you have of portions of the book. Share personal feelings about the book, especially any happenings which you might have experienced which caused you to remember the book. After your discussion reflect on O'Dell's statement. Did you find this true about the book which you discussed or do you think that he experiences stories more deeply because he is a writer?

B. Make up a free association quiz based on events or objects from classic tales. The following list is an example. See if you can add to it.

> a finger in the dike
> whitewashing a fence
> a pair of silver skates
> SOME PIG
> a boy who could fly
> hundreds of doughnuts
> an animal doctor
> a yellow brick road

Ask several persons to take the quiz, jotting down quickly the first phrase that comes to their minds about the story—other than the title of the book. When the quiz is finished, compare the statements and discuss the thoughts that were central in the minds of the quiz takers. Did the quiz stir the memory bringing to mind personal recollections related to the book incidents? Were any of the memories of different persons similar in relation to the book?

C. Compare some versions of folktales for the difference in treatment, searching for examples of mythic lore that might introduce children to immortal themes. "Cinderella" has numerous translations and adaptations. Some versions that would make good comparisons are found in Chase's *Grandfather Tales*, Lang's *The Blue Fairy Book* and Perrault's *Cinderella* as retold by LeCain.

D. Read some of the books that decidedly have a national rather than a universal setting. Suggested readings are the regional books of Lenski such as *Strawberry Girl* and the Little House series by Wilder as well as contemporary books such as *John Henry McCoy* by Chaffin, *Skinny* by Burch, *Philip Hall*

Likes Me, I Reckon Maybe by Greene and *The House of Dies Drear* by Hamilton. Are there evidences of modern objects, rituals, or events that might very well be compared with similar happenings in ancient myths? For example, the symbolism in *John Henry McCoy* brings to mind the family feuds of literature when the author chooses to give the hero that particular name and places him in Hatfield Branch, Kentucky. Does this contemporary story recall other feuding families in literature, such as the Montagues and the Capulets of *Romeo and Juliet?* Did Shakespeare draw on still other family feuds that led to disaster when certain family members fell in love or formed friendships? Peruse the books you have selected for examples of what seem to be national customs and rituals, but are easily comparable to mythic events of long ago.

2. The Classic Hero

CRITICAL COMMENT

Carr analyzes the characterization of Taran as a classic hero according to DeVries' set of ten motifs. The hero of the Chronicles of Prydain is exemplified in eight of the ten motifs. Alexander alters the classic hero's outcome drastically. Usually the hero must die in order to achieve immortality. Taran, however, remains a mortal—a fact that Carr considers "the most fascinating of all of Taran's relationships to the classic motifs."

Helson also uses the hero as a category in her analysis of fantasy tales. She notes that her main characters "learn courage, fortitude, and resourcefulness."

WAYS OF RESPONDING

A. Analyze the hero tales from Helson's study according to DeVries' scheme. These tales were *The Hobbit* by Tolkien, *The Lion, the Witch, and the Wardrobe* by Lewis, *Elidor* by Garner, and *The Mouse and His Child* by Hoban. How nearly do these books match the motifs noted by DeVries?

B. Read all of the books in Alexander's Chronicles of Prydain: *The Book of Three, The Black Cauldron, The Castle of Lyr, Taran Wanderer,* and *The High King.* Share the reading with a group of others who have also read the books. Find passages from the five books that illustrate the motifs that Taran exemplifies. As you discuss the books during this analysis, do you find your enjoyment of the books increasing? How much of this type of analysis do you believe would benefit children? Take a poll of the group's opinion on this question.

3. A New Mythology

CRITICAL COMMENT

The reader's own world is the setting for the new mythology that Carr suggests that Alexander has created. The critic states, "Our ideal is our myth." Taran's acceptance of responsibility for helping a fellow human being was the act that brought him from another age, that of the classical hero to our age. Carr also points out the human glories that were brought to light by Alexander, such as human handwork and human political skill, in contrast to magical feats and royal governments.

WAYS OF RESPONDING

A. Reread some of the classical hero tales. Examples of versions that would be appropriate to this project are *The Gorgon's Head* or *The Story of Perseus* by Serraillier or *Beowulf* by Sutcliff. How might you rewrite the tale in the style of the "new mythology" that Alexander used in writing about Taran? What adventures would the hero undertake that would be comparable to Taran's building the seawall? What heroic deed would the epic hero perform on the level of Taran's attempt to save Craddoc, the man who was supposedly his father and therefore the negator of Taran's dreams of royal birth?

B. Study some of the less central characters in other hero tales, such as *Journey Outside* by Steele, *A Wrinkle in Time* by L'Engle, and *Enchantress from the Stars* by Engdahl. Do any of these characters exemplify decidedly human values that are capable of being achieved only through love, hard work, and inner human resources? List these values and then, with a group of colleagues, try to rank the items in order of importance. After attempting to do so, reflect on your discussion of these values. Would children see them in the same order of importance? Are these the values true classical heroes would lay down their lives to protect?

C. Create some vignettes for a hero of the new mythology, including references to contemporary values. Perhaps the hero might be a woman, the virtues based on technological advances, and the feats attainable without the use of magic. Select the most promising theme and develop it, creating certain characters and situations to show some of the human values you consider worthy of mention in a hero tale. You may want to search through current magazines, newspapers, and television coverages to find items from today's news that could be adapted for a hero tale.

4. The Wish Fulfillment Tale

CRITICAL COMMENT

Helson's analysis of certain fantasies resulted in one category concerned with "wish fulfillment, with wonderful discoveries or strokes of luck which bring riches, success, good things to eat, excitement, adventure, or the heart's desire." The books are classified in an older descriptive categorization as comic. These are usually humorous stories that contain some conflict and aggression, but usually end happily, with the help of a magical power.

WAYS OF RESPONDING

A. Examine the same six books that Helson used in this category of her study: *The Twenty-One Balloons* by DuBois, *Half Magic* by Eager, *The Phantom Tollbooth* by Juster, *Higglety Pigglety Pop!* by Sendak, *Many Moons* by Thurber, and *Time at the Top* by Ormondroyd. Select illustrative examples of events from the books that are representative of the wish fulfillment motif. Use these examples to support your opinion on whether the books seem to you to be closely related as one might expect from the manner in which they are classified.

B. Analyze some other books to see if they contain elements of the wish fulfillment theme as described by Helson. In what ways, if any, are these books alike? In what ways, if any, are they similar to Helson's sample? *The Smartest Man in Ireland* by Hunter, *The 500 Hats of Bartholomew Cubbins* by Seuss, *Tal and the Magic Barruget* by Wuorio would be interesting to use for this analysis.

5. The Initiation Archetype

CRITICAL COMMENT

Both Helson and Carr wrote of the acts a young hero had to accomplish en route to manhood. Jung's categorization for this motif was the initiation archetype. It appears in much of literature.

WAYS OF RESPONDING

A. Three books by Joseph Krumgold were written as an initiation trilogy. The main character in each book undergoes many painful experiences as he grows into maturity. Miguel in . . . *And Now Miguel* learns, after many heartaches, that older persons are far wiser than he is; Andy's problem in *Onion John* is the search for identity; and Henry's difficulty in *Henry 3* is in moving from abstraction to understanding what is real. Two of Krumgold's trio of books were written in the 1950s. Read some children's books of realism written in the 1970s which might also be considered as initiation archetypes. Compare these with Krumgold's books. Do you see different ways of performing the same rituals in just a twenty year period? Possible selections are Blume's *Are You There God? It's Me, Margaret,* compared with . . . *And Now Miguel;* Snyder's *The Changeling* compared with *Onion John;* and Sachs' *The Truth about Mary Rose* compared with *Henry 3.*

B. The theme of growing up is common in children's literature. In many cases this theme might be considered to be an initiation archetype. Use the chapter, "Growing Up" from *Reading Ladders to Human Relations.*[1] Read one of the books noted in the compilation, giving attention to aspects of the initiation archetype. With your colleagues, state some of the motifs that you consider depict initiation rites. Quote specific passages from the book to support your generalization. You may want to compare the rituals such as "the willingness to attempt, to fail, and to imagine," and show the various actual incidents that are depicted that illustrate that rite.

6. The Shadow Archetype

CRITICAL COMMENT

One of the major archetypes noted by Jung is the shadow. This archetype refers to the part of the unconscious self that is unpleasant and bad. It is the por-

---

1. Virginia Reid, ed., *Reading Ladders for Human Relations,* 5th ed., (Washington, D.C.: American Council on Education, 1972).

tion of the self that we want most to suppress. Helson refers to the shadow as the evil powers in *Elidor* by Garner and the dragon in *The Hobbit* by Tolkien. The shadow is an important part of Jung's theory of individuation, which is central to Helson's study.

WAYS OF RESPONDING

A. Find evidence of the shadow archetype in other children's books. These may take the form of evil persons, the devil, fierce animals, and sometimes the baser qualities of a normally kind person. Some books that are varied in genre but might be fruitful for such a study are *Talargain* by Gard, *Duffy and the Devil* by Zemach, *Shadow of a Bull* by Wojciechowska, and *The Wolves of Willoughby Chase* by Aiken.

B. Find out if children can identify the shadow archetype in literature of varying subtleties. Choose several books and give a summary accompanied by selected readings from each book. Some examples of books that would be appropriate are *My Name is Lion* by Embry, *The Courage of Sarah Noble* by Dalgliesh, *The Witches of Worm* by Snyder, *The Bear's House* by Sachs and *Let the Balloon Go* by Southall. Give children a list of characters and have them divide the list into two groups: good and bad. Evaluate their lists. Were they able to distinguish the shadow archetype in books where it is subtly presented? Compare your findings with those of a teacher at another grade level. Does age make a difference in children's identification of the shadow archetype?

7. The Divine Child Archetype

CRITICAL COMMENT

Helson points out that one category of fantasy tales has the divine child as its hero. This is one of Jung's common archetypes. In this archetype Jung explains the divine child as being wholly divine and therefore not yet integrated into a human being. The divine child is usually characterized as having had a miraculous birth and having suffered many adversities. It affords the historic childhood view of the collective unconscious but it also offers anticipation of the future. This archetype is an early phase of the individuation process in which the person is developing fully into maturity after coping with many of the childhood archetypes.

WAYS OF RESPONDING

A. Examine one of the books from Helson's study for evidences of the divine child archetype. Some of the books used were *Charlotte's Web* by White, *The Little Prince* by Saint-Exupéry, *The Animal Family* by Jarrell, *Tistou of the Green Thumbs* by Druon, and *A Grass Rope* by Mayne. State some examples of the tenderness Helson refers to in her essay.

B. Is a book based on the divine child archetype easily understood by children? The group of books analyzed by Helson for this archetype is rather difficult from the standpoint of children's comprehension, with the notable exception of *Charlotte's Web*. In other instances, critics have stated that children probably read certain books and simply pass over the archetypes. Are the books of the divine child archetype of such a different nature, with a deeper emotional base and less active plot line, that they are seldom read by children? Make a survey of children's reading to determine if these books are frequently read. Share your findings and you generalizations with your colleagues.

8. Fantasy: An Expression of the Emotions

CRITICAL COMMENT

Helson states that a child can gain "context and expression for his feelings and emotional experiences" from a good fantasy, whereas adults can penetrate even deeper into the emotional relations between the fantasy motifs in their own lives. She describes the Jungian principal of individuation which involves working through some of the childhood archetypes that appear in fantasy literature.

WAYS OF RESPONDING

A. Can you be sure that children are finding expression for their emotional feelings in fantasies? Have your students keep a record of their reading for a period of six weeks and at the same time keep a journal. At the end of the time ask them to make a list from their journals of the concerns they have had. If you are in the habit of reading their journals, you could make this list yourself, perhaps with greater insight and accuracy. With the list compiled, do a content analysis of the fantasies they have read. Do these books meet the emotional needs of these particular children? What are the most significantly matched emotions that are shared by the books and the journals?

B. Read the chapter, "From Eight to Fourteen," in Cook's The Ordinary and the Fabulous.[2] In this chapter the author discusses meanings of many myths and tales and relates them to children of varying ages. Reflect on Helson's comments about individuation after reading Cook's chapter. Does this rather extensive coverage suggest that the deep themes of life are inherent within fantasy tales? What is your view on the abilities of adults to gain greater self-understanding by reinvolving themselves with these archetypes?

9. Allegory

CRITICAL COMMENT

Brady states that the Narnia tales are allegorical, encompassing "creation, sin, time, eternity, death, incarnation and resurrection." He praises the Narnia tales and suggests that the series can take its place beside Kipling's The Jungle Book and the Tolkien trilogy. He notes, however, that some critics have cast disfavor on the use of allegory. These critics compare allegorical writing with symbolic writing, arguing that allegory is used in a surface or artificial way whereas symbolism is used for depth meanings.

---

2. Elizabeth Cook. The Ordinary and the Fabulous. (Cambridge: Cambridge University Press, 1969).

WAYS OF RESPONDING

A. Read some children's novels that are allegorical. You might choose *Dorp Dead* by Cunningham, *Watership Down* by Adams, *A Wind in the Door* by L'Engle, *The Boy Who Had Wings* by Yolen, and *Forest of the Night* by Townsend. Do you find yourself drawn into the books intellectually or emotionally? Would you or wouldn't you ally yourself with Brady on the issue of allegories, especially the use of allegory in children's books?

B. One of the classic allegories is *Pilgrim's Progress*. The story was rewritten for children by Mary Godolphin. Read her version and share your reactions with your colleagues. Do you find a strong plot and a commanding story or are you constantly tripping over allegorical forms, trying to rationally determine their meaning?

10. Medieval Christian Symbolism

CRITICAL COMMENT

C. S. Lewis, the author of the Narnia series, was a renowned Anglican theologian. Brady describes the series as being filled with heraldic or medieval Christian symbolism even though the plots are written on varying levels so that children could read them as simply intriguing stories. Although Brady notes that it is not necessary for children to understand the symbolism, he notes, "it is still better that they do."

WAYS OF RESPONDING

A. Read some of Narnia books by Lewis, especially *The Lion, the Witch, and the Wardrobe; The Magician's Nephew;* and *The Last Battle.* Look specifically for the Christian symbolism. What is your opinion of the value of such symbolism for children? Discuss the symbols with some of your colleagues. Do you all interpret the symbols in the same way?

B. How would you go about teaching religious symbolism to children without practicing the religion? Check into some of the teaching methodologies and points of view about the teaching of religion in the public school suggested as guidelines by the professional education organization concerned with this task: The Public Education about Religion in the School Center.[3]

11. Parodies of Classic Tales

CRITICAL COMMENT

The Legend of Sleepy Hollow was suggested by Bruner as being a parody of ancient Greek myths. She notes that the author, Washington Irving, at one time defended his right to use popular traditions as the basis for his stories and she indicates that he probably felt the same way about the use of myths.

---

3. For information write to: The Public Education about Religion in the School Center (PERSC), Wright State University, Dayton, Ohio 45431.

WAYS OF RESPONDING

A. Select a Greek myth with which you are relatively familiar, such as a story about Pandora, the Muses, Pygmalion, and Jason. Write a modern day adventure that is a parody of the myth you select. The *Motif-Index of Folk Literature*[4] might be a useful reference tool for noting specific items that are used as parts of rites and rituals.

B. Read *Petronella* by Williams. How much of this book is drawn from ancient myths and how much is parody? Study the illustrations and make a judgment about whether they relate to the traditional myth form or to the parody element.

12. The Rebirth Archetype

CRITICAL COMMENT

One of Jung's major archetypes is that of rebirth, in which the person is transformed in one of a number of ways—some magical, some emotional. Psychologically, Jung saw this as a step in the process of individuation—a means of attaining a mature knowledge of the self. Jung suggested five forms of rebirth: transmigration of souls, reincarnation, resurrection, renewal, and indirect rebirth through transformation when one participates in a rite. *The Legend of Sleepy Hollow* is designated by Bruner as being an example of the rebirth archetype.

WAYS OF RESPONDING

A. Do children's books make use of the rebirth archetype? Study some of the books that show a great change taking place in the main character. Are these books reminiscent of any of Jung's forms of the rebirth motif? You might want to read *The Mountain and the Summer Stars* by Baker, or *Call it Courage* by Sperry. Point out distinctive elements to your colleagues.

B. A number of children's books deal with rituals. Read one of these and determine whether the book's theme could be classified as a rebirth archetype because of the rituals performed. Some books appropriate to this project are *Jennifer, Hecate, Macbeth, William McKinley, and Me, Elizabeth* by Konigsburg, *Lavender-Green Magic* by Norton and *Island Through the Gate* by Swahn.

C. Frye suggests that literature is created around four phases of a natural or seasoned cycle. These four phases might be adapted to *Charlotte's Web*, which touches on all the points. The first phase is that of the dawn, spring, and birth. It includes not only myths of birth, creation, and resurrection, but also the defeat of death. *Charlotte's Web* by White is one of the books used as the basis for a unit in the curriculum guide, *A Curriculum for English: Grade 4.*[5] Read the unit for suggestions on teaching, noting the comments that deal with

---

4. Stith Thompson, *Motif-Index of Folk-Literature*, Rev. Ed. (Bloomington, Ind.: Indiana University Press, 1955–58).
5. Nebraska Curriculum Development Center. *A Curriculum for English: Grade 4.* (Champaign, Illinois: National Council of Teachers of English, 1966).

discussing the mythical analysis of the book with children. What methods might you use for helping children observe the rebirth archetype of the story?

13. The Quest Archetype

CRITICAL COMMENT

Terry defines quest tales as stories with an external as well as an internal search. The first search concerns an exciting journey, but the internal search is one in which the character searches and finds inner depths to his person.

WAYS OF RESPONDING

A. Read *Stuart Little* by White in the light of Terry's definition of a quest tale. Does it fit the category? Terry illustrates her definition with examples of several books. Each of her examples, however, were stories in which the character succeeded in his quest. In what way, if any, does this fact alter your view of the quality of *Stuart Little* as a quest tale?

B. You might be interested in noting whether the quest archetype is as common in children's literature as it is in adult literature. Do a survey of the basic form of a preselected group of books, such as the Newbery Award books, the Lewis Carroll Shelf Award books for one year, or the books listed in compilations such as *Juniorplots* by Gillespie and Lembo.[6] Note the ratio of quest literature to other types of themes. Is the number high enough to lend support to Northrup Frye's assertion that all literary genres are derived from the quest-myth, a statement which he made in *Fables of Identity*.[7]

C. Analyze one or two of the books in Terry's bibliography. Do you find that these books are episodic in form as a journey often is? Does it seem to be a necessity of form that quest tales are episodic?

14. Values in Quest Literature

CRITICAL COMMENT

Children assimilate values from quest tales, according to Terry. She cites several incidents in quest literature old and recent that show human values of goodness overcoming evil. Her belief is that children will accept the moral judgment of the author.

WAYS OF RESPONDING

A. Make up a list of opposing statements concerning the characters or events in several quest tales. For example, you might use the Capping in *The White Mountains* by Christopher, and the hero in *Kiviok's Magic Journey* by Houston. Build a series of statements such as:

---

6. John T. Gillespie and Diana Lembo. *Juniorplots* (New York: R. R. Bowker, 1967).
7. Northrup Frye, *Fables of Identity* (New York: Harcourt Brace Jovanovich, 1963).

good_____bad
loving_____hateful
happy_____sad
noble_____base
intelligent_____ignorant
pretty_____ugly

Have a group of your colleagues assign a scaled mark for each pair of statements under each of the literary items. Share the results of this semantic dif-
ferential exercise and notice the amount of agreement for the various items.
On the basis of this test, do you agree with Terry concerning the assimilation
of values from the quest tales?

B. Several persons might combine their efforts to do a content analysis of
quest literature for its inherent values. Terry's bibliography would be a good
starting point. Other books might include Babbitt's *The Search for Delicious,*
McDermott's *Arrow to the Sun,* or Kendall's *The Gammage Cup.* What types
of values are apparent? Are any of these similar enough to be categorized together?

FURTHER READING

Alexander, Lloyd. "High Fantasy and Heroic Romance." *Horn Book* 47, no. 6 (December 1971): 577–84. The award-winning author of the Prydain books considers the mythic elements he used in his tales.

Anderson, William. "Fairy Tales and the Elementary Curriculum or, 'The Sleeping Beauty' Reawakened." *Elementary English* 46, no. 5 (May 1969): 563–69. The Brothers Grimm's tale is analyzed for its archetypes which are, in turn, related to older myths. A suggestion is made that these elements can be discussed in the elementary grades.

Cohen, Phyllis. "A New Look at Old Books: Coming of Age." *Young Readers' Review* 1, no. 1 (September 1964): 12. . . . *And Now Miguel, Call It Courage,* and *Onion John* are discussed as examples of the initiation rite archetype.

Colbath, Mary Lou. "Worlds as They Should Be: Middle-Earth, Narnia and Prydain." *Elementary English* 48, no. 8 (December 1971): 937–45. Tolkien's, Lewis', and Alexander's series of books based on fantasy worlds are analyzed in terms of three limitations: their depiction of a subcreation or secondary world, their relationship to man's mythological heritage, and their ability to be stimulants to the imagination.

Crago, Hugh and Maureen. "A Cupful of Diamond Juice." *Growing Point* (January 1972), pp. 1866–69. Preliminary thoughts are noted about a historical study of the recurring images in children's literature.

Evans, W. D. Emrys. "Illusion, Tale and Epic: Suzanne Langer's *Feeling and Form* and Four Books for Children." *The School Librarian* 21, no. 1 (March 1973): 5–11. Langer's theories of illusion, tale, and epic are discussed in relation to *The Hobbit* by Tolkien, *The Voyage of the Dawn Treader* by Lewis, *A Wizard of Earthshead* by LeGuin, and *Elidor* by Garner.

Grob, Shirley. "Dickens and Some Motifs of the Fairy Tale." *Texas Studies in Literature and Language.* 5 (1964): 567–79. The archetype of the fairy godmother is traced in greater and lesser degrees in Dickens' novels.

Heisig, James W. "Pinocchio: Archetype of the Motherless Child." *Children's Literature: The Great Excluded* 3 (1974): 23–35. A combination of psychological and archetypal criticism results in some interesting theories about this classic story.

Hooper, Walter. "Narnia: The Author, The Critics, and The Tale." *Children's Literature: The Great Excluded* 3 (1974): 12–22. The critic discusses the Christian symbolism in C. S. Lewis' Narnia series.

Hyman, Stanley Edgar. "Some Bankrupt Treasuries." *The Kenyon Review* 10, no. 3 (Summer 1948): 484–500. Twelve books of folklore are reviewed, including several children's books that have since become familiar sources. The critic decries the work of many of the collectors and discusses at length the field of folk criticism and its use of archetypes.

Krumgold, Joseph. "Archetypes of the Twentieth Century." *School Library Journal* 15 (October 1968): 112–15. The Newbery Award winning author discusses his trilogy of books based on the initiation archetype.

McDermott, Gerald. "On the Rainbow Trail." *Horn Book* 51, no. 2 (April 1975): 123–31. The Caldecott Award winning illustrator and film maker describes several of his folk tales as hero quests. Much attention is given to the symbolic meanings of *Arrow to the Sun*.

Olson, Paul A. "Religious Writing in Nebraska Curriculum." *Religious Education* 67 (July 1972): 69–74. The junior high curriculum of the Nebraska literature curriculum is described with an emphasis on its many mythic archetypes.

REFERENCES

Adams, Richard. *Watership Down*. New York: The Macmillan Company, 1972.

Aiken, Joan. *The Wolves of Willoughby Chase*. Illus. Pat Marriott. Garden City, New York: Doubleday, 1962.

Alexander, Lloyd. *The Black Cauldron*. New York: Holt, Rinehart and Winston, 1965.

————. *The Book of Three*. New York: Holt, Rinehart and Winston, 1964.

————. *The Castle of Llyr*. New York: Holt, Rinehart and Winston, 1966.

————. *The High King*. New York: Holt, Rinehart and Winston, 1968.

————. *Taran Wanderer*. New York: Holt, Rinehart and Winston, 1967.

Andersen, Hans Christian. *The Nightingale*. Illus. Harold Berson. Philadelphia: J. B. Lippincott, 1962.

Babbitt, Natalie. *The Search for Delicious*. New York: Farrar, Straus and Giroux, 1969.

Baker, Michael. *The Mountain and the Summer Stars*. Illus. Erika Weihs. New York: Harcourt Brace Jovanovich, 1968.

Blume, Judy. *Are You There God? It's Me, Margaret*. Englewood Cliffs, New Jersey: The Bradbury Press, 1970.

Bunyan, John. *Pilgrim's Progress*. Retold by Mary Godolphin. Illus. Robert Lawson. Philadelphia: J. B. Lippincott, 1939.

Burch, Robert. *Skinny*. Illus. Don Sibley. New York: The Viking Press, 1964.

Chaffin, Lillie D. *John Henry McCoy*. Illus. Emanuel Schongut. New York: The Macmillan Company, 1971.

Chase, Richard, ed. *Grandfather Tales*. Illus. Berkeley Williams, Jr. Boston: Houghton Mifflin, 1948.

Christopher, John. *The White Mountains*. New York: The Macmillan Company, 1967.

Cunningham, Julia. *Dorp Dead*. Illus. James Spanfeller. New York: Pantheon Books, 1965.

Dalgliesh, Alice. *The Courage of Sarah Noble*. Illus. Leonard Weisgard. New York: Charles Scribner's Sons, 1954.

Druon, Maurice. *Tistou of the Green Thumbs*. Trans. Humphrey Hare. New York: Charles Scribner's Sons, 1958.

Du Bois, William Pène. *The Twenty-One Balloons*. New York: The Viking Press, 1947.

Eager, Edward. *Half Magic*. Illus. N. M. Bodecker. New York: Harcourt Brace Jovanovich, 1954.

Embry, Margaret. *My Name is Lion*. Illus. Ned Glattauer. New York: Holiday House, 1970.

Engdahl, Sylvia Louise. *Enchantress from the Stars*. Illus. Rodney Shackell. New York: Antheneum, 1970.

Gard, Joyce. *Talargain*. New York: Holt, Rinehart and Winston, 1964.

Garner, Alan. *Elidor*. New York: Henry Z. Walck, 1967.

Greene, Bette. *Philip Hall Likes Me. I Reckon Maybe*. Illus. Charles Lilly. New York: The Dial Press, 1974.

Hamilton, Virginia. *The House of Dies Drear.* Illus. Eros Keith. New York: The Macmillan Company, 1968.

Hoban, Russell. *The Mouse and His Child.* Illus. Lillian Hoban. New York: Harper & Row, 1967.

Houston, James. *Kiviok's Magic Journey.* New York: Atheneum, 1973.

Hunter, Mollie. *The Smartest Man in Ireland.* Illus. Charles Keeping. New York: Funk & Wagnalls, 1963.

Jarrell, Randall. *The Animal Family.* Illus. Maurice Sendak. New York: Pantheon Books, 1965.

Juster, Norton. *The Phantom Tollbooth.* Illus. Jules Feiffer. New York: Random House, 1961.

Kendall, Carol. *The Gammage Cup.* Illus. Erik Blegvad. New York: Harcourt Brace Jovanovich, 1959.

Kipling, Rudyard. *The Jungle Book.* Illus. Philip Hays. Garden City, New York: Doubleday, 1964.

Konigsburg, E. L. *Jennifer, Hecate, Macbeth, William McKinley, and Me, Elizabeth.* New York: Atheneum, 1967.

Krumgold, Joseph. *. . . And Now Miguel.* Illus. Jean Charlot. New York: Thomas Y. Crowell, 1953.

_____. *Henry 3.* Illus. Alvin Smith. New York: Atheneum, 1967.

_____. *Onion John.* Illus. Symeon Shimin. New York: Thomas Y. Crowell, 1959.

Lang, Andrew, ed. *Blue Fairy Book.* Illus. Ben Kutcher. Foreword by Mary Gould Davis. New York: David McKay, 1948.

L'Engle, Madeleine. *A Wind in the Door.* New York: Farrar, Straus and Giroux, 1973.

_____. *A Wrinkle in Time.* New York: Farrar, Straus and Company, 1962.

Lenski, Lois. *Strawberry Girl.* Philadelphia: J. B. Lippincott, 1945.

Lewis, C. S. *The Last Battle.* Illus. Pauline Baynes. New York: The Macmillan Company, 1956.

_____. *The Lion, the Witch, and the Wardrobe.* Illus. Pauline Baynes. New York: The Macmillan Company, 1950.

_____. *The Magician's Nephew.* Illus. Pauline Baynes. New York: The Macmillan Company, 1955.

Mayne, William. *A Grass Rope.* Illus. Lynton Lamb. New York: E. P. Dutton, 1962.

McDermott, Gerald, adaptor. *Arrow to the Sun.* New York: The Viking Press, 1974.

Norton, André. *Lavender-Green Magic.* Illus. by Judith Gwyn Brown. New York: Thomas Y. Crowell, 1974.

Ormondroyd, Edward. *Time at the Top.* Illus. Peggie Bach. Berkeley, California: Parnassus Press, 1963.

Perrault, Charles. *Cinderella, or The Little Glass Slipper.* Trans. Adaptor, Illus. Errol LeCain. Scarsdale, New York: Bradbury Press, 1972.

Potter, Beatrix. *The Tale of Peter Rabbit.* New York: Warne, 1903.

Sachs, Marilyn. *The Bears' House.* Illus. Louis Glanzman. Garden City, New York: Doubleday, 1971.

_____. *The Truth About Mary Rose.* Illus. Louis Glanzman. Garden City, New York: Doubleday, 1973.

Saint-Exupéry, Antoine de. *The Little Prince.* Trans. Katherine Woods. New York: Harcourt Brace Jovanovich, 1943.

Sendak, Maurice. *Higglety Pigglety Pop!* New York: Harper & Row, 1967.

Serraillier, Ian. *The Gorgon's Head, The Story of Perseus.* Illus. William Stobbs. New York: Henry Z. Walck, 1962.

Seuss, Dr. *The 500 Hats of Bartholomew Cubbins.* New York: The Vanguard Press, 1938.

Snyder, Zilpha Keatley. *The Changeling.* Illus. Alton Raible. New York: Atheneum, 1970.

————. *The Witches of Worm.* Illus. Alton Raible. New York: Atheneum, 1973.

Southall, Ivan. *Let the Balloon Go.* Illus. Ian Ribbons. New York: St. Martin's Press, 1968.

Sperry, Armstrong. *Call It Courage.* New York: The Macmillan Company, 1940.

Steele, Mary Q. *Journey Outside.* Illus. Rocco Negri. New York: The Viking Press, 1969.

Stevenson, Robert Louis. *Treasure Island.* Illus. N. C. Wyeth. New York: Charles Scribner's Sons, 1911, 1939.

Sutcliff, Rosemary (reteller). *Beowulf.* Illus. Charles Keeping. New York: E. P. Dutton, 1962.

Swahn, Sven. *Island Through the Gate.* Trans. Patricia Crampton. New York: The Macmillan Company, 1974.

Thurber, James. *Many Moons.* Illus. Louis Slobodkin. New York: Harcourt Brace Jovanovich, 1943.

Tolkien, J. R. R. *The Hobbit.* Boston: Houghton Mifflin, 1938.

Townsend, John Rowe. *Forest of the Night.* Illus. Beverly Brodsky McDermott. Philadelphia: J. B. Lippincott, 1975.

White, E. B. *Charlotte's Web.* Illus. Garth Williams. New York: Harper & Row, 1952.

————. *Stuart Little.* Illus. Garth Williams. New York: Harper & Row, 1945.

Wilder, Laura Ingalls. *Little House in the Big Woods.* Illus. Garth Williams. New York: Harper & Brothers, 1953.

Williams, Jay. *Petronella.* Illus. Friso Henstra. New York: Parents' Magazine Press, 1973.

Wojciechowska, Maia. *Shadow of a Bull.* Illus. Alvin Smith. New York: Atheneum, 1965.

Wuorio, Eva-Lis. *Tal and the Magic Barruget.* Illus. Bettina. Cleveland: The World Publishing Company, 1965.

Yolen, Jane. *The Boy Who Had Wings.* Illus. Helga Aichinger. New York: Thomas Y. Crowell, 1974.

Zemach, Harve (reteller). *Duffy and the Devil.* Illus. Margot Zemach. New York: Farrar, Straus and Giroux, 1973.

chapter four

Structural Criticism

Structural criticism is concerned with the form of the literary work; it uses an analysis of the structure of the work in order to understand the meaning of the work. Several other names are given to this type of criticism: formalism, New Criticism, and textual criticism.

This form of criticism grew, in part, from a dissatisfaction with emphasis on elements that were external to literature, such as the biography of the author or the sociological setting of the novel. The structural critic believes that the literary work itself contains all that is needed for the work's interpretation. Critics use the form of the work itself, that is, the language, imagery, stanzaic patterns, meter, and rhythm, and the content—the tone, theme, etc.—all working together to show the precise meaning. According to the critics, the principle that develops from close analysis of these factors allows the work to reveal itself. It is the principle that keeps content and form inseparable.

Some techniques used by structural critics include giving multiple definitions to terms, judging one literary work in relation to other literature, and noting the use of paradoxes, that is, contradictions in metaphors.

Pros and Cons of Structural Criticism

Probably the greatest influence structural criticism had on the field of literary criticism was its return to the literary work itself as the focus for the criticism. Psychological, sociological, and archetypal criticism were concerned with external elements of the literature; structural criticism looked internally at the words themselves, noting their distinctive meanings and their artful arrangement that in itself illuminated the content. Structural criticism made a great distinction between the scientific and literary use of language.

The methodology of close reading offered a style of criticism that could be tedious, yet sought to uncover meaning in every possible way. The reader-critic learned to read with the use of many dictionaries, searching for various meanings and nuances, even studying the etymology of words for greater insight into the poet's message.

The poem-reader relationship was another valuable contribution of structural criticism. The reader was able to bring his own background of experience to bear on the poem as he selected the meaning which, due to his experience, seemed most appropriate.

Much negative criticism has been bestowed upon structural criticism. Because so much attention was given to poetry rather than any other art form, the criticism of narrowness in range was made. Another negative criticism was that there was the possibility of too great an emphasis on analysis to the point of losing sight of the whole meaning of the literary work. Some critics felt that the structural critics were trying to draw the analysis to a point where an absolute statement of meaning would be made, suggesting that such intense study of form would lead to "truth" when in actuality the meaning would still be only relative no matter how deeply analyzed the literary work might be.

The methodology of closely analyzing features such as diction and meter was considered by some to be an advantageous feature of structural criticism, and by others as amateurish at times. The term *mechanical* was also used in a negative sense to describe the method of analysis. The terminology that grew out of the structural theories was highly criticized, chiefly because it was not universally understandable—even by some fellow practitioners. Perhaps the most stinging criticism was that structural criticism was not humanistic. It was said to have separated literature from life so that the relationships and even the values of literature to man's problems—both current and past—were neglected.

Structural Criticism of Children's Literature

Structural criticisms of children's literature are the least numerous of the four types of criticism discussed in this book. A number of parodies include structural methodologies, but few serious structural analyses exist in published form when compared with those done in the other critical styles. An interesting observation is that those structural studies that are published are the work of educationists far more frequently than of critics in other fields, whereas the latter was the case in the selections from psychological, archetypal, and sociological criticism. Searches through journals that primarily reflect the New Criticism, such as *Yale Review, Kenyon Review,* and *Hudson Review* result in few criticisms of children's books. A genre that has had attention from the structural critics is folk tales. The work of Vladimir Propp, after its translation in 1958, prompted a number of studies of structural analysis of folk tales, albeit these are not the folk tales that have been adapted or retold for children's use.

Speculations as to why few structural studies have been done include the hunch that critics other than educationists might be unaware of the multiple levels of meaning to be found in children's books, particularly at the internal level. The highly patterned form of many children's picture storybooks is intuitively known by teachers who use books a great deal. These sometimes simple, highly repetitive elements of form may have caused would-be critics to see less of a challenge in the children's books than in adult literature.

The vocabulary of children's books may have kept structural critics from turning to this source when they were especially concerned with word choice and the multiplicity of meanings that the words connote. Other critics may read much of their meaning into children's books, but structural critics must initially rely on the specific words that make up the content and draw meanings from these. Even though the majority of children's trade books are not written with controlled vocabularies, the fact remains that vocabulary in children's books is less complex and erudite, than in adult literature. This is a reality that differentiates children's literature from adult literature.

Poetry is probably the most analyzed genre in structural criticism. When the poems of established poets are anthologized in collections of children's poetry, the simplest works are the ones selected. Structural critics would be likely to select more complex poems to allow greater depth in their analyses.

Thus, it is likely that the form of children's literature may be the very feature that causes formalist critics to avoid its use in critical analyses. If structural criticism were ever to have been prominent in children's literature, it probably would have been during the 1960s when curriculum-centered educationists sought to find the core ideas of each subject area, led by Bruner's thesis that children could learn certain basic features of the structure of any discipline. No particularly sizable surge toward structural criticism was evident at that time, however.

The technique of close reading is apparent during the reading of all the following essays. Each critic uses textual analysis, carefully studying the shape of the literature and the way it was developed. Form and meaning are the two areas of the literature that are focused upon. The critics point out some features unique to children's literature as they analyze the structure.

The concept that visual patterns can create the form that carries the story is central to Cianciolo's discussion of the wordless picture books. The author analyzes these books for their fundamental examples of literary elements, giving examples of the use of visual metaphors, visual irony, and visual features of plot development.

Picture books are the focus of Guttery's article. She notes the use of detail words such as size, number, specific name, shape, and color that help a child visualize the story more clearly. The sound of the story, as denoted in the rhythm and balance, is also significant. Guttery depicts the repetitious structure of many picture storybooks with a diagram showing the movements.

Perhaps the greatest concern specifically for words in any of the essays is found in Gilpatrick's analysis of *Peter's Tent*. Alliteration is pointed out more than once. Paradoxical metaphors are highlighted in instances such as the privacy concerns of the young boy versus the old man. Again, the use of the pictures is noted as a means of visually emphasizing the story feeling.

Neumeyer uses Propp's technique of describing the story according to the functions that occur. In doing this, Neumeyer depicts the sequence of the story. He suggests that such analyses of many books might result in seeing related structural patterns in children's literature.

The Owl Service is the only full-length novel analyzed in this collection. Cameron points out that the plot is based on three triangles of characters who occur in three different periods of time. She is critical of Garner's descriptions and his dialogues for what she considers to be a harsh rhythm, a phonological emphasis central to the technique of structural criticism. Cliches used in the dialogues are pointed out as being paradoxical; the characters speak negatively of other characters but the cliches they use to describe the others show their own lesser qualities.

Poetry is analyzed in Tichi's essay on "Hiawatha." She suggests that Longfellow used the form of his poem to show the Indians' progress toward civilization, thus making a sociological/political statement through the structure.

READINGS

Use Wordless Picture Books to Teach
Reading, Visual Literacy and to Study Literature

Patricia Jean Cianciolo

There is an interesting development taking place in the juvenile trade book publishing arena. It is the appearance of story books which consist only of pictures and have no written text. This innovation permits the book artist to function at a very high level; he can use a graphic form to tell his story to the extent that his knowledge, imagination, and talents permit.

I discovered the wordless picture book about four years ago when I read *The Magic Stick* created by Kjell Ringi. The illustrations in *The Magic Stick*, as in the other wordless picture books I have discovered to date, carry the completed load in the way of literary connotation. The sequence of the illustrations tells a story without the use of the written word yet the story is told rapidly, accurately, and as convincingly as the reader is able to interpret or speak the language of these visuals. At the time I first saw Ringi's wordless picture book, I thought it a superb example of the fact that pictures do speak a language. A *universal* language, if you will. But one must be visually literate in order to speak (or read!) that universal language. In other words, one must be able to bring meaning and significance to the shapes, positions, and movements that are depicted by the book artist as he tells his stories in pictures.

New as the books without words may be to the field of children's literature, there are many of them readily available in school and public libraries. They vary considerably in quality of artistic accomplishment. Happily, there is a respectable dissimilarity in format, content, and style of art from book to book. Some are addressed to the very young child; others are far more appropriate for the sophisticated and mature youth or adult.

The creative teacher can use the wordless picture books in any number of learning experiences. Implementing some of the techniques peculiar to the language experience approach they may be used to teach reading to those beginning to read, to illiterate adults, and to children in need of remedial reading instruction.

Reprinted from *Top of the News* 29, no. 3 (April 1973): 226–34.

They may be used to teach such visual literacy skills as literal translation of objects or situations presented in a visual or a sequence of illustrations arranged to transmit a fictional narrative and interpretation of figurative expressions presented visually. They may be used to help students of literature recognize and evaluate the author/artist's ability to develop in his fiction-in-pictures such basic components as plot development, characterization, theme, setting, and style.

Reading Instruction. In the language experience approach the child's real or vicarious experiences are used, the child's dictated stories or those he has written himself reflect these experiences. The compositions serve as a basis for his reading materials. The written compositions and recorded oral compositions constitute the learner's reading vocabulary and it is the words used in these compositions that are used to teach phonetic and structural analysis skills, or any other reading skills, when the learner evidences a need for instruction or practice in them. When the wordless picture books are used to provide the experience (vicarious) upon which the compositions are based, the compositions may be created by an individual or by groups of students. The experience upon which the composition is based is that which is offered by the sequence and details presented in the wordless picture books. The younger the child the more closely allied to the child's here-and-now world must be the content and experience presented in the wordless picture book. As the learner becomes more mature and acquires a broader background of experience the content and experience depicted in the illustrations may be more removed from his here-and-now world; they may be more sophisticated in theme and fanciful in nature. The kindergarten-primary school child would appreciate the fun-filled adventure depicted in the little books by Mercer Mayer, *Boy, a Dog, and a Frog* and its sequel *Frog, Where Are You?* The child in the third grade and beyond would find *Journey to the Moon* by Erich Fuchs much more to his liking for this picture book without words follows the day by day progress of the Apollo II mission, the launching, the flight, the landing, and the return to earth of the three astronauts. This narrative is presented in twelve stunning double-spread paintings and if the reader wants to verify his "reading" of these illustrations he may refer to the explanatory captions provided by the author; they are located on two pages preceding the paintings.

Visual Literacy

Growth in visual literacy depends upon exposure to visual literacy experiences and an awareness that visuals speak a language. It has been hypothesized that there is a hierarchy of visual skills. A visually literate person would be able to (a) read visuals with skill; (b) write with visuals expressing himself effectively; (c) know the grammar and syntaxes of visual language and be able to apply them; (d) be familiar with the tools of visual literacy and their use; (e) appreciate the masterworks of visual literacy, and (f) translate from visual language and vice versa.[1]

Literal Interpretation. The ability to read on the literal level the sequence of visuals arranged to identify assorted objects or transmit a fictional narrative is one of the first skills one must have if he is visually literate. One example of a book which could be used to help nursery-kindergarten aged children recognize and name the illustrations is *Shapes and Things* by Tana Hoban. In it everyday objects such as tooth-brushes, a comb, toys, buttons, safety and stick pins, and eyeglasses are shown against black and white and children are introduced to the beauty of form. The visuals are done with photograms—photographs taken without the camera.

Not a wordless picture book in the strictest sense of the word for there is a slight amount of verbal text, *Nothing Ever Happens on My Block* is one that might be used to teach visual literacy skills to the kindergarten or early primary grade child. Ellen Raskin has included so much action in the illustrations that a rather involved plot has been developed for this narrative fiction. Carefully close scrutiny of the little pictures is necessary if one is to appreciate the full impact of all that is taking place in this ironic story. While Chester sits on the curb stone in front of his staid Victorian house and complains that his life is dull, a series of numerous amusing and dramatic events are going on around him—a criminal is arrested, a house burns and is restored, children play tricks on an elderly lady, an armored truck is involved in an accident and $50 bills fly in all directions. Comparable to *Nothing Ever Happens on My Block*, but for older visual readers are the books by Frank Asch. *George's Store, Linda,* and *Yellow, Yellow* have very brief texts, are action-filled, and detailed illustrations superabound. The plots in each of these books are simple enough but each is filled with surprises and zany fun. They constitute the efforts of a talented and sophisticated graphic artist. A capable and experienced visual literate would enjoy them.

Kjell Ringi uses color to lead the reader of *The Magic Stick* to the world of imagination. The real world in which the main book character lives is portrayed in black and white; the boy's make-believe world is portrayed through brilliantly colored pictures. The little boy imagines he can become a pirate with a telescope, a weight lifter, a general leading a parade, and so on. Six and seven-year-olds would in all probability be able to interpret and respond to this use of color and black and white. They would respond with the same feelings and emotions as did the boy in the story—that of delight in finding and using the stick to bring about magic and then the obvious unhappiness when his friends approach him and cause him to toss away the stick and leave his world of make-believe.

Figurative Expressions. There are some wordless picture books that aptly present what John Debes called "visual puns" and "visual metaphors."[2] *One, Two, Where's My Shoe* and *Snail Where Are You?* by Tomi Ungerer and *Topsy Turvies: Pictures that Stretch the Imagination* by Mitsumasa Anno are examples of the "visual pun." Both of the Ungerer books are done in simple cartoon-type drawings. *One, Two, Where's My Shoe* is a playful pictorial search for a shoe. Likewise, in *Snail, Where Are You?* the reader searches for the snail. In each case the shoe and snail are found in the most unlikely places. The bodies of the birds in flight are shoes, as are the dog's snout, the man's torso, the ship's hull, the alligator's body, the Egyptian's mustache, the fish's mouth, the cannon's barrel, and so on. The snail shape is repeated in pictures of the waves, a violin, and a birthday party "blower." The pictures in *Topsy Turvies: Picture Books that Stretch the Imagination* are deceptively simple. Mitsumasa Anno presents optical illusions which form structures in which people can go upstairs to get a lower place, hang pictures on the ceiling, and walk walls. This book exemplifies a series of "visual puns" for children in the upper primary or middle grades.

An extended visual metaphor is evident in George Mendoza's *And I Must Hurry for the Sea Is Coming In.* The ironic ending of this book about a ghetto boy whose toy boat becomes a ship that rides the waves will surprise the children. Once they come to that point in the story they will be able to realize full well why the boy fantasized the events and circumstances that he did. The colored photographs were done by Wayne Dalrymple and tell this author's story superbly well. Older children and even adults will understand and react to (but not necessarily agree with perhaps) the theme of *And I Must Hurry for the Sea Is Coming In* which is that there exists an "urgency in providing lives of dignity and strength for all children—'for the sea is coming in' and we had all better hurry."[3] This book is a good example of a "multi-level" book. The young reader can enjoy on the literal level the visual metaphor that is presented via the photographs. The more mature, knowledgeable person who is aware of the realities of life, one who is an experienced and thoughtful reader of visuals will grasp the powerful message expressed in the theme and will respect the skill with which the visual metaphor is expressed.

Literary Devices. There is much that the reader of literature would benefit from if he were able to recognize the devices that an author/artist makes use of to develop a plot. Knowledge of this nature would help the reader to become more sensitive to the elements of good writing and book illustrating; thus, he could appreciate more fully future reading. It would help him to see the work from the standpoint of the author and think as an author thinks when he creates his own stories. Some literary devices that might be identified in the wordless picture books and also commonly used by authors of verbal fictional narratives include devices used to develop the plot (backflashing and foreshadowing); the point of view from which the story is told (first person, second person, third person, and omniscient point of view); the mood of the story (fanciful, realistic, satirical, ironical, serious, or humorous); and the style in which the story is told.

In order to read the pantomime story that is told in *Bobo's Dream* by Martha Alexander, the child must first recognize that the actions portrayed in the balloon pictures represent dreams. It would appear that the reader of this story about a grateful dachshund's dream of returning his master's kindness would need to have at his command a rather advanced visual literacy skill; this manner of telling the story by depicting the dog's dreams in balloons would probably be comparable to the device of telling a story from the omniscient point of view. This same point of view is used by the creator of *The Inspector.* Only the reader of this exciting but macabre picture book is fully aware of the inspector's plight, the hound's delight when consuming the monstrous creatures and its gradual but certain growth from a small apparently harmless dog to a huge, destructive, and hideous monster himself. Neither the hound nor the inspector is fully knowledgeable about his own or the other's state, but the reader is.

An example of a story that seems to exemplify the first person point of view is present in *Vicki* by Renate Meyer. In unusual full color paintings the reader is told by the little girl in the story how it feels to experience a spell of friendlessness. Her resolution to her problem, by the way, may surprise the readers but they probably would not debate the fact that it is a realistic and logical answer for her, yet not the one that they would resort to were they suddenly find themselves alone and in need of a friend.

The Study of Literature

Elementary school children can be taught to distinguish between good and inferior stories. However, in order to make these distinctions they must have some understanding of the basic components of literature, namely, setting, theme, characterization, plot, and style. One may make use of the wordless picture books to gain understandings of these components of fiction.

Literary Style. Style as a component of fiction is a rather nebulous element to deal with in the study of literature. Yet, the style of art used by the book artist, his use of color and space are among the basic factors that one must note and make some judgment about if one were to appraise the "literary style" of a wordless picture book.

Consider not only the manner or extent to which his style effects the unfolding or the development of the plot but how it creates a mood, portrays characters, and presents details about the setting of the story that is told in the picture book. For example, the line drawings done by Peter Parnall to tell the story of *The Inspector* are as macabre as the story and are very detailed. Only the visually literate person would benefit fully from all the artist has included in his illustrations. Attention to all the details in each of the illustrations would lead the reader to a wealth of visual statements about the thoughts and feelings of the inspector and the dog as they traipse ever onward over flat lands, mountains, and waterways all of which are infested with fantastically ugly monsters. Furthermore, the visually literate reader of this book knows the setting in which the story takes place every bit as well, perhaps better, than does the myopic inspector! No doubt about it, Parnall's style of art, his use of detail, his talented use of lines and shading and space produced a masterful piece of graphic art, told a good story, skillfully created a mood of horror, developed unique and emotional characters, and depicted a setting that was real. The many facets of Parnall's style together create a vitally unique story-in-pictures.

The carefree pastel sketches that Ruth Carroll did in *The Chimp and the Clown* are beautifully compatible with the fun-filled adventures of these circus animals. Likewise, the quaint pen and ink sketches done by Mercer Mayer establish the naive but action-packed experiences of the little boy, his dog, and their new mutual friend, the frog. The adventures of this threesome are found in *Boy, a Dog, and a Frog* and *Frog, Where Are You?* The intricate detail in Mitsumasa Anno's *Topsy Turvies: Pictures to Stretch the Imagination* reinforces the fact that this is not a book for the inexperienced student of visual literacy. And so on. Examples which might serve to demonstrate that the art work in large measure affects the "literary style" of a wordless picture book abound.

Literary Theme. The wordless picture books offer a rather unique and effective means by which one may help elementary school children to be able to recognize the theme of a literary selection. It is all well and good that they recognize the plot of a story and usually this is no problem if they can read the visuals at least on the most elementary level, namely, the literal level. But the reader must be a more competent reader of visuals, a more thoughtful reader of visuals if he is to move to the stage where he can identify the theme of the literary selection.

Not too many of the youngest readers would fail to recognize the theme presented by Edward Ardizzone in *The Wrong Side of the Bed*. There are few situations presented in this book that the reader would fail to identify with for Ardizzone, in his readily recognizable pen sketches, has offered the reader a "think" in each and every illustration.

I suspect it would take a somewhat mature child, probably eight or nine years of age, to be fully cognizant that one-upmanship is the message of Kjell Ringi's *The Winner*. Illustrations depicting a small girl, mischievous, snoopy goblins determined to right social inequities, and a flying saucer full of spaghetti together tell a droll story in Fernando Krahn's book *A Flying Saucer Full of Spaghetti*. The plot in this story would be easily followed by the kindergarten-primary-school-aged child. The characters are portrayed distinctively enough for them to keep straight, but the theme is one that would not be easily identified and understood until the child was nine years old or so, at which point he would be likely to be more knowledgeable and perceptive about or even sympathetic with social inequities.

The Inspector created by George Mendoza and illustrated by Peter Parnall is a controversial book. Some readers of this macabre picture book may be able to recognize a theme in the story—don't become too bogged down with the little details in life, take the broader view if you want to get a true perspective of what is happening to you. Other readers will insist there is no message presented in *The Inspector*. There is much happening in each of the illustrations in this book. One will have to look very carefully to see what is happening to the inspector, his hound, and the grossly wild and improbable monsters. This is not a book for kindergarteners. It is a good book I think, for the nine to thirteen-year-old who is beginning to like detective stories or horror stories.

Conclusion and Summary

I am not so certain that what I have said about using wordless picture books to develop visual literacy skills has not been said before. To paraphrase Madeleine L'Engle, if I thought I were expected to say it better than anybody else I would have been more than a little disinclined to start![4] The important issue is that some more thoughts should be given about this aspect of visual literacy and I have tried to present some of these above. The wordless picture books are available in ever growing quantity and quality. They constitute an excellent type of literary material through which children might be taught to read, to become visually literate, and to study aspects of literature, especially fiction.

BIBLIOGRAPHY OF WORDLESS PICTURE BOOKS

Alexander, Martha. *Bobo's Dream*. New York: Dial, 1970.

————. *Out! Out! Out!* New York: Dial, 1968.

Amoss, Bertha. *By the Sea*. New York: Parents, 1969.

Anno, Mitsumasa, *Topsy Turvies: Pictures to Stretch the Imagination*. New York: Walker/Weatherhill, 1970.

Ardizzone, Edward. *The Wrong Side of the Bed*. Garden City, N.Y.: Doubleday, 1970.

Asch, Frank. *The Blue Balloon*. New York: McGraw-Hill, 1971.

Baum, Willi. *Birds of a Feather*. Reading, Mass.: Addison-Wesley, 1969.

Bolliger-Savelli, Antonella. *The Knitted Cat*. New York: The Macmillan Company, 1973.

Carle, Eric. *Do You Want to be My Friend*. New York: Thomas E. Crowell, 1971.

————. *One, Two, Three. To The Zoo*. New York: World, 1968.

————. *The Very Hungry Caterpillar*. New York: World, 1970.

Carroll, Ruth. *The Chimp and the Clown*. New York: Henry Z. Walck, 1970.

————. *The Christmas Kitten*. New York: Henry Z. Walck, 1970.

————. *What Whiskers Did*. New York: Henry Z. Walck, 1965.

Espenscheid, Gertrude. *Oh Ball*. New York: Harper & Row, 1966.

Ets, Marie Hall. *Talking Without Words. I Can. Can You?* New York: The Viking Press, 1968.

Fuchs, Erick. *Journey to the Moon*. New York: Delacorte, 1969.

Gilbert, Elliot. *A Cat*. New York: Holt, Rinehart and Winston, 1963.

Goodall, John S. *The Adventures of Paddy Pork*. New York: Harcourt Brace Jovanovich, 1968.

————. *The Ballooning Adventures of Paddy Pork*. New York: Harcourt Brace Jovanovich, 1969.

————. *Shrewbettina's Birthday*. New York: Harcourt Brace Jovanovich, 1971.

Hoban, Tana. *Look Again*. New York: The Macmillan Company, 1971.

————. *Shapes and Things*. New York: The Macmillan Company, 1970.

Hutchins, Pat. *Changes, Changes*. New York: The Macmillan Company, 1971.

Krahn, Fernando *How Santa Had a Long and Difficult Journey Delivering His Presents*. New York: Delacorte, 1968.

————. *A Flying Saucer Full of Spaghetti*. New York: Dutton, 1970.

Mari, Iela. *The Magic Balloon*. New York: S. G. Phillips, 1969.

Mari, Iela and Enzo. *The Apple and the Moth*. New York: Pantheon, 1970.

————. *The Chicken and the Eggs*. New York: Pantheon, 1970.

Mayer, Mercer. *Boy, a Dog, and a Frog*. New York: Dial, 1967.

————. *Frog, Where Are You?* New York: Dial, 1969.

Mendoza, George. *And I Must Hurry for the Sea is Coming In*. Photos, DeWayne Dalrymple. Englewood Cliffs, N.J.: Prentice-Hall, 1969.

————. *The Inspector*. Garden City, N.Y.: Doubleday, 1970.

Meyer, Renate. *Vicki*. New York: Atheneum, 1969.

Mordillo, Guilermo. *The Damp and Daffy Doings of a Daring Pirate Ship*. New York: Harlin Quist, 1971.

Miller, Barry. *Alphabet World*. New York: The Macmillan Company, 1971.

Olschewski, Alfred. *Winterbird*. Boston, Mass.: Houghton Mifflin, 1969.

Ringi, Kjell. *The Magic Stick*. New York: Harper & Row, 1968.

————. *The Winner*. New York: Harper & Row, 1969.

Shick, Eleanor. *Making Friends*. New York: The Macmillan Company, 1969.

Simons, Ellie. *Cat*. New York: McKay, 1968.

————. *Dog*. New York: McKay, 1967.

————. *Family*. New York: McKay, 1970.

Steiner, Charlotte. *I Am Andy*. New York: Knopf, 1961.

Ungerer, Tomi. *One, Two, Three*. New York: Harper & Row, 1964.

————. *One, Two, Where's My Shoe?* New York: Harper & Row, 1964.

————. *Snail, Where Are You?* New York: Harper & Row, 1962.

Wezel, Peter. *Good Bird*. New York: Harper & Row, 1966.

Wondriska, William. *A Long Piece of String*. New York: Holt, Rinehart, and Winston, 1963.

REFERENCES

1. John L. Debes, "The Loom of Visual Literacy—An Overview." *Visual Literacy.* Clarence M. Williams and John L. Debes eds. Proceedings of the First National Conference on Visual Literacy, (New York: Pitman Publishing Co., 1970), pp. 13–14.

2. Ibid.

3. Lynne Stewart, "The Book Review" *School Library Journal* 17:106 (September 1970).

4. Madeleine L'Engle, *A Circle of Quiet*, (Farrar, Straus and Giroux, 1972).

Style in Children's Literature

Jean Guttery

If an author has the ability to make vivid the colors of an August sunset against the distant blue outline of mountain tops, or the wild sound of a winter storm on a lonely, forgotten beach, he is an artist with words, whether he is writing for children or adults. If, through his sensitivity to the sound and meaning of words, he is able to transfer to his reader a picture, an emotion, or an idea, he is writing with what we call "style," no matter whether his reader is young or mature. Anyone, then, who can appreciate the beauty and design in Pater's prose ought to be able to appreciate the rhythm and wording in the best of children's literature—from Rudyard Kipling's *Just So Stories* to Kenneth Grahame's *Wind in the Willows*. In contemporary juvenile literature, children and adults alike should respond to the memorable phrasing of Elizabeth Goude's *Smoky House*, Hilda van Stockum's *Kersti*, Elizabeth Orton Jones' *Maminka's Children*, and of many other modern stories written particularly for the child.

There are certain characteristics, however, which are not by any means found only in children's literature, but which seem to be particularly important in style designed for children. Many authors, for instance, adapt their style to the young reader by using a very informal and intimate approach. The author puts himself on the level of the child and speaks to him on personal, friendly terms as if they had shared secrets many times before. There is nothing sentimental about this style; it is just an occasional twist of a phrase that seems to establish understanding between the author and the reader. A conversational tone or an unexpected use of the second person can make the young reader at home with the author and give him the feeling that he and the author know just a bit more about the world than anyone else. It is this approach which Elizabeth Goudge uses so effectively when she breaks into the narrative of *Smoky House* every so often with such an observation as, "For children, of course, are much more sensible than grown-ups and dogs more sensible than children." E. Nesbit in *Wet Magic*

Reprinted from *Elementary English* 18, no. 6 (October 1941): 208–12, 240.

uses the same tone: " 'I don't believe they'll let you take it all,' said Bernard—and if you know anything of grown-ups you will know that Bernard proved to be quite right." A. A. Milne and Kenneth Grahame are particularly skillful with this approach.

A child's imagination is extremely visual, having little patience with abstractness or vagueness. When a child listens to a story, he wants to be able to fix in his mind in orderly and concrete fashion every detail of the setting and the action. A child's mind is like the mind of a stage director, seeing every play vividly but insisting on knowing exactly where every piece of stage setting is located and what type of property is used. So authors who write for children use a style rich in minute details and set their stories carefully in a well-planned background. When Margery Bianco introduces the hurdy-gurdy man to town in her book, *The Hurdy-Gurdy Man*, she tells about the weather, the season of year, and describes what all the townpeople are doing at the time. It is a vivid picture that Elizabeth Goudge paints of the village Faraway in *Smoky House*. Before meeting any of the main characters of the story, the reader knows that the people of Faraway are gay and kind, that they live in cottages "built of white-washed stone and thatched with golden straw," that they keep gardens filled with bushes of scarlet fuchsia and purple veronica, and that the "moors closed in this lovely land on three sides, and on the fourth side was the sea." In telling a child a story verbally, a story-teller knows that if he describes a meadow filled with flowers, the child will demand to know what *kind* of flowers. In writing for children, then, an author anticipates such questions. When Elizabeth Orton Jones describes the little boy in *Maminka's Children* as running out the door with a bucket in his hand, it is not just a bucket that she gives the boy but a "red-striped" bucket, and immediately the entire scene becomes visual. The color of a bucket in this case satisfies a child's curiosity about details just as in Emma Brock's *The Greedy Goat* the fact that the goat eats not just an unspecified amount of garden flowers but eats "all the purple asters and *four* of the sunflowers" appeals to a child's love of exactness. Although it is also incidental to the plot of Clare Newberry's *Babette*, it is important to the child reader to have an itemized list of all the Christmas presents Charity receives, and so the reader learns that besides Babette, the cat, Charity receives a doll, red mittens, a pink tea set, hankies, and the like.

A style rich in detail is usually rich in color. Although a colorful style is the goal of many an author writing for any age level, it is particularly important for children who are especially sensitive to the color element. Color is used generously and artistically in contemporary literature for children. Notice how colorful and attractive Elizabeth Orton Jones makes a bowl of chicken food appear in *Maminka's Children*:

> She filled a bowl with chicken food, and slipped a long red apple peeling, a lovely blue prune, a bright green pepper, a light green cabbage leaf, a purple beet, and some white, white rice into her pocket.

When Emma Brock describes *Little Fat Gretchen* running into a barnyard, she fills her path with color. "She ran into the sunlight that shone across the striped green and yellow fields and into the barnyard."

Notice how carefully words are chosen and how artistically color is used in the following quotations:

> Winter's feather-duster had swept the last remnants of gold off the earth—*Kersti*, Hilda van Stockum.
>
> A white duck was waddling in the willow pool in the pale morning light—*Little Fat Gretchen*, Emma Brock.
>
> He wore a mulberry-colored coat and exquisite lace ruffles terribly torn, and the powder flew in a silver cloud from his bright red hair–*Smoky House*, Elizabeth Goudge.

The color red seems to play an interesting and picturesque part in stories for children. When Snipp, Snapp, and Snurr, in Maj Lindman's book, *Snipp, Snapp, Snurr and the Red Shoes* want to buy their mother a present, they want not only slippers but they must be red slippers. When Dorothy Kunhardt tells a story of an old man who likes junket in the book *Junket is Nice*, the old man has a red beard, wears red slippers, and eats out of a red bowl. In Elizabeth Goudge's *Smoky House* the highwayman and adventurer is remembered as "The-Man-with-the-Red-Handkerchief."

Use of well-chosen figures of speech adds to the interest of any style, and it is interesting to note how authors adapt figures of speech to the experience of children. Style is enriched by the use of similes, but the similes are always more colorful in children's books when they spring naturally from the life of children and from those specific experiences with which they are most familiar. When Hilda van Stockum wants to impress the idea of "youngness" on her reader in *Kersti*, she draws upon all the illustrations of "newness" and "youngness" closest to the life of a child. She says in describing a new-born baby, "He is younger than a new moon, younger than the buds on the trees, younger than the eggs we found in the nest this morning, younger even than the hole in your stocking." Peggy Bacon appeals to the imagination of children in her description of a kitten in *Mercy and the Mouse*, "She was soft like the dust under the bed, with eyes like huckleberries and whiskers like a thistle." Elizabeth Goudge uses the simile with unusual effectiveness as is apparent in the following quotations from *Smoky House:*

> The golden thatch on the roof was so thick that they were as warm under it as a teapot is when you put a tea-cosy on top.
>
> Dancing with him was like dancing with a whirlwind on its afternoon out.
>
> Making a noise like a cork-coming-out-of-a-bottle, which was her favorite after the cats-on-the-roof-noise.

Just as an author adapts a figure of speech to the experience of a child, so he must adapt his expressions of time, size, and distance to a child's experience and his desire for concrete imagery. Style itself becomes more vivid when abstract measurements are replaced with more realistic measurements which a child can visualize. Lucy Embury in *The Listening Man* does not describe age in abstract terms of the number of years, but she says, "Already for more than a lifetime of eight elephants it has endured." W. H. Hudson creates a picture of early morning in *Tales of the Pampas* when instead of naming the hour of day, he says, "The stars were still shining when we set out on our journey." Again a realistic description of the time of day is found in Elizabeth Orton Jones' *Maminka's Children* when Aunt Patsy is said to arrive "just at Old Cow's milking time." The reader of Doris Gates' *Blue Willow* discovers that the little girl, Janey, is very short when Janey looks down at her shadow which was "a very short shadow even for a ten-year-old." Another little girl, Sally, in Cornelia Meigs' *Mother Makes Christmas* is described as being big enough now to see herself in the mirror when she sits at table. W. H. Hudson in *Tales of the Pampas* makes a tree trunk seem very large, indeed, by saying that "five men with their arms stretched to their utmost could hardly encircle it."

Good literary style is distinguished not only by its color, choice of words, and visual appeal, but also by its ability to please the ear, its rhythm, balance, its sentence and story pattern. Writers of children's literature show a definite consciousness of rhythm and an appreciation of children's sensitivity to it. Particularly noticeable is the fact that they capitalize on children's love of repetition. Just as young children will repeat a sentence or a phrase over and over in a sing-song way fascinated by the sound of the words, so authors writing for children will establish a definite sentence pattern by repeating action with only a slight variation in wording. Partly for the sake of simplicity, partly for the sake of rhythm, partly for the sake of building to a climax, an author will repeat as Marjorie Flack does in *Angus and the Cat*—

> "Angus came closer"—and the cat sat up.
> "Angus came closer"—up jumped the cat.
> "Angus came closer"—that little cat boxed his ears.

Miss Flack uses this same technique again very effectively in *Wait for William*, when Charles and Nancy must both repeat everything that is said to William.

> Charles said, "Hurry up, William, put away your scooter and we will take you down Maine Street to see the Circus Parade."
> Nancy said, "Hurry up, William, put away your scooter and we will take you down Maine Street to see the Circus Parade."

Repetition in sentence structure is carried through an entire story in "The Poppy Story," one of the *Arabella and Araminta Stories* by Gertrude Smith. Here everything that Arabella does must be repeated because her twin, Araminta, does it too. "Arabella lived in a white house on a green hill, and Araminta lived in a white house on a green hill."

Repetition not only of sentences but of individual words is used effectively. When Alice Dalgliesh writes a story about *The Little Wooden Farmer*, the reader expects the story to center about a lot of wooden things. It starts off with a nice rhythm of repetition: "There was a little wooden farmer who lived with his little wooden wife in a neat wooden farmhouse." In Marjorie Flack's *Angus Lost* the repetition of the word *same* gives not only rhythm but strengthens the mood of boredom for Angus who is sick of the *same* house, the *same* cat, and the *same* things. Repetition in *Wait for William* also is used as a special method of emphasis. It achieves an emotional response when it is used in connection with

William standing alone. If William were merely standing "alone," it would elicit little reaction, but he is a very pathetic figure when he is "standing alone, all alone." Notice how well great space is expressed by simple repetition when Miss Flack says, "William looked down, way down. Their friends looked up, way up."

The use of repetition achieves other purposes as well in children's literature. It contributes to story pattern in addition to sentence pattern and it helps the reader to anticipate what is coming in the story. Children enjoy guessing what is going to happen next and discovering that their guesses were correct. An author who uses the device of repetition subtly enough and simply enough can very successfully foreshadow the next step in the story for his young reader. One reason why *Little Black Sambo* has always proved so popular is probably that it is designed on just this pattern. After Little Black Sambo has once forfeited an article of his clothing to a tiger, it is easy to foresee that as the story progresses he will gradually give up one piece of clothing after another. More recently in Peggy Bacon's *The Lion-Hearted Kitten*, once the kitten evolves her strategy to outwit the wolf, the reader knows that she will use this same strategy on the tiger and the snake. In Margery Bianco's *The Hurdy-Gurdy Man*, the hurdy-gurdy man meets with the same experience of being turned away from all the neat looking stores. This is repeated so often that when the hurdy-gurdy man finds a tumble-down shack among all the neat shops, even the youngest reader is instinctively sure that here he will be welcomed. In Grace Paull's *Peanut Butter's Slide* the design is established at the beginning of the story for Peanut Butter, the goat, to do everything the boys do, and this is followed throughout. Sometimes in these stories a refrain is built up by having one character at regular intervals repeat the same idea. A child reading Lois Lenski's *The Easter Rabbit's Parade* learns to look for the growling remarks of Old Graybeard the Goat as time after time he may always be counted on to look on the dark side of any suggestion. After the first few times, one also expects Marjorie Flack's sheep in *Up in the Air* to repeat his reminder that they must all be "brave together."

It is interesting to note that many of these stories building on repetition use almost the same design. The initial action takes place in three or four moves varying only slightly. The main character reaches an impasse here or introduces a new action which takes up three or four similar moves. Finally, of course, there is the concluding move of a problem solved and a happy ending. The movement translated into diagram form looks something like this:

First Movement

_____
_____
_____
_____

Second Movement

_____
_____
_____
_____

Conclusion

_____

Notice how this is followed in Dorothy Kunhardt's *Junket is Nice* and how easy it is to anticipate the next move. Each movement builds to its own climax.

> *First Movement*
>> First come all the fastest runners to see the old man.
>> Then come all the moderate runners.
>> Then come all the walkers.
>> Then comes the little boy.
> *Second Movement*
>> Some people make a wrong guess as to the man's thoughts.
>> Others make a wrong guess.
>> Still another wrong guess is made.
>> But the little boy guesses right.
> *Conclusion*
>> Junket is nice!

This same pattern is used in *Peanut Butter's Slide* when first the story follows the various things the boys and Peanut Butter do together. The next move starts in saying that best of all, they like to find a place quite satisfactory. The various sliding places are listed with the climax that they find the right place on the back of Father's new car. Father, himself, brings the story to a happy conclusion by buying them a slide. This story design with minor variations may be see in *The Hurdy-Gurdy Man* by Margery Bianco, *Angus Lost* by Margery Flack, *Snipp, Snapp, And Snurr and the Red Shoes,* by Maj Lindman, *The Lion-Hearted Kitten* by Peggy Bacon, and many others.

Style, then, in children's literature requires all the skill, planning, artistry that are used in writing for any age. Simplicity, color, rhythm are as important, if not more important, in children's literature as in literature for adults. The most interesting observations in studying style in children's literature come in noting how these same qualities of style are adapted to children's taste and experience, making the reading matter not only more colorful, musical, and interesting but making it more colorful, musical, and interesting for *children*.

REFERENCES

Bacon, Peggy. *The Lion-Hearted Kitten*. New York: Macmillan, 1927.

―――――. *Mercy and the Mouse*. New York: Macmillan, 1928.

Bianco, Margery. *The Hurdy-Gurdy Man*. New York: Oxford, 1933.

Brock, Emma. *The Greedy Goat*. New York: Knopf.

―――――. *Little Fat Gretchen*. New York: Knopf, 1934.

Dalgliesh, Alice. *The Little Wooden Farmer*. New York: Macmillan, 1930.

Embury, Lucy. *The Listening Man*. Garden City, N.Y.: Julian Messner, 1940.

Flack, Marjorie. *Angus and the Cat*. Garden City N.Y.: Doubleday Doran, 1931

―――――. *Angus Lost*. Garden City N.Y.: Doubleday Doran, 1932.

―――――. *Up in the Air*. New York: Macmillan, 1935.

―――――. *Wait for William*. Boston, Mass.: Houghton Mifflin, 1935.

Gates, Doris. *Blue Willow*. New York: Viking, 1940.

Goudge, Elizabeth. *Smoky House*. New York: Coward McCann Geoghegan, 1940.

Hudson, W. H. *Tales of the Pampas*. New York: Knopf, 1916.

Jones, Elizabeth Orton. *Maminka's Children*. New York: Macmillan, 1940.

Kunhardt, Dorothy. *Junket is Nice*. New York: Harcourt Brace Jovanovich, 1933.

Lenski, Lois. *The Easter Rabbit's Parade*. New York: Oxford, 1936.

Lindman, Maj. *Snipp, Snapp, Snurr and the Red Shoes*. Chicago: Whitman, 1932.

Meigs, Cornelia. *Mother Makes Christmas*. New York: Grosset and Dunlap, 1940.

Nesbit, E. *Wet Magic*. New York: Coward McCann Geoghegan.

Newberry, Clare. *Babette*. New York: Harper's, 1937.

Paull, Grace. *Peanut Butter's Slide*. New York: The Viking Press, 1939.

Smith, Gertrude. *The Arabella and Araminta Stories*. New York: Small, Maynard, 1937.

van Stockum, Hilda. *Kersti*. New York: The Viking Press, 1940.

Power of Picture Book to Change Child's Self-Image

Naomi Gilpatrick

An effort is here made, perhaps for the first time, to apply to a picture book the tenets of the New Criticism, as advocated by Ransome, Tate, and Warren, *i.e.*, giving a close reading to the text itself, analyzing the special kind of language in it for its literary strategies, and tracing the structure of meanings through the counterplay of symbols and images.

Too often a child's book is judged on the basis of whether or not he "liked" it and in terms of what the child can get at through his own limited language, as if this exhausted its possibilities for him. But there is a tacit dimension at work in a child's knowing that permits him to take in much beyond the periphery of his own vocabulary. Because a child knows more than he can ever know he knows, he can get at the richness of literature through implications rising from the words before him, outside of the "intentional fallacy" (what the author wanted to say) and the "affective fallacy" (how the work affected the reader in terms of like or dislike). As literature, the picture book is not too small to be treated qua story, as an object in itself, worthy of meaning analysis.

Can a child who reads a picture book for the sheer enjoyment of the story itself emerge with his own self-image enlarged and reinterpreted? No moralizing or author's comment mars the swift flowing of action in Norah Smaridge's *Peter's Tent* (Viking Press, 1965). Equally direct and to the point are the illustrations by Brinton Turkle. Yet a second reading reveals the magic in this book that has the power to touch a child's self-image.

In the very first sentence, we meet a Peter who "ran in from the yard, cross as a bear—" which alerts us that not only is he a person of mammoth feelings (borne out throughout the story) but that he is going to fall into the broad category of a universal. This simile is preparing us deftly and simply for a story told with the direct line of action and application of a fable. As in all good fables, each reader can creatively find his own application within the latitude allowed.

Reprinted from *Elementary English* 46, no. 5 (May 1969): 570–74.

Describing Peter as having the crossness of a bear gives him the single trait that fable characters have (half human, half animal). It also gives him a towering nature with the promise he will dominate the story about him. The importance of the cue "bear" is picked up in the alliteration of three "b's" in the second sentence: " 'Barbie burst my balloon.' " We feel further his kinship with "bear" when we read of his preoccupation with food (something human begins share with animals) not as it is on the table but as it may be found growing, accompanied by his indignation at the encroachment of a predator (the chief cause of anger in an animal): " 'And Sammy dug up my carrots and ate the fat one!' "

He strikes an attitude, arrogant, huge: he won't play with his friends. At this, "Mother made big eyes"—which in one stroke gives us not a person who acts, but a person who responds. She is the strings upon which Peter will vibrate. He has a sounding board in her—and we know now where he acquired the hugeness of a "bear." The importance of his every pout to his mother has been such nourishment to his pride that it has magnified him into a giant, awkward in his premature, gangling eminence. He is king of his lair (father never enters the story). Realizing this has swollen his ego to the point that he can share no part of the earth he dominates with anyone else. Many youngsters reading this may sense they share this out-of-proportion importance with Peter. Identification is necessary if the self-image is to be touched. "What happens to Peter may happen to me" is their unspoken thought.

" 'Pooh to friends,' said Peter."

His importance is tonally indicated by the alliteration of "p's" and the slight adverting of the mind to Winnie the Pooh (who is also involved with a bear) links him to another fable-like character. In his actions, the ear picks up the alliteration of "k's" (a metallic, dehumanized sound): "too cross to care. He kicked the stairs."

The noncomplex tone of the "bear" is picked up in his thought: "Boys are better." The final line on the first page (that has accomplished all this to establish mood and intention artfully) by its triple "p's": "I need a private place, thought Peter" draws the interest to this particular person—Peter (if I may use the author's device) and at the same time gives us the central problem about which the plot will pivot.

We know now what his unique need, his quest, is. Angered at the whole human race (because two destroyed his property)—and how easy it is for the immature to extend to everybody the resentment they feel for a few, he craves to be alone. The capitalization of "WHERE?" makes a monument of his search.

In Brinton Turkle's illustration, a boy filling the whole page with hands behind his back (to indicate his frustration) is pacing with broad steps, his head jutting forward with single-minded determination, his lips pursed with the seriousness of his problem, his sharp proud nose lifted with the disdain that perpetually fills him. The rest of the page is stark white to show his preoccupation with himself alone, unassuaged by any awareness of trees or flowers. The colors borrow from two sources—brown for "bear" and white for isolation. The stark, black lines outlining his figure indicate the economy of the single emotion delineated. What

saves him from being a precious prig is the hair falling irregularly over his fore-
head. Underneath, he is a dear boy with a problem.

The ambling, sense-loving nature of the "bear" is in his aimless hunt for a
private place ("Not my room, because Mother is mopping it"), in his foraging
bumblingly in the linen closet among the sheets for something to use as a tent
("They were cool and smelled sweet"), and in getting the best sheets snatched
from him by a panicky mother. All of this foraging and smelling is very much
like a cub's exploration of what is available. In the illustration, Mother with
broad copper bangs to her eyebrows looks like a teen-ager—who can cope with
her desperate little boy only by giving him a substitute for her "GUEST sheets"
—"two old green bed covers that will be just right for a tent." The color green
ejects the little boy into the out of doors where semi-wild creatures belong. Because "GUESTS" is capitalized, we know Mother places great importance upon
having company in her home, that she wants them to have the best, and that
she has no desire to be private like her little boy. The illustration shows this
tranquil, girl-faced mother handing over the bed covers to her glowering son
whose lips are now sucked in and whose eyes have the inward quality of a fixa-
tion to them.

Next, Peter demands the mopstick, broomstick and clothes line to support his
tent. His mother's protest that she needs these "to clean and sweep and hang out
the wash' " is preemptorily brushed aside by Peter who tells her: " 'You can have
a holiday.' "

In his use of "holiday" for "vacation," we know he is a British child—or the
creation of an author who travels frequently to England. Like all good people on
the continent, Mother smiles at hearing of a holiday and acquiesces immediately.
Only employers or people in high position can award a "holiday" from work; so
once again we are profoundly aware of the position of dominance that Peter has
in his home in his relation to his mother. We see this not by the author's telling us
in so many words but rather by means of graphic scenes pertinent to the action
where Mother must barter green bed covers to get back her "pink GUEST sheets"
and where the son loftily dispenses his mother from work when he makes off
with her essential tools.

He makes his private tent, but no one is truly private until someone else has
observed one's position of isolation and feels left out. Then one's triumph is
complete. In the illustration, Mr. Grey next door is sitting on one of those flared-
back chairs that retired people elect. In these two, contrapuntally, we see the
privacy that is forced on the old and the privacy the young seize by force. We are
not told, but he would have to be retired to be able to sit and observe the
machinations of a small boy in the yard next door during the daytime.

The picture of the tent covering both pages conveys the freedom from striving
of the boy within. Although it is dark in there where he just fits, we smell the
grass and hear the flies and feel the ants tickling and a spider dancing up his arm
(all excellent use of sense imagery). Although Peter has with him all the material
things that he wants ("Stones. Bottle caps. Ice cream spoons. And a little box for
worms"), the eternal restlessness that is at the heart of every boy who will be a
man seized him and he wondered, " 'Now what shall I do?' " There rose in him

the awareness that came to the first lone man in the human race: it is not good for man to live alone.

Peter had not sought his solitude for any creative purpose or for the purpose of getting a prayer said, a work done, or a wound healed. He had sought it purely for the sake of being alone. His aloneness was not to commune with the Great Alone—God. It was sought as a defiant announcement of separateness. As such, once attained, it had no blessing for Peter, no contribution to make him, no satisfaction. It was quite sterile. Like a "bear," he is hibernating in the snug dark—but for a human little boy, it proves a hollow experience. This is the turning point for him, for the story.

After arriving at hibernation, the goal of the "bear," he now starts to turn from the "bear"—to cast it off, to lose his similarity to it, and to take on human attributes. He went into hibernation as a "bear"—he is going to come out of it as a "boy"—a human boy. But it is, as Leland B. Jacobs states, the "hypothetical other" that points up our being human. When another boy pokes his face into the tent, Peter, trying to keep his past identity, shouts, "Keep out!"

The other boy with quite a literal mind told Peter that there was no sign that said the tent was private. Matt had a mind controlled by linguistics. He felt the word "Private" would make it private—that words had power over things. He ran to get paper and crayons to effect this—need bringing forth the act of writing on the part of a little fellow. When he told Peter that his mother could see him if she calls, this introduced a third "hypothetical other" that was a potential threat —and Peter capitulated. "Then you'd better come in,' Peter said. So Matt crawled into the tent."

He wasn't welcomed for himself, or for his contribution of a written word that defined—but because he represented two boys' solidarity against an outside force. However, the two boys ran into an unforseen linguistic problem. Neither could spell "Private." Barbie, true to girls' advanced language skills, came along not only with the ability to spell "Private" but to print it very well.

When she was admitted, children might gather that knowledge of spelling and printing will gain one entré into choice places! They had grown now to the pro-portion of a tribe and in true tribal fashion, they resented the arrival of Sammy who had eaten the fat carrot. Sammy donated his polo shirt as a tent flag. When Peter saw Sammy shivering in his bare torso, there was nothing to do in terms of his new humanity (developing bit by bit as his needs became more complex and refined and less oriented in frustration) but to invite the once outrageous Sammy in.

Now everyone "belonged." Everyone was "in." No one was excluded from the inner circle.

But boundaries are made to collapse if humanity and institutions are to ex-pand—yet this tent did not give way until they all experienced the salutary effect of pushing to make room. Mother's seeing "a green whale flopping on the grass" recalls Jonah's whale that contained a man. Mr. Grey, saying with empathy, " 'Save us'," helped Mother "fish" the children out of the bed cover. The use of "fish" here sustains the whale-Jonah metaphor. The former safe darkness of the tent is now dimly felt as a retreat to the cool, liquid darkness of the womb where one once was truly alone—a search for a past security where coping with "the hypothetical other" was no problem. There the developing person was private— not then in the second best "green bed covers"—but in the primary and best "cool, sweet, pink linen" of the mother's womb.

This peace, this security within the tent could also stand for the Church which alternately keeps people out or admits them at the decree of the head, Peter, finding room for artisans like Matt, scholars like Barbie, and the most unlikely people like the over-sized Sammy who contributes the significance of an enduring symbol (the tent flag) as well as his larger than life humanity.

Or Peter could be the symbol of the self-seeker who found a portion that became a country that takes in or excludes refugees seeking harbor. Sammy with his big bat arrogantly poking the vulnerable sides of the curtained tent suggests the aggression of a Communist country like Russia—and yet the same Sammy who gobbled down the fattest carrot is the one who stripped himself of his red polo shirt (down to the skin) to donate a meaningful flag. Children reading this slim picture book see human nature in all its many guises changing before their eyes and get some glimpse into the potentiality for change within themselves. They become less fearful of the world around them—for they see it, too, has potentiality for change. They begin to get some idea of the plastic nature of character. They see that they do not have to hold to their old mistaken views of their place in the universe and that their relationship to others need not be static and fixed. They see that they are not only master of their tent but master of themselves and that they have the power to exclude or admit those thoughts or those ideas that poke their faces within view. They get a sense of their power of choice. Reading this book with its character changes helps strengthen and enrich their self-image.

Peter's tent can be seen as a miniature of the United Nations, testing and weighing the motives of each newcomer—a touchstone of his integrity and an evaluator of his contribution. Such a tent has a purpose; for it draws amorphous humanity together from all corners of the earth and defines their need for togetherness, inspiring in each a will to contribute for the benefit of all.

As the children gather to hold their parley, deciding to build bigger and better next time with a sign in small print admitting friends (a need larger than the need to be alone even if it is shyly admitted only in fine print), Mother and Mr. Grey listen to the words that in drawing the children closer together, draw them farther from Mother and Mr. Grey. In the picture, Mother has a little puff of age beneath her eyes that she hadn't before. Mother has lost the animalistic tyrant that dominated her life and gained in its place a boy who has joined the human race.

As a child experiences the layers of meaning in a picture book, the stereotypes in his mind drop away. He knows a new freedom. In a picture book that tells its story directly blow by blow with no editorial comment whatsoever as *Peter's Tent* by Norah Smardige does, the young reader can find inviting spaces between the lines to form constructs and images over and above the narrative line itself. On the sheer strength of its implications, the picture book has the power to build new self-images for the young child. *Peter's Tent* traces the growth of a child's relationship to others from the savage to the civilized: now he is willing to share, to value the artistic and symbolic contributions of others, and to accept individual differences. The young reader grows right along with Peter. In perceiving Peter's growth, the young reader recognizes and learns to live with his own. The picture book of the stature of *Peter's Tent*, delightful in its swift, direct surface telling of everyday events, is replete with overtones that strike up vibrating chords in the mind where self-images have their "private" dwelling place.

For symbols in a book to affect a child's self image, it is not necessary that he be able to identify them or even advert to their presence. It is unlikely that he would. Rather, their greatest power lies in their subliminal influence. All the unnamed, often unguessed hidden symbols and literary devices act below the threshold of overt knowing. The child benefits through tacit knowing—his ability at all times to know more than he can ever say or ever know he knows. The best that literature has to offer comes to him through his tacit knowing.

A Structural Approach
to the Study of Literature for Children

Peter F. Neumeyer

The problem:

Although there exist admirable studies of children's reading preferences, and although these studies contain and lay bare much potentially valuable raw data, the studies and the data seem peculiarly unrelated to each other and are less helpful than one might hope in leading to further experimentation and subsequent practice in the classroom.[1] Though the best of the studies were conducted on large samples, and used exemplary interviewing techniques, the results are limited either in that they are confined to examining closely the responses of *one* child to various "types" of books, or in the nature of their conclusions as to the "types" of books liked by children of given ages. Thus we are left with such over-generalized vacuities as children's liking stories of adventure, or stories of animals. And these simplifications, in turn, become the basis for the many lists of suggested readings for children.

In addition to the fact that they do not suggest further avenues of exploration into the nature of either children or books, the data and the conclusions seem unhelpful in another respect. For even if children do like adventure stories or animal stories, it is improbable that they should like *all* stories falling into those categories. It seems obvious that there must be bad, poorly written, inadequate animal or adventure stories that don't appeal to children at all. Similarly, it is obvious that lists of specific books preferred by children do not give a satisfactory base from which one would confidently make generalizations. That youngsters like *Peter Rabbit* or *The Swiss Family Robinson* may mean no more than that these two books are written in just the way that happens to hit it off with children.

If one is to begin talking intelligently about books and children, one must set about making true and testable statements about books and children—statements

Reprinted from *Elementary English* 44, no. 8 (December 1967): 883–87.

that are neither so sanctimonious and vague as to be useless, and statements which, though specific, are derived from procedures that are both replicable and pregnant with implication for further development.[2] One may begin the investigation, as previous workers must have discovered, using as the focus either the individual child, or the body of literature.

If one begins with the literature itself, it remains to find a critical instrument suitable for giving one a hand-hold in the vast and seemingly diverse mass of books which children enjoy. For this purpose the usual tools of literary criticism, though they seem occasionally to lead one to true statements about specific works, are not the most useful. One may, if one is so inclined, pursue a sophisticated "new critical" reading of *Winnie the Pooh*, or, as has on occasion been ventured, a Freudian, sexual interpretation of *Alice in Wonderland* (down the hole after the rabbit), or even a Marxist reading of *The Three Little Pigs*, but notwithstanding whatever light these readings can shed on the specific works, they do not lead us much further than we were before toward having an instrument with which to talk definitively about which books the eight-year-old urban child likes. Yet that is precisely the sort of knowledge which, if reliable, would be of great practical help to parents, teachers, and librarians.

The clue to a direction in which to begin may lie in the word "type" in the last paragraph. What follows is a suggestion for an approach to children's literature —or, books children read—which, though limited, seems critically sound, and may permit us to begin grouping children's books in categories that are not so elusive as to be useless.

"Elusive categories" are something with which students of folklore have become familiar, and so when I propose a way out, the proposal will be in the vein of some current thought among folklorists.

A possible solution:

As early as 1910, the Finish folklore scholar, Antti Aarne, attempted to establish a taxonomy of types of the folktale. This work was later expanded into the standard work, the most useful index of Stith Thompson.[3] There one may find folktales classified under schema such as the following:

A. Mythological Motifs
    A 100—A 499 Gods
    A 200—A 299 God of the upper world
    A 200 God of the upper world
    A 210 Sky-god
    A 220 Sun-god
    A 240 Moon-god
    A 250 Star-god
    A 260 God of light
    A 270 God of dawn
    A 280 Weather-god
  or
L. Reversal of Fortune
    L 200—L 299 Modesty Brings Reward

L 200   Modesty brings reward
L 210   Modest choice best
L 220   Modest request best
L 250   Modest business plans best

But immensely helpful as it has been to have tales from all over the world so classified, certain drawbacks are apparent. Vladimir Propp noted the frequent overlapping of motifs in the motif indexing method. Citing the common division of folktales into fairy tales, tales of everyday life, and animal tales, Propp asked questions such as "Don't tales about animals sometimes contain elements of the marvelous to a very high degree? And conversely, don't animals actually play a large role in fairy tales?"[4] More recently Propp's objections, and his direction in looking for an answer have been taken up by Alan Dundes.[5] In arguing the case for a "structural study" of folktales, Dundes began to develop and elaborate a technique and approach having its roots not only in the suggestions of Vladimir Propp, but in the interesting, if short-lived, Russian school of Formalist Criticism.[6]

In essence, it is maintained by the structuralist critic that there are common denominators within stories. One may look for sequences of action or reaction that, no matter how much the superstructure may vary, remain always the same. Thus, said Propp, it does not really matter whether the hero is assigned a difficult task by the king, or by a genii. It *does* matter that he is assigned a task. And if the hero receives money, that fact *too* is important, just as it is a critical distinction whether the money is given him and he then buys a magic horse, or the money is given him as a reward for an act of bravery.[7] In addition to defining certain "functions" that seemed basic to the tales he considered, Propp found, surprisingly, that—at least in his limited sample of stories—*the functions invariably followed an identical set sequence*, though of course in any given tale some functions might be excluded. That Propp's "functions" are not what the English teacher generally calls "themes," that the functions are, in essence, more like verbs than like nouns, that they are *sequences* of action and reaction, rather than "underlying ideas," must be understood.

As was suggested some paragraphs back, what is needed if we wish to learn about the interaction between children and books is a critical instrument that allows us to talk consistently about either children or books. If we talk about the books, then we must, at least at the outset, talk about them the same way, heeding similar and identifiable aspects of the story, and referring to these aspects in agreed-upon terms. And likewise when we later move on to the most difficult consideration of varying responses of different children to different books, we must hold constant as many factors as possible.

Holding constant the aspects of the story necessitates first identifying those aspects. The Proppian enumeration of "functions" is remarkably serviceable even beyond the limits of the hundred folktales examined by the originator, though there is no reason at all why one might not attempt a similar, though different, labelling or identifying schema if it would be more applicable.[8]

By way of demonstrating the first step, one might schematize *Peter Rabbit* according to the following Proppian functions:

I. Initial situation absence: One of the members of a family is absent from home.

Symbol: β

(β' departure of elders)

Mrs. Rabbit says "I am going out." (Goes to buy five currant buns, presumably one for each little rabbit).

II. Interdiction addressed to the hero.

Symbol: γ

As in ". . . do not venture forth from the courtyard."

Actually, in *Peter Rabbit*, Peter is told not to go into Mr. McGregor's garden just before we are informed that his mother is going away.

III. The interdiction violated.

Symbol: δ

(Functions II and III are twin elements.)

"At this point . . . the villain enters the folktale. . . . He comes on fast, sneaks up on. . . ."

(Propp)

Peter goes to Mr. McGregor's garden, eating his vegetables. Accidentally comes on Mr. McGregor, who chases Peter.

XVI. Struggle

Symbol: H

The hero and the villain join in direct combat.

Mr. McGregor's repeated attempts on Peter's life (with sieve, treading on him, and with rake in picture).

XXII. Rescue

Symbol: Rs^1

"The hero is rescued from pursuit (sometimes he is saved by lightning fast running)." (Propp) (Rs^4 the hero hides in flight.) (There is a vestigial Rs^8, "rescue from attempt at being devoured," since Mrs. Rabbit had, during the opening injunction, warned Peter that his Father had an accident and was put in a pie by Mr. McGregor.)

Peter escapes because of his smallness and quickness, having first hidden himself in various places.

Unfortunately there exists no Proppian symbol signifying the hero being given camomile tea and being put to bed, while his siblings eat blackberries. Perhaps if one designs symbols to schematize children's cautionary tales, one would need one to designate "Expiation for violation of initial injunction." But to summarize, for our simple initial purposes, we are able to represent a story like *Peter Rabbit* as

$$\beta$$
$$\gamma'$$
$$\delta$$
$$H$$
$$Rs^1$$
$$(Rs^4)$$

Anyone familiar with our method can reconstruct the "deep structure" of the tale though his dramatis personae might be very different. We have, then, an objective counterpart of one dimension of the story, and—so it seems to me—for the first time there is the opportunity for conducting replicable "experiments" with children and literature, for example by holding all elements (functions) constant but one, and proceeding to investigate whatever we are investigating. (One might stipulate a Peter Rabbit who ends up in Mr. McGregor's stew pot, or a Peter Rabbit going on an errand to Mr. McGregor's for his mother. And then, by means yet to be devised, one may test the responses of the children.)

No doubt the generalizations we will be able to make will be very modest at the beginning, but on the other hand we will be saying *real* things about children's books, and we will be seeing *real* similarities and differences. We might find, to our surprise, that the popularity of *Peter Rabbit* lies not at all in the fact that Peter is an animal, but rather in that a) he is enjoined from a certain action, b) he violates the injunction, and c) he escapes the dire consequences—just barely. And if we consider certain versions of *Babes in the Woods, Little Red Riding Hood,* or *Hansel and Gretel,* we may indeed see a very similar structural sequence. And we may at least hypothesize—and test further—whether it is not certain *structural* sequences that appeal to children at certain ages.

Attractive as the relative manageability of a structural approach is, there are difficulties and objections which have not yet been answered.

The first of the difficulties is that, though one may write a structural analysis of a full-length novel (see note 8), to juggle merely one of the functions as one is testing with a class of children would seem an unwieldy enterprise. The length of the novel would surely preclude any youngster's reading it twice in only slightly differing form. Moreover, the time it takes to read a novel would allow for the introduction of so many variables (even if two classes of children were used for comparison, that the reading would only be done once), that again the results would be suspect. But that there exists this difficulty does not invalidate the idea that functions are of signal importance in determining children's responses, and it may be that one must merely begin with shorter works than novels.

The second and more substantive objection was implied by the seminar student who asked why, in testing with children, is was necessary to use novels or stories in the first place. Why not use merely the bare-bones functions?

The answer to this question lies in the fact that one must realize that functions are *only one* (relatively controllable) ingredient of stories. There still remain all such elusive manifestations as characterization, diction, rhetorical assumptions, and the evanescent matters of "tone" and "texture." And yet, if we understand functions, we may begin to learn about the interaction between stories and children. The warm heart of the story, and the even warmer one of the child, may still be eluding us—and I, personally, hope they will continue to elude us. And yet, if we teach literature to children, and if we do talk of sequence and articulation in curriculum, it behooves us to understand what is understandable, and to attempt to bring some order into an area governed perhaps needlessly by intuition.

NOTES

1. Among the better known reading-interest studies are May Lazar, *Reading Interests, Activities, and Opportunities of Bright, Average, and Dull Children* (New York: Teachers College, Columbia, 1937); George W. Norvell, *What Boys and Girls Like to Read* (Morristown, 1958) and by the same author *The Reading Interests of Young People* (Boston, 1950); and Carleton Washburne and Mabel Vogel, *Winnetka Graded Book List* (Chicago, 1926).

2. It is noteworthy that the children's reading preference lists by no means agree with each other, and that Norvell, in fact, takes violent issue with the findings of others.

3. Stith Thompson, *Motif-Index of Folk Literature*, revised ed. (Bloomington, Indiana, 1955).

4. Vladimir Propp, *Morphology of the Folktale*. (Bloomington, Indiana, 1928) p. 5.

5. Alan Dundes, "From Etic to Emic Units in the Structural Study of Folktales," *Journal of American Folklore*, (April-June, 1962): 95–105.

6. For a history and brief synopsis of the tenets of Russian Fromalism, see Victor Erlich, *Russian Formalism: History-Doctrine*, second rev. ed. (The Hague, 1965). Also *Russian Formalist Criticism: Four Essays*, ed. Lee. T. Lemon and Marion J. Reis (Lincoln: University of Nebraska Press, 1965).

7. Propp, p. 20. A similar direction of thought about "fairy tales" was suggested by Buchanan in a lecture published as *Pamphlet No. 79, The English Association*, July 1931.

8. In fact, though, Mr. Miles Wichelns, one of the students in my seminar, has found the Proppian schema fully satisfactory for representing the sequence of action in *Treasure Island*. Not only are there symbols for all the actions, but the sequence of action follows that described by Propp as being constant in his Russian tales.

The Owl Service: A Study

Eleanor Cameron

Alan Garner's *The Owl Service*, Britain's 1967 Carnegie Medal winner and the writer's fourth book, reveals that he is not a man to rest on the laurels awarded him by those enthusiastic children who read with pleasure *The Weirdstone of Brisingamen, The Moon of Gomrath,* and *Elidor.* For *The Owl Service* (a set of dishes, not a train run) is entirely different from his other three, having in common with them only that it is fantasy and takes off from legend. But because certain of Garner's tendencies as a writer are noticeable in all of his books and because these tendencies play an important part in the final effect of *The Owl Service*, it is rewarding to go back to the beginning and consider his work as a whole.

Garner is one who, from the start, has found his inspiration in Scandinavian mythology, Celtic legend, and Hebridean and British folklore. Rich is his knowledge of old spells, of the *Mabinogion,* and such volumes as Murray's *The God of the Witches,* Robert Graves's *The White Goddess,* and Watkins's *The Old Straight Track,* which has to do with prehistoric man's use of long-distance tracks marked by cairns, stones, and beacons. Old Britain and its ancient powers and presences waiting to be released over the English countryside are what are felt most strongly in the first two books. Garner has a splendid sense of place. When he shows Colin in *The Weirdstone* searching for the old straight track, and its eventual revelation by moonlight, he is at his best, involved purely in scene and feeling and overtone.

Nevertheless, even given Garner's knowledge and his particular qualities as a writer, neither *The Weirdstone* nor *The Moon of Gomrath* can begin to compare with the first fantasies of Lucy Boston, for instance, or Mary Norton or Philippa Pearce when it comes to subtlety and depth. It may be that the average child devoted to fantasy will prefer Garner's books for their movement, their tension, and continuous threat of evil about to be fully unleashed. But I am speaking of

Reprinted from *Wilson Library Bulletin* 44, no. 4 (December 1969): 425–33.

artistry from the point of view of the critical adult who is considering the following elements: a combination of cleanness and strength of structure, no matter how complex; sense of reality (and fantasy must have this); the communication of the visual perceptiveness of the writer; the way in which his mature thought and imagination compels and shapes action with full respect for his audience; originality in the handling of materials (all materials have been worked and reworked a thousand times); characterization; and style which, in its involvement with the whole impact of the book, cannot be separated from content.

Concerning the folk of his novels, there is in *The Weirdstone* a great bustling of all sorts of mythic and legendary beings, and in its sequel, *The Moon of Gomrath*, the bustling becomes positively overcrowded. In both of these books, all action stems from a fierce battle between the forces of Black Magic and the Old Magic, which works through feeling and intuition and which was driven into hiding when the Age of Reason arrived. The basis of action is a cops-and-robbers chase, the Bads after the Goods, and the Goods then turning and stealthily tracking the Bads. But no amount of curious creatures, svarts and trolls and goblins and elves, can offset the absence of memorable individuals whose qualities might play upon one another to create unique situations of more lasting value and interest than the excitement of constant action. In neither *The Weirdstone* nor *The Moon of Gomrath* do the children, Susan and Colin, evolve into individuals. Except for their superhuman courage, they are almost completely at the mercy of plot, possessing no other qualities with which to affect it.

Humans are full of idiosyncracies as most legendary creatures are not, i.e., dwarves and elves are apt to be good, trolls and goblins bad. And it is an important facet of J. R. R. Tolkien's genius, for example, that he *could* individualize his chief legendary protagonists to the extent that *The Hobbit* and the three volumes of *The Lord of the Rings* have become classics of their kind. What is more, chase plays a great part in Tolkien's novels, as it does in the last three volumes of Mary Norton's *Borrower* books. But in both cases memorable characterizations and involvements arising out of the interplay of the protagonists' personalities, rather than out of the demands of plot, make chase, as such, almost a secondary consideration.

Concerning *The Weirdstone*, Garner has written that it is "a fairly bad book," but that "there had to be a start somewhere."[1] Referring to his first drafts of the opening chapters, he notes, "At that stage I was indeed writing for children and the result was the usual condescending pap. Luckily I saw this in the first month, and thereafter wrote for myself." Earlier he had stated, "I don't write for children but entirely for myself. Yet I do write for children, and have done so from the very beginning."[2] What Garner was expressing in a rather ambivalent fashion was the conviction that his work for children demanded writing which he himself as critic could respect.

Elidor is a better book than the first two, not only because it is more original in its various conceptions of the impingement of magic upon the everyday world, but because both scene and action are no longer cluttered with too many beings, too many wills at cross-purposes. Here, again, the Bads are tracking the Goods and the Goods are then turning and searching out the Bads to save Elidor from extinction. But Garner's disclosure of a realm of existence, invisible to us but interpenetrating ours, is typical of his sensitivity to place, his imaginative power of seeing, and his ability to reveal what he sees to his reader. He is no longer describing the English countryside, but his own country of the mind. And in his conjuring of a desolate landscape, menacing, drained of all color, intensely seen as in a nightmare or in some surrealist film in stark black and white, we again experience Garner's gift of poetic overtone released by certain kinds of circumstances. I was reminded of that sequence in Ingmar Bergman's film *Wild Strawberries* in which the elderly protagonist dreams of his own funeral carriage moving along a warped and deserted street where a giant watch hangs overhead pointing to some doomed moment. For it is exactly this premonitory sense of dream, in which events seem insanely warped yet exude, as one progresses through the dream, a kind of arcane logic, that is best in *Elidor*. It is there as Garner prepares for and carries off the instant when the four children, Helen, Nicholas, David, and Roland are, through apparently their own decisions, led to that fateful crossroads of incidents which ejects them from our plane of existence into that other that has awaited their coming since the days of the starved fool. It is there when Roland discovers the empty fingers of Helen's recently lost mitten clutched in layers of smooth-growing turf and, underneath, the cuff frozen in ancient quartz. It is there when the children are shown an ages-old parchment on which the fool had foretold their coming and painted their small pictures in figures of medieval beauty. (Here, in these last two details, are the first hints of Garner's captivation by the idea of past, present, and future existing in a timeless moment which comes to fuller fruition in *The Owl Service*.) It is there, this arcane, dreamlike logic, in those later events in which the children are besieged by men of the other world who are attempting to reclaim the treasures of the four kingdoms that the children are preserving until Elidor shall be safe and light shines in Gorias again.

In many of these last chapters, Garner makes use of one of the principles of physics, yet in doing so in no way sends his fantasy over into science fiction. Here we are reminded of William Mayne's *Earthfasts*. Garner's fantasy was first published in Britain in 1965 and Mayne's in 1966, so that both must have been brooding their own special uses of scientific knowledge within the context of fantasy at about the same time. But there is an interesting difference between the two men's employment of science. Garner makes direct use of the effects of static electricity upon the children and all electrically run objects within the force field surrounding whatever place the children have hidden the treasures. But Mayne mingles poetic and scientific insights and awarenesses throughout *Earthfasts* not only to make more precisely felt by the reader the experiences of his two boys in a situation of released magic in the twentieth century, but to pinpoint those qualities and points of view which differentiate David and Keith. It is a much richer and more subtle use than Garner's.

Character portrayal, a deficiency in Garner's writing which was apparent in his first two books, is again a problem. For in *Elidor* too there is a lack of characterization of the children, with the exception of Roland, the child most concerned with all that is unbelievably happening to the Watsons. It is through his eyes that we see the landscape of the other world, and through his thoughts that we experience most of the action and emotion of the book. It is he who in the human world remains faithful to the idea of Elidor in the face of the flip, slangy cynicism of his two brothers, set down in a more staccato style than the conversations of the two previous books. Yet what we have of him, simply because we are "seeing" through his senses, does not approach the complexity and felt humanity of either David or Keith in *Earthfasts*. And I cannot in recollection separate Garner's Nicholas from his brother David, nor remember anything about Helen except that she is a girl.

Having finished *Elidor*, one wonders, was it at this stage that Garner's idea of audience changed for him or, rather, expanded? It would seem that *Elidor* was written for children, any child who could read, no matter what age. But once again Garner has something to say about audience, and the number of times he brings it up would seem to indicate some private tussle with the idea. "Only recently have I come to realize that, when writing for myself, I still am writing for children—or, rather, for adolescents. By adolescence I mean an arbitrary age of from, say, ten to eighteen. This group of people is the most important of all, and, selfishly, it makes the best audience. Few adults read with a comparable involvement."[3]

In *The Owl Service* Garner again takes off from legend, specifically from the fourth book of the *Mabinogion,* and relates the effects of this legend upon a small group of people living in the valley of Ardudwy in Wales. Susan Sontag, in her essay "Against Interpretation," advises that in order to do any creative work the highest justice, the critic must never show what a work means, but rather "show how it is what it is," and "even that it is what it is."[4] Nonetheless, Garner himself has placed in the front of *The Owl Service* a quotation from the *Radio Times* concerning possessive parents and selfishness, and there in the fewest possible words is the minor theme of the book, one that determines, actually, the progression of the major theme, which the reader can scarcely avoid seeing as an explication of how the evil that men do lives after them.

The particular story from the *Mabinogion* upon which Garner bases his action is that of the betrayal of her husband by Blodeuwedd, whom the magicians Math and Gwydion had fashioned out of flowers. Blodeuwedd's infidelity is an act for which she is punished by Gwydion when he transforms her into an owl, whom all birds attack and insult wherever they find her. Blodeuwedd's husband, Lleu Llaw Gyffes, had been the chief concern of the magician Gwydion since Lleu Llaw's childhood, and every event of the boy's life, because of Gwydion's pride, leads fatefully and inevitably to that moment when Math and Gwydion "took the blossoms of the oak, and the blossoms of the broom, and the blossoms of the meadowsweet, and produced from them a maiden, the fairest and most graceful that man ever saw. And they baptized her, and gave her the name of Blodeuwedd."

And Blodeuwedd, to whom Gwydion and Math have given, as magicians taking too much upon themselves, a thinking mind and the capacity to love, is the one who suffers. The evil thereafter countinues, for she everlastingly brings suffering to others in her unabaiting struggles to escape her hateful imprisonment within the form of the owl. One might even, in considering the *Radio Times* statement and its relationship to the book, point out how, from the very beginning, it was Gwydion's parentlike concern for Lleu Llaw and his unyielding determination to forcibly shape the boy's life, that actually brought Blodeuwedd into being.

One sees within the structure of *The Owl Service* a series of three triangles. The first triangle was formed in legendary times by Blodeuwedd, her husband, and her lover. The second triangle was formed centuries later, before the action of the book, by Huw Halfbacon and Nancy, servants in the house which is the main scene of the book, and Bertram, Nancy's lover. The third triangle is formed in present time by the teen-agers Gwyn (Nancy's son), Alison, and Roger, who is Alison's stepbrother. The story begins with the act by which Blodeuwedd's accumulated agony is given power and direction when Gwyn and Alison recover the owl service from its hiding place, a service decorated with a design which could be either owls or flowers. When Alison chooses to see the design as owls and acts accordingly, she brings upon herself the concentrated hatred of Blodeuwedd and at length becomes her emotional and spiritual captive. Only through a fresh "seeing" of the design can both Blodeuwedd's and Alison's release be affected after continuing discoveries by Gwyn and Roger concerning the past. Nancy acts always as the impassioned obstacle to these revelations, and Huw Halfbacon as the fateful voice of timelessness.

Garner's method in this book (the first time he has used it to such an extent) is to allow almost all information regarding place, previous events, character, and plot to be revealed through the actions and the words of the protagonists rather than through explanations by the author. And it is a tribute to his craftsmanship that with a few deft strokes these relationships are all made clear, though in the interests of tension and suspense the legendary ones come through by degrees.

As in his three previous works, Garner is at his best in the evocation of place, but there is little actual description in *The Owl Service* and what is given is laid on in almost pointillist strokes, now here, now there, in single sentences or short paragraphs having to do with feeling and action. Presently one realizes almost by osmosis, that it is the same valley, Ardudwy, where the legendary lover, Gronw Pebyr, met his death at the hands of Lleu Llaw Gyffes. Wales as place is a necessity, given the Welsh origin of the legend, and the ancient Cantref of Ardudwy in particular. But Garner takes advantage of Wales as the small, insular bit of the British Isles, where the inhabitants are even more deeply aware than in the rest of Britain "of time as an eternal moment rather than as something with a separate past and future,"[5] to make of *The Owl Service* a time tale. And not only because of Welsh nature and its awareness of the Globe of Time, but because the spirit of Blodeuwedd, a creation of magic, exists in timelessness. He also takes advantage of the fact of Ardudwy as a valley to conceive of it as a reservoir in which force, power, energy (Blodeuwedd's wild agony at being imprisoned) builds up until it must find release through whatever humans are in a particular emotional state with regard to one another. Under extreme duress, they must find it possible to give comfort instead of express hate and so bring to an end the evil that Gwydion had begun. Both Blodeuwedd's imprisonment and the desolation of the valley have continued over the centuries because hatred and murder have been the choice.

With respect to character portrayal, we are struck by Garner's aesthetic growth since his first and, indeed, since his third book, where only the child Roland came through as an individual. In *The Owl Service* Garner works not only with the relationships of the teenagers Gwyn, Roger, and Alison, but with the bitter resentments generated between parent and child and between servant and employer, between classes, backgrounds, and these resentments are continuously laced through the progression of the main theme.

Huw Halfbacon, caretaker of the house and man of all work, who would seem to have existed in the valley since time immemorial, is in his own mind both the magician Gwydion and the betrayed husband Lleu Llaw Gyffes; to the English Roger and his father Clive, he is nothing but an especially moronic type of Welsh clod, "a great hairy Welsh freak"; but to the inhabitants of the valley he is their master, their father, their lord. He it is who holds within himself the weight of the legend, who has taken on its burden, who must protect his people from it, and see that Gwyn does not escape the inheritance of that burden.

Nancy, the housekeeper, who was once, according to Huw, "the winds of April," is now lean and knotted with hard work and bitter with memory, with frustrated destiny; one sees and feels her strongly, as one does Huw and Gwyn, purely through their own words and actions. She hates the valley and what it represents of her own low beginnings, and thus still nurses her hatred of Huw, not only because of their previous relationship, but because he is the spirit of the valley: "I own the ground, the mountains," he says, ". . . the song of the cuckoo, the brambles, the berries, the dark cave is mine." And yet all these years Nancy has been instilling in Gwyn such an intimate vision of the valley that, though he has never been there until now, he knows every inhabitant, every house, every path and turn and rise and vista and meadow.

As for Gwyn, he is torn between his love of Welsh earth, Welsh singularity, and his fierce determination to better himself away from Welshness in the face of English self-possession, English "superiority," the kind that so takes itself for granted that it is scarcely conscious of its own power to enrage those who suffer under it. And while Gwyn loathes, not his mother's Welshness, but her crudity and illiteracy, he at the same time detests these thick-skinned Birmingham snobs, who come here simply to be able to boast to their friends that they own a Welsh cottage.

Furthermore, this loathing of his mother's class, her commonness, and what it means for his own future, is all entangled with his fury at her blind, raw, selfish power over him, a fury so intense that his moment of revenge on "the old cow" is one of the jolting scenes of the book. Neither Roger nor Clive are any more capable of sensing Gwyn's terrible, self-devouring sensitivity than they are capable of seeing Huw for what he really is. Gwyn says of his own future that he ought to be in Parliament, but Roger calls him a Welsh oaf, and is amused that he wants to better himself. Clive says of his kind that they turn out to be nothing but "barrackroom lawyers. . . . They're the worst . . . brains aren't everything, by a long chalk. You must have background." Clive blandly takes for granted that he and Roger have background, mistaking the possession of a comfortable income for breeding. And Roger shares with his father the morality that, "You'll not go far if you don't learn to bend with the wind." Yet he can say of his father, "Anything for a quiet life; that is why he never gets one." Nancy sees right through Clive. She calls him Lord Muck, the man who looks on pebbledash, a kind of cheap stuccoed surface, as being "rather tasteful," and who is delighted with a hideous little "Kelticraft" object made, revealingly enough, in England. Neither Roger nor Clive are aware of the fact that the clichés that litter their utterances are symbols of their own too-easy, unreflecting attitudes toward life and human relationships.

Alison seems an echo of them. Though she can say to Gwyn in a moment of comradeship that it doesn't matter how he speaks, and that she likes his way because it is Gwyn and not "ten thousand other people," still, she, like Clive and Roger, bends with the wind (Mummy's desires) and, as part of her effort not to upset Mummy, deals Gwyn a mortal hurt in such a way as to reveal herself as either incredibly stupid or incredibly insensitive. We cannot be sure which because we don't know enough about Alison.

I have gone into these character portrayals at some length because Garner's ability to imbue with felt life (Henry James's phrase) his three Welsh protagonists, and his lesser ability to do so for his three English protagonists, is interesting and has a bearing on the final effect of the book. By "felt life" I mean the depths and complexities, the cross-currents of desire and repulsion communicated to the reader from fictional persons. Garner's three English characters are vapid and superficial, and are no doubt meant to be so. But were they meant to be merely *types* of English, or rather *a* type of English? Were they meant to be lacking in interesting qualities, in uniqueness? They are, and here we are faced not only with the communication of their superficiality, but also with this quality in the rendering of them. It is true certainly that something of their personalities can be caught, but there is really not a great deal more to be said of them than what is reported here, except possibly the fact of Clive's stinginess. Were they minor characters, this would be sufficient, but they are not. The book therefore suffers as it would not have done had Garner depicted the vapidness of those three English people as acutely as he has the qualities of his three complex Welsh protagonists. Assuredly the portrayal of an uninteresting or ordinary person can, in the hands of an artist, prove just as fascinating and revelatory of crosscurrents as the portrayal of an extaordinary one. There are simply no human beings who do not possess their fascinations, even including those like Roger and Clive and Alison. Alison, to a disappointing degree, is reminiscent of Susan in Garner's first book: the puppet of plot.

One of the weaknesses of Garner's presentation of his English characters is the lack of past. We see backward along the vistas of Huw's and Nancy's and Gwyn's lives, but Alison and Roger and Clive seem scarcely to have existed before the action of the book begins. In Garner's portrayal of Gwyn we even discern with sadness his possible future in London where he will become like those Welsh artists Dylan Thomas speaks of, who "ape the narrow 'a.' They repudiate the Welsh language, whether they know it or not." They stifle "their natural ardour so that they may disparagingly drawl, and with knowledgable satiety, of the paintings, the music, the guests, their host, corseting their voices so that no lilt or inflection of Welsh enthusiasm may exult or pop out."[6] We know enough of Gwyn, however, to suspect that there will be a time beyond that when he will become himself again.

Dialogue, which can be the means of communicating individuality above all else, raises a question here: can the too faithful echoing of reality result in an injury to art? In *The Owl Service* the dialogues are even more staccato in rhythm than in *Elidor*. And the number of cliché phrases and expressions is truly astonishing: "Once bitten twice shy," "How now brown cow," "Too much clean living —I'll cut down on the yoghurt," "Holy cow," "How super," "We'll make a packet on the telly," "You can say that again," "We've had a basin-full," "His head's screwed on," "Pull the other—it's got bells on," "For crying out loud." Smart-aleck retorts made their appearance to some extent in *Elidor*, but here their use is carried to such an extreme that they strike us as almost an ingratiation with that ten-to-eighteen age group Mr. Garner says he is writing for: as if he were slanting his book, and this is a regrettable impression. It is no use protesting, "But this is the way people—especially teenagers—talk." Art is selective; the artist *must* select, for strict naturalism is a dead end. Oddly enough, Garner says that he learned Welsh in order not to use it, to avoid the "superficial in characterization—the 'Come you here, bach' school of writing." And he says of the possible insertion here and there of "a gratuitous, and untranslated, line of the language" that "This is reality laid on with a trowel, and it remains external and false."[7] He clearly understands the danger of strict naturalism, and might well have looked farther into the gratuitous use of another kind of language, using the word 'gratuitous' in the legal sense to mean something given without receiving any return value. It is true that these clichés reveal one quality of Roger and Clive, and that Gwyn tries always to be less Welsh. But what Garner has succeeded in doing in his use of this TV type of dialogue (in the unsparing and unselective use of worn phrases in the utterances, quite often *as* the utterances, of those of his characters who would use them) is to lessen the number of opportunities he has to convey facets of individuality and to cheapen the texture and therefore the content of his work.

As well, Garner makes tedious his pages of dialogue by his persistence in using a rhythm which could just possibly be used among his particular characters but which, in art, in a created work, strikes insistently on the inner ear to the point of exhaustion. Two persons, devoted to fantasy, upon finishing *The Owl Service*, accused it of being "confusing," "choppy," of failing to hold together as a unified structure. And I believe that while the effect of confusion could have resulted from the fact that the books is so lean and spare that one must note each small detail, each pointillist stroke in order to understand the whole, it is the staccato beat of the dialogue which may give the effect of choppiness rather than the progression of the action. Furthermore, the tedium of the often unrelieved beat results in weariness on the part of the reader and an ensuing lack of attention and therefore of understanding.

Two questions occur to me in the last pages of *The Owl Service*. The first arises out of the fact that Garner's third triangle is composed of teenagers, young teenagers, though of their exact ages we cannot be certain. One reader thought they could be around thirteen. I felt they were fifteen or sixteen and might well have been older: three persons capable of mature sexual passion and love in order that the full drama inherent in the releasing of Blodeuwedd's agony in the valley of Ardudwy might have been more powerfully realized. Assuredly a novel of teenage struggle can be as full of drama and emergence in any direction as the creator is capable of making it. Possibly here it is the seethe and leap of old fires, still burning fiercely in timelessness, that renders the relationships of these particular young people pale by comparison. Alison appears to have no particular feeling for anyone: for Roger a vague friendliness, and in Gwyn a brief interest. Roger, as far as emotions are concerned, entertains only one: scorn for both Huw and Gwyn. Only Gwyn, of them all, seems capable of passion in the large sense, though his love of Alison (it may simply be an attraction because she is feminine and appealing and is aware of him as a human being as Clive and Roger are not), sinks once he discovers how passively and completely she is at the mercy of her mother. Gwyn suffers. Who else does, of the three? One questions Garner's purpose in determining the members of his triangle to be immature teenagers, two of them uninvolved, if he desired to bring to their fullest fruition the potentialities of his conception. One recalls Rosemary Sutcliff choosing, after a series of novels on early Britain written for youth, to put the story of Arthur and Guinevere and her lover into a novel for adults, because in no other way could she come at its deepest imaginative truth. My question is this: Has Garner wasted his material in thus debilitating it? If one agrees that he has, the question could then be asked if it is wise, having conceived one's idea, to tailor it to an audience of teenagers rather than to allow the material itself to dictate the way in which it shall be handled.

This weakness, this lack of passion and power and force from the depths (what one feels to be an emphasis on the working out of plot: "My concern for the reader is not to bore him"),[8] brings me to a second question, that of the ending. Given Garner's implied necessity that only forgiveness can release Blodeuwedd from her imprisonment, one finds the concluding lines of The Owl Service conveying mere prettiness of conceit, a disappointing ease of solution. In fact Roger says, "Is that all it is? As easy as that?" And it turns out to be a matter not of inner struggle but of the repetition of words, the repetition of a single word. Nor is it Gwyn, the inheritor of Huw's burden, who forgives, who comforts. It is Roger, who has suffered nothing—and what does he forgive? A few angry words of Gwyn's. And when one considers the degrees of forgiveness man has wrung out of himself in the face of the most appalling indifference, hypocrisy, and brutality since history began, we find ourselves again faced with weakness, with not nearly enough brought to bear if Garner is concerned, as he declares himself to be, with layers of meaning.[9]

By way of contrast, I keep thinking of another fantastical work, one that has at its heart, as does The Owl Service, the brazen act of a magician taking upon himself too great a power, daring too much, and bringing into life a being who should never have existed, an act out of which only suffering can come. I am referring to Ursula K. Le Guin's A Wizard of Earthsea, one of the finest books to have been published in 1968, but one that found no place in the runners-up for the Newbery Award. It is a work that is never satisfied simply with the act of magic, but goes beyond to the truth behind it, to the battle of human beings, surrounded as they are by a doom wrought of misapprehension and indiscipline. The final effect of the book is built up through gradual realization and not any easily brought about magical change. It is a work that reveals the human condition as calling for the painfully slow effort to understand one's self and others and then to act upon that understanding, something inevitably as difficult as all that has gone before. As for *The Owl Service*, my second question is this: Isn't it possible that the ingeniousness of conceit which commences it, the fact of Alison seeing one thing rather than another in the design of the plates, may fatally have led to a mere ingeniousness of conceit in the last pages?

For myself, though I appreciate what is best in the craftsmanship of the book, neither the texture nor the final effect is such that I shall go back to it again as I have been compelled to go back to *Earthfasts* and *A Wizard of Earthsea* for that almost indefinable aesthetic reward which arises out of implications, out of the whole ambience of a work, which is always more than a sum of the meanings of the words.

FOOTNOTES

1. Alan Garner, "A Bit More Practice," London *Times Literary Supplement,* (June 6, 1968): 577.

2. Ibid.

3. Ibid.

4. Susan Sontag, *Against Interpretation* (New York: Farrar, Straus and Giroux, 1966), p. 23.

5. John Ackerman, *Dylan Thomas: His Life and Work* (New York: Oxford, 1964), p. 6.

6. Dylan Thomas, *Quite Early One Morning* (New York: New Directions, 1954), pp. 146–47.

7. Garner, "More Practice," pp. 577–78.

8. Garner, "More Practice," p. 577.

9. Ibid.

Longfellow's Motives for the Structure of Hiawatha

Cecelia Tichi

The critical disesteem of Longfellow's verse was perhaps a certainty upon the decline of the poet's inflated reputation shortly after his death in 1882. Despite Edward Wagenknecht's sympathic mid-twentieth century reappraisal of Longfellow through biography, and Newton Arvin's more recent effort to establish him without apology as a minor figure in American literature, still it is quite likely that few readers yet confront a poem like "Hiawatha" with an attitude approaching disinterested openness. Howard Nemerov, for one, assures us he cannot, having "between the halves of a football game . . . heard great swatches of 'Hiawatha' droned out over the public address system while several hundred drum-majorettes twirled their batons."[1] Yet if the suggestion of Minnehaha electrically amplified seems today as bizarre as the retrospect of controversy raging over the propriety of Longfellow's unrhymed meter (adopted from the Finnish epic *Kalevala*), still there are other aspects of the poem that ought not to be obscured by current inclinations to banish it to the grade school classroom, to contemporaneous realms of *kitsch* and camp, or to the special province of the cultural historian of the nineteenth century.

For if the poem seems today beyond the pale esthetically, hedging anthropologic truth and misguidedly working, in Longfellow's terms, to "clothe the real with the ideal and make actual and common things radiant with poetic beauty," still it is possible that a significant literary motivation for the structure of "Hiawatha" has been overlooked.[2] For more than a century since its 1855 publication criticism of the poem has focused either on the romance between Indian composite cultural hero Hiawatha and the Minnehaha of Longfellow's fictive fancy or on Longfellow's perpetuation of Henry R. Schoolcraft's ethnological error in stating that Manabozho and Hiawatha were one.[3] Yet it seems plausible that Longfellow's design for "Hiawatha" pertains less to his softening

Reprinted from *American Literature* 42 (1970): 548–53.

of hard truths for the sake of the picturesque than it does to his attitude toward cultural continuity between the old world and the new.

It was Henry James who found Longfellow "interesting for nothing so much as for . . . the way in which his 'European' culture and his native kept house together." James pondered whether Longfellow's personal harmoniousness derived from "his having worked up his American consciousness to that mystic point . . . at which it could feel nothing but continuity and congruity with his European." He concluded that if "something in [Longfellow's] liberal existence . . . seemed a piece of the old world smoothly fitted into the new, so it might quite as well have been a piece of the new fitted, just as smoothly, into the old."[4] Longfellow himself has left ample evidence of the importance he attached to evolving cultural continuity. If one may equate his position with that of his character Mr. Churchill in the passage dealing with American literary nationalism in the prose tale *Kavanagh* (1849), then Longfellow certainly anticipated a future time when the "thoughts and feelings . . . of all nations . . . finally mingle in our literature." The culmination of such mingling would be "a kind of universality" in American literature resulting from "culture and intellectual refinement" achieved "not in the growth of a day," but over centuries.[5]

With processes of literary assimilation established in his mind as a desideratum for the growth of American literature, Longfellow appears, consciously or not, to have designed "Hiawatha" as a groundwork of native materials in a land whereon European culture could plausibly be grafted. Newton Arvin calls attention to an early (1825) essay in which Longfellow suggests that Indian materials will so engage men's imaginations that "our land will become, indeed, a classic ground."[6] But his "Hiawatha" source materials, replete with polygamy, torture, lust, adultery, scalpings, and white men paradoxically bearing the standard of a higher civilization, yet altogether villainous—these were not in Longfellow's nineteenth century regarded as viable components of an American classicism.[7] They did not intimate the "culture and intellectual refinement" appropriate to "mingle in our literature." Certainly they could not induce either for poet or reader the rich poetic associations Longfellow used so frequently in poems whose settings are European. Thus, if the Indian in America was to evoke qualitatively the same kind of poetic associations as historical-legendary places and personages of Europe, then it was for Longfellow to make the evocation possible by creating a work that would give native American materials some parity with those of Europe, and further make plausible an Indian-Euro-American cultural continuity in America. To do this, he structured his plot so as to reveal American Indians becoming progressively civilized up to the appearance at the end of the poem of the white Christian missionaries, presaging the Caucasian immigration and further indicating a prospective cultural suffusion of Europe into America.

Briefly considered, the plot of "Hiawatha" begins with the promise of a unified social order among tribes scattered or at enmity. The Master of Life, Gitche Manito, smokes the calumet and admonishes the tribes that

> All your strength is in your union,
> All your danger is in discord;
> Therefore be at peace henceforward,
> And as brothers live together.[8]

He promises to send a Deliverer (Hiawatha), who later in the poem reinforces social unity when he, an Ojibway, vows to marry Minnehaha of the enemy Dacotahs,

> That our tribes might be united,
> That old feuds might be forgotten,
> And old wounds be healed forever. (p. 135)

Still in young manhood, Hiawatha enables his people to escape the vagaries of hunting and foraging for their food. "Must our lives depend on these things?" he asks in a plaintive refrain that prefaces ritual fasting and fighting which culminate in agrarianism signalled by the arrival of Mondamin, corn (pp. 124–126). Hiawatha's next deliverance of his people is his development of picture-writing (pp. 145–147) for sending messages, recording history, and communicating love. Subsequently in the poem he travels abroad

> Teaching men the use of simples
> And the antidotes for poisons,
> And the cure of all diseases. (p. 149)

In sum, the plot of the poem, entwined as it is with legends and romance, moves nonetheless from social unification through agrarianism and literacy to medical knowledge. Civilizing progress is marked in each step of a pattern in which the Indians increasingly master their environment. Thus in a poem structurally implying progress, Longfellow manipulates his plot to make the advent of Christianity the civilizing apotheosis of an Indian nation now prepared for it. He is not so fatuous as to suggest for the Indians a future unclouded by miseries, for surely the liquidation of Indian reservations between 1829 and 1843 with its "trail of tears" debacle of western removal beyond Missouri of the Shawnees, Delawares, and Wyandots, among others, made clear to Longfellow the fate of the Indian peoples in America. His poem "To the Driving Cloud" evinces his full awareness of it. Yet Christianity at the end of "Hiawatha" is the common touchstone for whites and Indians. Hiawatha's final admonishment to his people as he departs for the Land of the Hereafter is to pay heed to the missionary Black-Robe chiefs, to

> Listen to their words of wisdom,
> Listen to the truth they tell you,
> For the Master of Life has sent them
> From the land of light and morning. (p. 164)

From Hiawatha's view the white men in ships represent vast armed power, though even in his darker vision of tribes scattered "like the withered leaves of Autumn" (p. 162), he does not blame the Europeans for his peoples' fate.

It seems, moreover, that toward the end of the poem Longfellow interjects his own view in rather Whitmanesque terms within the consciousness of Hiawatha when the Indian hero recounts a vision:

I beheld, too, in that vision,
All the secrets of the future,
Of the distant days that shall be.
I beheld the westward marches
Of the unknown, crowded nations.
All the land was full of people,
Restless, struggling, toiling, striving,
Speaking many tongues, yet feeling
But one heart-beat in their bosoms. (p. 162)

That "one heart-beat" of the European immigrants hints at a cultural unity in America which, applied to belles lettres, prefigures the ultimate "university" Longfellow himself envisioned for American literature. If the Indians seem in the lines above too readily set aside for another social order making incursions on their lands, it might be recalled that Longfellow's "Hiawatha" deals with Indian legend, not history. He infuses the poem with just enough detail of daily life to establish a reality in which the appearance of white missionaries seems plausible. Longfellow at the end of "Hiawatha" conjoins the eternality of Indian legend with historical time. His connecting bridge, built all along, is a limited amount of anthropological detail about circumstances of eating, canoe building, etiquette, flora and fauna, etc. But having shaped the various legends in a unified work that presents the Indians as advancing in civilization, Longfellow is able at the last to suggest a continuity of cultures in America from the primitive yet dignified indigenous to the sophisticated migratory transplanted from the old world. His structural implication is that if whites are to supplant the Indians, still the latter are as he presents them worthy in their own native culture of a historic European on-grafting in America.

Possibly it was the design of Longfellow's plot structure that led him correlatively to prettify Indian life—or mercerize it, as C. F. Fiske describes the poet's sacrifice of earthiness for a surface sheen nowhere to be found in his sources.[9] Evidence suggests that Longfellow was personally receptive to the original accounts, for his journal entry of July 31, 1854, mentions reading to his boys the Indian story of the Red Swan, a legend in which a detached scalp figures prominently. Yet for Longfellow emphasis on the consanguinity of Indian civilization meant necessary deletion of the brutally sanguine. And if it is true that in "Hiawatha" he violated Indian myths by "insisting upon sentiments which form little or no part of Indian feeling, but which do appeal to the civilized reader,"[10] it might be suggested that Longfellow's attitude toward cultural and literary continuity between the old and new the worlds was his poetic motive for doing so.

NOTES

1. Howard Nemerov, "Introduction," *Longfellow* (New York, 1959), p. 9.

2. Quoted in Edward Wagenknecht, *Longfellow* (New York, 1955), p. 63.

3. See Stith Thompson, "The Indian Legend of Hiawatha," *PMLA*, 37 (March 1922: 128–40. The essay clarifies Indian legends about which Schoolcraft erred and discusses liberties Longfellow took in shaping the poem. For discussion of Hiawatha's Indian antecedents in American literature see Wilbur L. Schramm, "Hiawatha and Its Predecessors," *PQ*, 11 (October 1932): 321–343.

4. Henry James, *William Wetmore Story and His Friends*, 1 (Boston, 1903): 311–12.

5. Henry W. Longfellow, *Kavanagh*, ed. Jean Downey (New Haven, 1965), p. 87.

6. Newton Arvin, *Longfellow* (Boston, 1962), p. 19. Arvin offers evidence that Longfellow's attitude did not change with time. He writes that "in his old age (Longfellow) wrote to Louise Chandler Moulton, who was about to sail for Europe: 'Please don't get expatriated. Ah, no, life is not all cathedrals and ruined castles, and other theatrical properties of the Old World'" (p. 23n).

7. Discussion of Longfellow's sources and his use of them can be found in Arvin (pp. 154–80), Wagenknecht (pp. 202, 335), and Cecil B. Williams, *Henry Wadsworth Longfellow* (New York, 1964), pp. 156–158. Firsthand perusal of the works of John Heckewelder, John Tanner, George Catlin, and especially of Henry R. Schoolcraft makes clear why it is that virtually all critics (favorable and otherwise) of "Hiawatha" discuss at length Longfellow's remarkable shaping of a unified work from an incoherent mass of material. Taken together, the sources are a farrago of disparate legends, of Indian history, Christian moralisms, and rudimentary sociology and anthropology. Schoolcraft himself would likely have objected to Longfellow's remark that his writings were ill-digested; yet he had an eye toward the American literary imagination that might shape his Indian lore. He remarks in *Oneota, or Characteristics of the Red Race of America* (New York, 1847) that he hopes, "herein (to) be the medium of presenting the germs of a future mythology, which, in the hands of our poets, and novelists, and fictitious writers, might admit of being formed and moulded to the purposes of a purely vernacular literature" (p. 246). Schoolcraft's criteria for such a literature are "simplicity, conciseness, and brevity," and he deplores literary works which cast Indians as "English figures, drest in moccasins, and holding a bow and arrows" (p. 347). Nevertheless, Longfellow, according to his Introduction to "Hiawatha" intended the poem for those "who love a nation's legends/Love the ballads of a people," and many of the Indian traits, customs, and incidents Schoolcraft and the others record were far from being lovable, or even acceptable to many readers.

8. Citations from "Hiawatha" in my text are to *The Complete Poetical Works of Longfellow*, ed. Horace E. Scudder (Cambridge, Mass., 1893), p. 116. Hereafter page references are listed in the text.

9. C. F. Fiske, "Mercerized Folklore in 'Hiawatha,'" *Poet-Lore*, 31 (December 1920): 538–575.

10. Thompson, p. 139.

Responding to Structural Criticism

1. Understanding Literary Style Through Wordless Picture Books

CRITICAL COMMENT

Cianciolo believes children can be taught to distinguish between good and bad stories after they have learned to understand certain elements of literary style. She suggests that wordless picture books are a good medium for beginning that understanding.

WAY OF RESPONDING

A. Use the close reading technique to study the effect of artistic style on plot development in the wordless picture books. Goodall's books about Paddy Pork, for example, use the unique device of a half page that, when turned, creates a next step in the adventure. Does this always add a surprise element or does the surprise and excitement come with the turning of the larger page? What effect has Goodall created? In Ringi's *The Winner*, the characters are placed off center on the pages. What does this tell the reader about story progression? Select some other books from Cianciolo's list and analyze them with similar care.

B. Do you and your peers agree about the effect a book's literary style has on its plot development? For example, discuss some books from Cianciolo's list that, because of their style, might be considered controversial. Ungerer's *One, Two, Where's My Shoe?* in which a shoe shape is "hidden" within the picture might be contrasted with the same author's *Snail Where Are You?* which shows the more natural form of a snail secreted among various objects. Contrast two books of realism: *And I Must Hurry for the Sea Is Coming In . . .* by Mendoza and *Journey to the Moon* by Fuchs. Are these books illustrated appropriately?—One is done in a series of photographs, while the other is in rather modernistic trapezoids and rectangles. Which one depicts its plot better? What are your peers' reasons for their opinions?

2. Levels of Meaning in Visual Literacy

CRITICAL COMMENT

Cianciolo contends that some of the higher levels of meaning of wordless picture books are contained in the irony of the pictured situations. Not all children who would enjoy looking at the pictures could understand the incongruities within them. Cianciolo suggests that some wordless picture books, such as the books by Frank Asch, are for children with advanced visual literacy, while others, such as the books of photographs by Tana Hoban, are understandable at a preschool level.

WAYS OF RESPONDING

A. Select several wordless picture books that seem to you to necessitate decidedly different levels of visual understanding. For example, *Elephant*

Buttons by Ueno, *The Good Bird* by Wezel, and *Wheels* by Simmons might represent a simple level of understanding, while *The Winner* by Ringi, and *Apples* by Hogrogian might be at a higher level necessitating abstraction. Show the stories to children individually and record their responses to a controlled set of questions. Compare the verbal understanding scores and reading comprehension ability scores of these children with their performance on this simple experiment. Was there a difference in their ability to respond to the different levels of books?

B. Humor and children's ability to understand its various forms was studied by Monson. Read her findings.[1] Study the humor in several of the wordless picture books. Do you think the factor of visual literacy Cianciolo discusses might instead be a factor of mental ability or inability to understand the humor within certain situations?

3. Close Reading of Pictures

CRITICAL COMMENT

Nothing Ever Happens on My Block by Raskin is suggested by Cianciolo for teaching visual literacy skills at the kindergarten level. She states, "Carefully close scrutiny of the little pictures is necessary if one is to appreciate the full impact of all that is taking place in this ironic story." The book pictures the hero sitting on the curb glumly facing the reader and complaining that nothing ever happens on his block, while in the background many exciting events, such as pranks, theft, fire, and the landing of parachutists occur.

WAYS OF RESPONDING

A. Use *Nothing Ever Happens on My Block* with kindergarten children to form your own opinion of the ability of a child this age to do close reading, even if the "reading" is of pictures. Are kindergarten children able to put order to visuals and interpret the pictures if they have not experienced such situations previously? Is it possible for them to hear a statement read, see a conflicting action in the picture, and interpret the event as ironic humor? You may want to extend this observation to the use of several other books, such as *Changes Changes* by Hutchins and *Bobo's Dream* by Alexander.

B. *The Silver Pony* by Ward is a wordless picture book intended for intermediate-age children. Read through the book to get the full story. Is it necessary to study the pictures with the technique of close reading as the term is used in structural criticism? Are there nuances in the story to be gained in the fine details of the pictures? in the ordered placement of the pictures from page to page? Develop a series of questions to check children's understanding of the story. Use the questions with several children and draw some conclusions about the use of close reading with materials for this age level.

C. Use Munari's *The Circus in the Mist* to determine if more of the story is told through the pictures than through the text. Has the author-illustrator cre-

---

1. Dianne Monson, "Children's Test Responses to Seven Humorous Stories," *The Elementary School Journal* 68, no. 7 (April 1968): 334–38.

ated a book that is dependent on its design to tell the story? Share the book with your colleagues and get their reactions.

4. Making Strange as a Critical Device

CRITICAL COMMENT

The literary device of *making strange* is common to structural critics. They believe that a greater sense of understanding is created when an author juxtaposes the familiar with the unfamiliar. Guttery points out the importance in children's stories of making every attempt to make the unfamiliar understandable by describing it in terms and experiences familiar to the children. This is done through the use of minute details, color words, expressions of time, size, and distance, and figures of speech that interest and are natural to the lives of children. One example was that an author who tried to get across the concept of youngness used such expressions as "younger than the buds on the trees," and "younger than the hole in your stocking." Guttery emphasized the importance of making the abstract concepts more concrete by the use of phrasings which children can visualize; thus, Guttery's technique is that of making familiar rather than making strange, just the opposite of the structural criticism methodology.

WAYS OF RESPONDING

A. Determine whether the device of making concrete statements that are within the experiences of young children still persists. You many want to select a group of representative picture books, since these are the books Guttery draws on most frequently. A usable source list would be the books considered for the Caldecott Award. Preliminary lists are published in *Language Arts* (formerly *Elementary English)* in the November/December issues. These might serve as good samples for the prevailing style of the present.

B. Consider whether the technique of making abstract statements more familiar by the use of figures of speech and phrasings relevant to the interest of children is a factor of the age level for which the book is written. Guttery writes about picture storybooks and gives no attention to books written at an intermediate level. Is it possible that authors writing for children nine years old and above would use the device of making strange rather than making familiar? Select a variety of books written for this age level and analyze them by the method of close reading. Newbery Award winners and honor books might be contrasted with books winning awards chosen by children. Listings of award-winning books are found in *Awards and Prizes.*[2] The factor of the style of the writing might have some effect on the children's enjoyment of the book and the two sets of samples could serve to note this factor. A study such as this could be time-consuming, but if done by a group of college students, the results could be shared without too great a time expenditure on the part of any one person.

---

2. Christine Stawicki, *Children's Books: Award & Prizes* (New York: The Children's Book Council, 1975).

5. Emotional Content Through Structure

CRITICAL COMMENT

An example of the use of structural forms to build emotional content is pointed out by Guttery in *Wait for William* by Flack. She notes how Flack used a repetition of the term "alone" to get across the aloneness of the character.

WAYS OF RESPONDING

Select several picture storybooks that use repetition. Determine if this style is ever used to get across emotional content. You may want to make a chart of the examples of repetition in three or four books such as *The Secret Hiding Place* by Bennett, *May I Bring a Friend?* by De Regniers, and *The Blue Nosed Witch* by Embry. After noting the several instances of repetition on the chart, identify those repetitions that are included apparently to emphasize the emotional content. Does this use seem to predominate the use of repetitions or could it just occur by chance?

6. Concern for Form

CRITICAL COMMENT

Many picture storybooks analyzed by Guttery were built on similar form patterns. In fact, Guttery was able to diagram the various portions of the story she termed *movements*. She pointed out several books following the same design and several others that contain only minor variations of the patterns.

WAYS OF RESPONDING

A. Analyze some other picture storybooks to note whether similar patterns occur. You might study such highly structured books as *Mr. Rabbit and the Lovely Present* by Zolotow, *Just Me* by Ets, and *Blueberries for Sal* by McCloskey. Make your own diagram for the books. Do you find recurrences of the same pattern or variations of the pattern?

B. Use the story pattern diagrammed by Guttery as a basis. Find other books that fit this pattern. Pick books at random from established sources, such as the listing of picture storybooks in *Adventuring with Books*[3] and *The Elementary School Library Collection*.[4] Are books with this same design found frequently? What generalization could you make about books with this design?

C. Study a group of picture storybooks for their patterns. Select a source that lists a sizable number of the picture books. You might turn to the catalogs for a year or two of *The Children's Book Showcase*,[5] a collection of graphically beautiful books. Select the picture storybooks and analyze them. Do these books have a tendency for a governing structural principle? What are the

---

3. Shelton Root, Jr. ed., *Adventuring with Books,* 2nd Ed. (New York: Citation Press, 1973).
4. Mary V. Gaver ed., *The Elementary School Library Collection,* 8th Ed., (New Brunswick, New Jersey: The Bro-Dart Foundation, 1973).
5. *The Children's Book Showcase* (New York: The Children's Book Council, 1972, 1973, 1974, 1975).

patterns? Are any of the patterns related? Other sources for picture story-books are the Caldecott Award and Honor books and the *Horn Book*'s Fanfare list of picture books.

D. Set up a small experiment to determine if there is a time when children do not respond positively to highly patterned stories. Use several books that have definite form, such as *Play with Me* by Ets, *Pelle's New Suit* by Beskow, and *Bedtime for Frances* by Hoban. Read the stories and record the responses to the stories by children at different grade or age levels. Does there seem to be an age beyond which children do not care for such stories?

E. If order is truly an aesthetic element, then it is likely to be found in books beyond the picture book stage. Study the structure of some intermediate grade books to note whether patterns exist. Are there specific types of novels that lend themselves to this format? For example, McCloskey's *Homer Price* is a book with an episodic plot. Compare other books of this style such as *The 18th Emergency* by Byars and *Runaway Ralph* by Cleary. Do books such as this have certain chapters that are based on patterns for their humor or drama?

Another organizing format that might be considered is the use of chronology as in O'Dell's *The King's Fifth* and Cameron's *The Court of the Stone Children*. Does there seem to be a conscious effort on the part of the authors to have a definite form for the books?

7. Simile and Metaphor

CRITICAL COMMENT

Gilpatrick takes the first simile in Smaridge's *Peter's Tent* and finds references to it throughout the tale. She points out allusions to the boy as bear in de-scriptions of the child's size, in his manner of movement, and in his habits. She discusses other metaphors in the story, not necessarily related to the bear theme. The analysis of similes and metaphors is a methodology commonly used by structural critics to explain the deep underlying meanings within the story.

WAYS OF RESPONDING

A. Read aloud a metaphorically rich passage of *Time-Ago Tales of Jahdu* by Hamilton or *The House of Wings* by Byars, to a small group of intermediate grade students. Immediately afterward, ask the children to individually tape record their descriptions of the characters that were discussed, telling as much about them as they think is true, not restricting them to actual words that were used in the text. As you listen to the tapes, note any extensions of the literal statements that might possibly have been brought about by the metaphors. Use this experience to form your opinion about the power of metaphors to give greater meaning to the young readers of children's books.

B. *The Witch of Blackbird Pond* by Speare is a book that makes a great deal of use of metaphors. After reading the book, analyze a portion of it for its deeper meaning. Do you sense a greater understanding after reflecting on the metaphors? Discuss your experience with your colleagues.

8. Symbols as a Subliminal Influence

CRITICAL COMMENT

Gilpatrick believes children understand much literary writing through their tacit dimension; that is, they know more than they can express. She asserts that certain literary devices, particularly symbols, enable children to interpret and understand the story at a depth of meaning they are unable to express.

WAYS OF RESPONDING

A. Examine some of the symbols in picture storybooks. You might use *We Were Tired of Living in a House* by Skorpen, *One Morning in Maine* by Mc-Closkey, and *Dandelion* by Freeman. Make a list of the symbols you find in the books. Discuss these symbols with people who are aware of the experiences of young children. Do the symbols refer to experiences that are likely to be within the realm of children who would hear the stories? Take a consensus of these people concerning whether they agree that symbolic references could be understood tacitly by children.

B. Work with two or more people on this project to determine the amount of intersubjective agreement on the meaning of symbols. Use a picture storybook such as *Where the Wild Things Are* by Sendak, *Frog in the Well* by Tresselt, or *Crow Boy* by Yashima. Have each person analyze the book through close reading, picking out the symbols from the story. Then have each person write a brief statement describing the meaning of the symbols. Compare the statements. Do the adults agree on their meaning of the symbols? Does the agreement or the lack of agreement influence any of the person's views on Gilpatrick's thesis?

9. Alliteration as a Literary Strategy

CRITICAL COMMENTS

Gilpatrick asserts that an emotional feeling or a mood can be evoked through the use of alliteration. She gives examples of a number of instances in *Peter's Tent* where Smaridge uses alliteration to help establish intent and feeling.

WAYS OF RESPONDING

A. Select examples of the use of alliteration from children's books. For example, you might use *Lyle, Lyle, Crocodile* by Waber or *Belling the Tiger* by Stolz. Read these examples to a group of your colleagues and ask them to state the kind of mood the passages evoke. From this experience, what conclusions can you draw about the use of alliteration for establishing emotional tone?

B. Listen to the recording of a children's book containing a number of cases of alliteration, rhythmic patterns, and assonance. Try to be particularly aware of these phonological devices. During a subsequent listening to the story, follow the text, marking the places where the phonological patterns occur. In the context of the story, do the sound patterns tend to occur at important places? Do they set moods in the story? After this experience, determine your opinion about Gilpatrick's assertion that alliteration establishes mood and feeling.

10. Analyzing Stories According to Actions

CRITICAL COMMENT

One technique of analyzing stories is by employing the method used by the Russian structuralist, Vladimir Propp. He defined certain actions, or "functions," that were basic to folktales and listed them according to their sequence in the story. Propp's study resulted in the finding that the functions followed the same sequence, although from story to story, certain functions were omitted. Neumeyer suggests that this same type of analysis can be used for children's fiction.

WAYS OF RESPONDING

A. Use a book such as Krauss' *The Carrot Seed* for an analysis in Propp's style. Identify each action. After listing the actions by giving them brief identifying terms or symbols, try to perceive the sequence. For comparison purposes, analyze *Lion* by Du Bois and note the similarities in actions with *The Carrot Seed*. From your analysis of these two books, what generalization can you make about the actions in children's picture storybooks in relation to the findings of Propp's study?

B. A recent study of one hundred picture storybooks resulted in designating eight individual actions as constants that appeared in at least fifty of the books.[6] These actions were journey, arrival, violence (received), observation (given), communication (given), communication (received), service (received), and achievement. Analyze some of the books from the study to note the use of these actions. A representative sampling includes: *Billy and Blaze* by Anderson, *The Little House* by Burton, *Bear Party* by Du Bois, *The Happy Lion* by Fatio, *Millions of Cats* by Gag, *Sam, Bangs, and Moonshine* by Ness, *Let's Be Enemies* by Udry, and *No Roses for Harry!* by Zion.

11. The Structural Design of a Novel

CRITICAL COMMENT

Cameron visualizes Garner's *The Owl Service,* a full length novel for intermediate age children, as having a structural design of a series of three triangles. She describes the book and the interrelations among the characters according to this format.

WAYS OF RESPONDING

Notice the structure of other children's novels to determine if there is a plan that can be visualized. In *Finn's Folly* by Southall for example, one might note the shifting of scenes from one incident to another combined with the use of flashback and characters' recollections of the past. *M. C. Higgins, the*

---

6. Mary Lou White, "A Structural Analysis of Children's Literature: Picture Storybooks" (Unpublished Ph. D. dissertation, The Ohio State University, 1972).

Great by Hamilton might be studied from the standpoint of the various moves the hero makes away from his secure home and the design these moves create.

12. Paradoxes

CRITICAL COMMENT

Certain of the characters in Garner's *The Owl Service* are fully developed and display many human foibles. Cameron points out the paradoxes between the criticisms some of the characters make about other persons while the very phrasing terminology which they use reveals similar faults in themselves.

WAYS OF RESPONDING

A. When children go through the growing up period they tend to make contradictions between their acting and speaking. Examples of these paradoxes are often found in children's books. Read through several novels or think back over recent readings, particularly those that deal with the maturation process. Books that might serve as good sources are *Zeely* by Hamilton, *The Truth About Mary Rose* by Sachs, and *The Friendship Hedge* by Norris. Select the specific phrases that show inconsistencies. In your opinion, why did the author include phrases that did not show progress in character development?

B. When structural critics study the use of paradox, they are frequently concerned with contradictions in metaphors. Study the use of metaphor in several children's books. Is it a true generalization to say that for most part, the literary language in children's books is straightforward and makes use of little irony? Cite examples to support your opinion. You may want to review books such as *Nightbirds on Nantucket* by Aiken and *Time Cat* by Alexander. It might also be worthwhile to notice the use of metaphor in books first written in other languages. In these cases, the literary language may be altered due to the translation. Some suggested titles here are *Don't Take Teddy* by Friis-Baastad, *Wildcat Under Glass* by Zei, and *The Late-Born Child* by Aleksin.

13. Phonological Aspects of Prose Literature

CRITICAL COMMENT

Cameron is concerned with the harsh rhythm of Garner's writing. Responding to criticisms of choppiness in the book, she suggests that this may be due to the beat of the dialogue. She contends that although the actual tone of the language used by real persons who lead lives similar to the characters may sound like this, the literary artistry of the book is hurt when the phonology of the phrasing is dissonant.

WAYS OF RESPONDING

A. Read aloud the portions of dialogue of Garner's *The Owl Service* you consider to be the ones of Cameron's concern. You may want to have an audience listen to your reading or judge it yourself. Do you agree that the rhythm is staccato and harsh?

B. Tape some conversations of teenage children who might be similar to Garner's characters. Is their language discordant? Would you have preferred to have Garner use reality in the tones of his dialogues for this fantasy or do you believe artistic license would have justified his making the dialogue more pleasing to the ear?

C. Listen to commercial recordings of children's books. For example, there are fine recordings of *The Little Prince* and the *Just So Stories*.[7] Judge the sound of the writing according to the scale below:

	Resonant	Dissonant
Dialogue	/——/——/——/——/——/——/——/——/——/	
Narration of action	/——/——/——/——/——/——/——/——/——/	
Description	/——/——/——/——/——/——/——/——/——/	

D. Cameron wrote about phonological aspects heard by the "inner ear," so to speak, not the actually produced sound. Compare this type of sound in books of various types: sports, mysteries, realism, fantasy, biography. What types of variations do you find in the rhythm and tone of the books?

14. Poetry: What It Is—Not What It Means

CRITICAL COMMENT

Tichi elects to look at the poem "Hiawatha" structurally. She notes that the poem shows a pattern of the Indian movement toward civilization. The Indians' progress toward the mystery of their environment paralleled their move toward the ultimate goal of Christianity. The final vision in the poem suggests a unity with the white man's culture.

WAYS OF RESPONDING

Study poems written especially for children and note their structure. Do they actually tell part of their theme or message through their design? Narrative poems might be used, such as *Amigo* by Schweitzer or *Listen, Rabbit!* by Fisher Concrete poems might also be used, such as in *Seeing Things* by Froman and *Out Loud!* by Merriam.

15. Poetic Metaphors

CRITICAL COMMENT

The phrase "one heart-beat" is studied by Tichi who suggests that Longfellow was using this to suggest a cultural unity that he hoped would occur. In the

---

7. Antoine De Saint-Exupéry, *The Little Prince,* read by Peter Ustinov (London: The Decca Record Company Limited, Argo Division, 1972) and Rudyard Kipling, *Just So Stories,* Vol. One, Vol. Two (London: The Decca Record Company Limited, Argo Division, 1973).

poem one of the final visions of the Indian is that the land will be full of people "Speaking many tongues, yet feeling/But one heart-beat in their bosoms."

WAYS OF RESPONDING

A. Poetry as an art form uses such precise language that many metaphors are found within it. Study a number of poems to notice their use of metaphors. What deeper meanings do you find as you look at the contrasts in the use of the words and unique phrasings that are employed? Books of poems that might be particularly interesting for study are *Sam's Place* by Moore and *What a Wonderful Bird the Frog Are* by Livingston.

B. Read some of the ballads that have been written in picturebook format for children. *The Ballad of the Burglar of Babylon* by Bishop and *The Charge of the Light Brigade* by Tennyson offer strong themes. As you read these, find examples of metaphors concerning the major theme of the poems that might have cultural meanings.

FURTHER READING

Cameron, Eleanor. "Of Style and the Stylist." *Horn Book* 40, no. 1 (February 1964): 25–32. A noted author and critics of children's books uses structural features of five outstanding books as examples of artistic techniques in writing.

Groff, Patrick. "Children's Literature Versus Wordless 'Books.'" *Top of the News* 30, no. 3 (April 1974): pp. 294–303. An argument against Cianciolo's article on wordless books (see text), this critic rejects the notion that visual literacy is a forerunner to reading.

_____. "The Most Highly-Esteemed Children's Poems." *Elementary English* 34, no. 6 (October 1962): 587–89. Thirty-six poems found in five leading anthologies are analyzed structurally. The use of rhyme, figures of speech, alliteration, assonance, and imagery is noted.

Guéron, Jacqueline. "Children's Verse and the Halle-Keyser Theory of Prosody." *Children's Literature: The Great Excluded* 2 (1973): 197–208. A new linguistic theory is explained and applied in an analysis of metrical patterns of English nursery rhymes and French *comptines*. The article is rather complex for the reader unfamiliar with the theory but is representative of a structural study of sound patterns in poetry.

Novak, Barbara. "Milne's Poems: Form and Content." *Elementary English* 34, no. 6 (October, 1957): 355–61. A portion of the article discusses Milne's use of spacing, repetition, parenthetical asides, and even variations in typeset, all of which add emphasis to his poetry.

Sendak, Maurice. "The Aliveness of Peter Rabbit." *Wilson Library Bulletin* 40, no. 4 (December 1965): 345–48. An outstanding illustrator details the structural features that add to the story content in the illustrations of Potter's *Peter Rabbit*.

Smith, James Steel. "Children's Literature: Form or Formula?" *Elementary English* 25 (February 1958): 92–95. Examples of structural patterns in fine literature for children are contrasted with books that are written imitating successful styles.

Stanek, Lou Willett. "The Junior Novel: A Stylistic Study." *Elementary English* 51, no. 7 (October 1974): 947–53. A structural analysis of Campbell's *Why Not Join the Giraffes?*, Zindel's *I Never Loved Your Mind,* and Stolz' *The Seagulls Woke Me* reveals that these novels, representative of adolescent books, are, respectively, formula, experimental, and classic in style.

Werner, Judy. "Black Pearls and Ebony." *School Library Journal* 15 (May 1968): 57, 67. A librarian criticizes negative uses of the term "black" in children's books and suggests that these stories may have a damaging effect on children. The article brought forth comment and correction in the September and November issues of the journal.

REFERENCES

Aiken, Joan. *Nightbirds on Nantucket*. Illus. Robin Jacques. Garden City, New York: Doubleday, 1966.

Aleksin, Anatolii Georgievich. *A Late-Born Child*. Trans. Maria Polushkin. Illus. Charles Robinson. New York: World Publishing, 1971.

Alexander, Lloyd. *Time Cat*. Illus. Bill Sokol. New York: Holt, Rinehart and Winston, 1963.

Alexander, Martha G. *Bobo's Dream*. New York: The Dial Press, 1970.

Anderson, C. W. *Billy and Blaze*. New York: The Macmillan Company, 1936, 1964.

Bennett, Rainey. *The Secret Hiding Place*. New York: World Publishing, 1960.

Beskow, Elsa. *Pelle's New Suit*. Trans. Marian Letcher Woodburn. Eau Claire, Wisconsin: E. M. Hale, n.d.

Bishop, Elizabeth. *The Ballad of the Burglar of Babylon*. Illus. Ann Grifalconi. New York: Farrar, Straus and Giroux, 1968.

Burton, Virginia Lee. *The Little House*. Boston: Houghton Mifflin, 1942.

Byars, Betsy. *The 18th Emergency*. Illus. Robert Grossman. New York: The Viking Press, 1973.

————. *The House of Wings*. Illus. Daniel Schwartz. New York: The Viking Press, 1972.

Cameron, Eleanor. *The Court of the Stone Children*. New York: E. P. Dutton, 1973.

Cleary, Beverly. *Runaway Ralph*. Illus. Louis Darling. New York: William Morrow, 1970.

DeRegniers, Beatrice Schenk. *May I Bring a Friend?* Illus. Beni Montressor. New York: Atheneum, 1964.

DuBois, William Pène. *Bear Party*. New York: The Viking Press, 1963.

————. *Lion*. New York: The Viking Press, 1955, 1956.

Embry, Margaret. *The Blue Nosed Witch*. Illus. Carl Rose. New York: Holiday House, 1956.

Ets, Marie Hall. *Just Me*. New York: The Viking Press, 1965.

————. *Play with Me*. New York: The Viking Press, 1955.

Fatio, Louise. *The Happy Lion*. Illus. Roger Duvoisin. New York: Whittlesey House, 1954.

Fisher, Aileen. *Listen, Rabbit!* Illus. Symeon Shimin. New York: Thomas Y. Crowell, 1964.

Flack, Marjorie. *Wait for William*. Boston: Houghton Mifflin, 1935.

Freeman, Don. *Dandelion*. New York: The Viking Press, 1964.

Friis-Baastad, Babbis. *Don't Take Teddy*. Trans. Lise Somme McKinnon. New York: Charles Scribner's Sons, 1967.

Froman, Robert. *Seeing Things*. New York: Thomas Y. Crowell, 1974.

Fuchs, Erich. *Journey to the Moon*. New York: A Seymour Lawrence Book; Delocarte Press, 1969.

Gág, Wanda. *Millions of Cats*. New York: Coward, McCann & Geoghegan, 1928.

Garner, Alan. *The Owl Service*. New York: Henry Z. Walck, 1967.

Goodall, John S. *The Adventures of Paddy Pork*. New York: Harcourt Brace Jovano-vich, 1968.

Hamilton, Virginia. *M. C. Higgins, the Great*. New York: The Macmillan Company, 1974.

————. *The Time-Ago Tales of Jahdu*. Illus. Nonny Hogrogian. New York: The Macmillan Company, 1969.

————. *Zeely*. New York: The Macmillan Company, 1967.

Hoban, Russell. *Bedtime for Frances*. Illus. by Garth Williams. New York: Harper & Row, 1960.

Hogrogian, Nanny. *Apples*. New York: The Macmillan Company, 1972.

Hutchins, Pat. *Changes, Changes*. New York: The Macmillan Company, 1971.

Krauss, Ruth. *The Carrot Seed*. Illus. Crockett Johnson. New York: Harper & Brothers, 1945.

Livingston, Myra Cohn (ed.). *What a Wonderful Bird the Frog Are*. New York: Harcourt Brace Jovanovich, 1973.

McCloskey, Robert. *Blueberries for Sal*. New York: The Viking Press, 1948.

————. *Homer Price*. New York: The Viking Press, 1943.

————. *One Morning in Maine*. New York: The Viking Press, 1952.

Mendoza, George. *And I Must Hurry for the Sea Is Coming In . . .* Illus. DeWayne Dalrymple and Herb Lubalin. Englewood Cliffs, N.J.: Prentice-Hall, n.d.

Merriam, Eve. *Out Loud!* Illus. Harriet Sherman. New York: Atheneum, 1973.

Moore, Lilian. *Sam's Place*. Illus. Talivaldis Stubis. New York: Atheneum, 1973.

Munari, Bruno. *The Circus in the Mist*. New York: World Publishing, 1968.

Ness, Evaline. *Sam, Bangs, and Moonshine*. New York: Holt, Rinehart and Winston, 1966.

Norris, Gunilla. *The Friendship Hedge*. Illus. Dale Payson. New York: E. P. Dutton, 1973.

O'Dell, Scott. *The King's Fifth*. Illus. Samuel Bryant. Boston: Houghton Mifflin, 1966.

Raskin, Ellen. *Nothing Ever Happens on my Block*. New York: Atheneum, 1968.

Ringi, Kjell. *The Winner*. New York: Harper & Row, 1969.

Sachs, Marilyn. *The Truth About Mary Rose*. Illus. Louis Glanzman. Garden City, New York: Doubleday, 1973.

Schweitzer, Byrd Baylor. *Amigo*. Illus. Garth Williams. New York: The MacMillian Company, 1963.

Sendak, Maurice. *Where the Wild Things Are*. New York: Harper & Row, 1963.

Simmons, Ellie. *Wheels*. New York: David McKay, 1969.

Skorpen, Liesel Moak. *We Were Tired of Living in A House*. Illus. Doris Burn. New York: Coward, McCann & Geoghegan, 1969.

Smaridge, Nora. *Peter's Tent*. Illus. Brinton Turkle. New York: The Viking Press, 1965.

Southall, Ivan. *Finn's Folly*. New York: St. Martin's Press, 1969.

Speare, Elizabeth George. *The Witch of Blackbird Pond*. Boston: Houghton Mifflin, 1958.

Stolz, Mary. *Belling the Tiger*. Illus. Beni Montresor. New York: Harper & Brothers, 1961.

Tennyson, Alfred Lord. *The Charge of the Light Brigade*. Illus. Alice and Martin Provensen. New York: Golden Press, 1964.

Tresselt, Alvin. *The Frog in the Well*. Illus. Roger Duvosin. New York: Lothrop, Lee & Shepard, 1958.

Udry, Janice May. *Let's Be Enemies*. Illus. Maurice Sendak. New York: Harper & Brothers, 1961.

Ueno, Noriko. *Elephant Buttons*. New York: Harper & Row, 1973.

Ungerer, Tomi. *One, Two, Where's My Shoe?* New York: Harper & Row, 1964.

————. *Snail, Where Are You?* New York: Harper & Brothers, 1962.

Waber, Bernard. *Lyle, Lyle, Crocodile*. Boston: Houghton Mifflin, 1965.

Ward, Lynd. *The Silver Pony*. Boston: Houghton Mifflin, 1973.

Wezel, Peter. *The Good Bird*. New York: Harper & Row, 1966.

Yashima, Taro. *Crow Boy*. New York: The Viking Press, 1955.

Zei, Aliki. *Wildcat Under Glass*. Trans. Edward Fenton. New York: Holt, Rinehart and Winston, 1968.

Zion, Gene. *No Roses for Harry!* Illus. Margaret Bloy Graham. New York: Harper & Row, 1958.

Zolotow, Charlotte. *Mr. Rabbit and the Lovely Present*. Illus. Maurice Sendak. New York: Harper & Row, 1962.

chapter five

Helping Children Respond to Literature

One goal for the use of children's literature that most persons would agree on is that books should be read for enjoyment. This goal is to be prized, but often its interpretation has led people to believe that adults should not intervene between the book and the child-reader—that the role of the adult—teacher, librarian, or parent—is to bring books and children together. Consider the act of enjoying. Is it passive? Does it involve varying degrees of response to the stimulus? Is the intensity of enjoyment heightened through expressing the joy? Can it be felt subliminally? Is it immediate? Can it be learned? Questions such as these have not been answered definitively. The *concept of enjoyment*, which seems to belong in the realm of the emotions, has not been explored with a thoroughness that can be used practically. The *concept of response to literature* offers greater direction for the teacher and librarian. This is the concept toward which teachers and librarians have turned primarily since the attention given to the topic at the Dartmouth Seminar in 1966.[1] Response to literature can be defined as *the rational or non-rational behavior of the reader resulting from his interaction with a piece of literature.* The response may be expressed openly in many forms or it may be a change within the inner reader. Response may occur at any time after the reading.

Whether response to literature can be taught is still a concern, although the research points to an affirmative answer to the question. Purves and Beach, after an extensive review of research on the topic, concluded in their 1972 report that the teacher and the instruction were important for attaining goals of reading that included growth in critical reading, interests, and the skills of criticism.[2]

1. Discussions of the proceedings of this conference are reported in James R. Squire ed., *Response to Literature* (Champaign, Illinois: National Council of Teachers of English, 1968).
2. Alan C. Purves and Richard Beach, *Literature and the Reader: Research in Response to Literature, Reading Interests, and the Teaching of Literature* (Urbana, Illinois: National Council of Teachers of English, 1972), p. 181.

The research is not specific in terms of individual situations, however, so that much of what is done with children must be based on intuitive beliefs. Thus, the teacher or librarian who chooses to develop children's ability to respond to books must be committed to certain hypotheses on the use of literature:

Response to literature can be developed.

Response to literature is an important behavior although it cannot always be measured simply, efficiently, and objectively.

Response to literature is personal, therefore not resulting in behavior that can be judged right or wrong.

The process of responding to literature can be understood and engaged in successfully by children of elementary school age.

Developing the ability to respond to literature is more important than the child's response to any one particular book.

These statements are not totally in the realm of hypothesis. They represent beliefs that cannot be verified explicitly and some of the statements are in opposition to the views of certain people who work with children and books. It is highly probable, however, that agreement about these statements could be reached among many people.

Teachers and librarians who accept these statements and choose to implement the concept of response to literature would work toward two objectives for children:

1. To develop attitudes, both rational and nonrational, for responding to books.

2. To develop techniques for responding to books—techniques that are varied and appropriate to the differing abilities of children.

Implementation of the first objective leads to an examination of the studies on critical thinking and affective behavior basic to many curricular programs. Many constructs of the critical thinking process are available. The frameworks of Bloom[3] and others lend themselves to teaching the processes of critical thinking. Bloom's formulation of the thinking process is probably most widely known. When the steps of the taxonomy are recast as processes, they are: knowing, comprehending, applying, analyzing, synthesizing, and evaluating. Prior to discussing a book, the teacher can develop questions and activities concerning literature that demand children's use of these processes. For example, third grade children, after reading *The Biggest Bear* by Ward, might be asked to list the mischievous acts of the bear and then determine: Could all the acts be categorized as silly pranks? Were some acts more destructive than others? Analyzing such a situation causes children to use their critical thinking processes and, during the process, to think more deeply about the book.

Nonrational attitudes need development in the same manner. The construct of the affective domain by Krathwohl, Bloom, and Masia notes these five major processes: receiving, responding, valuing, organizing, and characterizing.[4] Non-

3. Benjamin S. Bloom ed., *Taxonomy of Educational Objectives: Handbook 1: Cognitive Domain* (New York: Longmans, Green, 1956).

4. David R. Krathwohl, Benjamin S. Bloom, and Bertram B. Masia, *Taxonomy of Educational Objectives: Handbook II: Affective Domain* (New York: David McKay, 1964).

rational behaviors are more difficult to observe, but in relation to literature a teacher might try to provide opportunities for children to develop their affective behavior. For example, a learning station might be devised that would allow certain activities to be done by choice after reading a book. The children might enjoy doing a simple activity like placing their names and the book title on a card and selecting a happy, sad, or neutral face to represent their view of the book. In a library setting, another child might find satisfaction in responding (a higher degree of affective behavior according to the earlier mentioned taxonomy) by dramatizing a scene from Cleary's *The Mouse and the Motorcycle* with the use of puppets or toy animals.

Children need to know how to respond to books in order to express themselves in ways other than the traditional, "It was a good book," or, "I didn't like it." When the various modalities of learning are considered, activities can be provided that will enable children to respond to books in ways appropriate for them. For example, some children might work best through the psychomotor domain, using large movements of the body. In that case, opportunities could be offered for dance interpretations of certain portions of the books or dramatizations in pantomime. In the school setting, the teacher or school librarian needs to assess the abilities and needs of the students for literature, just as in other areas of the curriculum. Then activities can be planned to meet those needs individually. The teaching must also be done in a manner that motivates and gives the students incentive to learn. In a public library setting, the activities cannot be as easily individualized, but variety in types of book programs will allow children to make more personalized choices for their responses.

Teachers and librarians must realize that their objectives are to teach attitudes and processes so children can develop habits of responding to books. The immediate object of the response—the particular book being discussed—is not the primary concern of the teaching. Thus, tests on how much can be recalled and assessments of interpretations of the book, noting how well one student interprets in relation to the group consensus of interpretation, are not the goal, even though these activities might be easier to check than children's attitude and process development.

Critical Frameworks for Developing Children's Response to Literature

There are many ways in which literature can be studied. Generally, literature as a field of study in itself uses the basic components of literature as referents: characterization, plot, theme, setting, and style. The four critical approaches highlighted in the preceding chapters of this book are common to the field of literary criticism but not especially common to the teaching of literature, particularly at the elementary level in schools and libraries. These approaches are offered here as an alternative or additional framework for teaching literature in the elementary school and for developing programs in libraries. When used, these approaches would ultimately offer more ways for children to respond to literature.

Each of the forms of literary criticism pointed out in the preceding chapters has certain elements that characterize it as a style. These elements are sometimes techniques, sometimes terminology, sometimes point-of-view. Many of the elements, however, can be formulated as teaching constructs. The following items represent some of the more basic elements of the four critical types which have been recast in the form of constructs appropriate for teaching at the elementary level and for developing a sound program of activities in the children's library.

Constructs of Psychological Criticism

A. Determine if there is any relationship between a piece of literature and the reader's life.

B. Compare similarities in the life and the fiction works of an author.

C. Interpret the meaning of symbols used in the literature.

D. Determine the extent of realism in a character's life.

Constructs of Sociological Criticism

A. Select portions of the literature that are propagandistic in tone.

B. Confirm that certain segments of the literature are truly representative of the social, political, or economic views of the time depicted in the tale.

C. Make judgments as to whether the responses of the characters to issues, problems, and events were in keeping with the norms of the time and place.

D. Identify traits of characters who are depicted as ideal heroes.

E. Point out items within the story that add to its realism.

F. Identify groups of characters that are relegated to certain social classes.

G. Judge whether the author portrays different classes with equality.

H. Point out how the social, economic, or political forces of the time affected the lives of the characters.

Constructs of Archetypal Criticism

A. Recognize examples from contemporary literature that draw on archetypes from Greek and Roman mythology.

B. Explain the allegorical references in selected literary works.

C. Show relationships that could be considered universal among characters in various works of literature.

D. Point out elements from literature that are suggestive of basic archetypal themes, such as: the earth mother, initiation rites, journey, quest, river, sea, classical hero, shadow, divine child, birth, creation, rebirth, defeat of death, Christian-Judeo symbolism, cycles of seasons.

Constructs of Structural Criticism

A. Discern the structural form of a literary work.

B. Differentiate the various shades of meaning of particular words, phrases, and metaphors used in literature.

C. Define the meanings of certain words used in literature in order to determine the meaning that seems most appropriate to fit the author's intent.

D. Identify sound patterns in the literature.

E. Point out differences in literal and figurative meanings of phrases.

F. Recognize the use of irony.

G. Compare the relationship of a particular poem or work of literature with the traditional body of poetry or literature.

H. Point out the contradictions in metaphors.

I. Analyze the effect of certain words and phrases on the emotional tone of the literary work.

Planning the Literary Content

One of the unconfirmed tenets of teaching and librarianship is that the most successful programs are the ones the adult has most enjoyed preparing. In all activities there is a tendency to get most involved with activities that are intriguing and that, through their own dynamism, motivate even more work than might be required.

Selecting the content for teaching an element of literature draws on this principle. The most effective content will be selected by the person who will be teaching the lesson or directing the program, especially when attention is given to the interests of the children. The best beginning is through reading good books, using suggestions of titles from students, librarians and teachers. There are many sources for learning about new books. Nearly every educational journal has a column of new book reviews, such as the "Books for Children" column in Language Arts. Certain journals such as School Library Journal and Horn Book are devoted primarily to book reviews. Each year lists of the outstanding books published that year are drawn up. Libraries and bookstores often have displays of new books. Lists of award-winning books, such as Newbery and Caldecott winners, are usually publicized in libraries and bookstores. Book displays such as Books on Exhibit[5] and the Children's Book Showcase,[6] are frequently made available in school systems, universities, and libraries so that persons can examine the actual books.

After reading an especially enjoyable book that is reminiscent of the kind of topic or situation that intrigues the particular group of children, look for some central elements of the book that are outstanding. In essence, let the book be the guide to selecting the content for instruction and programming. If the book is an especially good character study, perhaps the focus could be on the extent of realism noted in the character's life. A mystery that is spellbinding because of the way in which the plot unfolds might be studied for its structural form. A unique title might serve as a focus for symbols or metaphors. These brief examples suggest possibilities, but they are intended only to show the direction in which to move; the actual lesson or program development should be the exciting and enjoyable task of the adult. A word of caution should be included here: Don't force the issue. Sometimes certain portions of books can be developed into geography, vocabulary, and science lessons, but that is not

---

5. Books on Exhibit, Incorporated, Mount Kisco, N. Y. 10549.
6. The Children's Book Showcase, Sponsored by The Children's Book Council, 175 Fifth Avenue, New York City 10010.

really the goal of teaching literature. If children are to enjoy books to a greater depth than they might achieve on their own, they need guidance in interpreting and responding to the literature, not instruction in other curriculum areas. For example, *Dinky Hocker Shoots Smack* by Kerr is the story of a young girl's frustration with and rebellion against the problems of growing up. In one incident, Dinky, who is quite fat, gets started but doesn't continue on a Weight Watchers program. A study of dieting, or the basic food groups, would be only peripheral to the theme even though relevant to the textual content of the book. Central concepts and issues within the book should be the stressed content.

Although the ideal lesson or program is the one developed from "scratch" by the teacher or librarian for a particular group of children, often an idea comes from the adaptation of other material. For example, setting as the central focus is used in a study of Armstrong's *Sounder,* in a literature unit developed by Scholastic Books.[7] A teacher might adapt the teaching ideas of the unit to other books that are strongly tied to their settings such as *My Side of the Mountain* by George, or *Viva Chicano* by Bonham. In these books the sociological implications of the settings might be studied to note how the eastern mountains or Dogtown might influence the actions of the characters.

For another example, a librarian might draw from the series of articles on puppetry in the January, 1975 issue of *Top of the News.* Several mentions are made of the use of fairy tales for puppet shows. Children might be shown tales that have contrasting views of women and girls and then be drawn into a discussion of this topic.

Planning the Process Dimensions

Children can be helped to respond to literature through many processes. Selecting the processes is important, however, because they are the methods through which children learn to respond. When the processes are always of the same nature, children fail to learn alternatives and to expand their abilities to respond. Sometimes they become bored with the processes. When processes are always other directed—either by an adult personally or by a book, tape, or set of papers that give directions, the child fails to learn independence. In these cases, the child doesn't practice relying on self resources; instead, the child practices following the directions of someone else. Thus, children need opportunities for planning activities individually and with groups of their peers. They need to feel free to respond independently to books and even, if they choose, to not respond at all, if they feel it is not a book worthy of much consideration. Selecting processes for helping children respond to literature should be done with attention given to the appropriateness of the process for the children's learning abilities. Assessment tests are often given to children in order to note their best modalities for learning. Some children learn faster and retain longer through listening, others through seeing, writing, or using large body

---

7. Robert C. Small, Jr. ed., *The New Fiction: Teaching the Junior Novel,* Unit 7, *Sounder* by William H. Armstrong (New York: Scholastic Book Services, n.d.).

movements. An awareness of the most successful modes of learning for individual children would be helpful in planning activities concerning literature. A wide variety of activities could be planned that would offer various means of responding, such as speaking, writing, and small and large body movements through games, art projects, interpretative dance, and dramatic performances. On occasion, these modes of responding could also be accompanied by forms of intake other than reading, such as listening and viewing of nonprint media. The possibilities are numerous for planning activities concerning literature that will meet the process needs and abilities of individual children. Original and creative programs can be planned that involve a variety of processes or ideas can be adapted from conferences, classroom visits, other adults or the many print sources that are available. An example of the adaptation of a process could be taken from the book *Workjobs,* which details numerous independent activities for the early childhood level.[8] One activity that deals with classification suggests that children sort pictures of animals into piles according to where the animals live: land, water, air. This classification task could be adapted to a project on books that are real and imaginary; characters that are primarily admirable, adventurous, or mischievous; topics based on journeys, accomplishing a goal, or becoming a hero; or time studies of books that take place in one day, one week, one month, one year, or more than a year. A panel of students could judge whether the classifications were correct.

Sample Activities

The emphasis in the preceding pages has been on the creation of new ideas or adaptation of other ideas for topics and processes. One of the facets of working with children and books that makes it a rewarding enterprise is the opportunity for creativity on the part of the adult. The suggestions for the activities that follow are not placed here in disregard of the earlier emphasis. They are suggested as idea starters and as samples that can be adapted. Because they are designed around the approaches to literary criticism that are the focus of this book, they serve as examples of applications of the literary criticism methods discussed throughout the book.

Psychological Criticism

1. *Construct:* Determine if there is any relationship between a piece of literature and the reader's life.

Discuss with children the concept of expressing feelings through dance or dramatic interpretation. The book *Sometimes I Dance Mountains* by Baylor is especially good for getting across this idea. Encourage a group of children to recall passages in books they have read that have created strong personal feelings within them. Some books telling of strong anger or frustration may touch cords in children. *Summer of the Swans* by Byars has some passages of very

---

8. Mary Baratta Lorton, *Workjobs: Activity-Centered Learning for Early Childhood Education* (Menlo Park, Calif.: Addison-Wesley, 1972), pp. 72–73.

real feeling for the preadolescent and *From the Mixed Up Files of Mrs. Basil E. Frankweiler* by Konigsburg offers opportunities for feelings of great exhilaration. Primary youngsters may respond to *Harvey's Hideout* by Hoban or *Too Many Girls* by Gaeddert. Encourage children to form small groups and present their personal feelings that were turned on by these books. Children may want to select their own musical accompaniment for a dance interpretation, or use mime to express their feelings about a certain passage in a book.

2. *Construct:* Determine if there is any relationship between a piece of literature and the reader's life.

Occasionally the teacher or librarian becomes aware that a certain book has made an impact on a child. When this occurs, it is usually a book with depth, such as *The High King* or one of the other Prydain series by Alexander, or a book with special significance to a particular reader such as *Good-by to Stony Crick* by Borland and Speicher. Talk with the child about how very special the feeling is when an unknown author can touch strands within the life of the reader. Encourage the child to write personal feelings and keep a private journal relating incidents in the book to the child's life. Invite sharing of the written account with one or two specially selected persons. An assignment such as this is rare, but it could be a very worthwhile experience for a special child.

3. *Construct:* Compare similarities in the life and the fiction works of an author.

The book *Owls in the Family* by Mowat is based on experiences from the author's childhood. Read the book to a group of children. Discuss the author's life and have the children pick out expressions and events that highlight the reality of the book. Next, have the children individually select books that are based on actual experiences of an author's life. Some suggested texts are *Caddie Woodlawn* by Brink, *Our Eddie* by Ish-Kishor, and *Black Is Brown Is Tan* by Adoff. Help the children find information in the library about these authors. Use the individual conference method following the reading of each book. Encourage children's thinking with questions such as: "Did the setting of the bok reflect the author's background?" "What were the author's interests outside of writing?" "Were there events in the author's life that were hinted at in the books?" Lead the children to make some generalizations about the ability and the inclination of authors to draw from their own lives for the content of their books.

4. *Construct:* Compare similarities in the real life and the fiction writings of an author.

Show the filmstrip "Meet the Newbery Author: Madeleine L'Engle."[9] After children have read at least one of L'Engle's books, such as *The Wind in the Door,* discuss the aspects of the author's life that are brought out in the filmstrip: her interest in books, her actor husband, her strong religious orientation. Have the children discuss aspects of books looking for evidences of realism from the author's life that are included in the book. Instruct the children on how to write an essay using the form of comparison. Then direct them to write

---

9. "Meet the Newbery Author: Madeleine L'Engle," MNA 1005-C (New York: Miller-Brody Productions, Inc., 1974).

such an essay, comparing the real life and the fiction writing of Madeleine L'Engle. In library settings, charts might be made showing these contrasts and comparisons.

5. *Construct:* Interpret the meaning of symbols used in the literature.

Have a child who has read a book that contains symbols show an understanding of their meanings by setting up realia representing the symbols from the books in a display shelf. For example, a white marble representative of the gift given in Zolotow's book *The White Marble* or any of the items that were used in multiples in *The Endless Pavement* by Jackson and Perlmutter. A brief statement interpreting the symbolic meaning of the item could be mounted on a card or taped on a cassette as a part of a display.

6. *Construct:* Determine the extent of realism in the character's life.

After several children have read *Julie of the Wolves* by George, have them engage in an activity to determine their opinions about the realistic portrayal of the character. Offer some possible activities, such as creating a hypothetical situation of danger in which Julie might be cast. Have each write a version of how Julie might have realistically reacted to the situation. Compare the versions and have a leader take a poll of how many portrayed Julie as acting in ways similar to her actions in the book. Younger children could adapt the same activity to books such as Steptoe's *Train Ride* and Loree's *The Sunshine Family and the Pony*.

Activities such as this could be part of the planned programs for small groups of children in public libraries. The groups might be formed for short periods of time to cover such topics as "Adventures Afar" or might be an ongoing project of the children's division of the library.

7. *Construct:* Determine the extent of realism in a character's life.

Display several copies of *That Was Then, This Is Now* by Hinton. After two or three children have read the book, ask them to interview at least ten persons who have not read the book, asking their opinions of what the major character would probably do following a specific story situation. Prior to the interview, the children should prepare a synopsis of the story that describes the characters similarly to the author's portrayal, perhaps selecting a small portion to read aloud. Plan questions to ask each interviewee so that all interviewed are given the same questions and directions. When the taped responses are compared, have the interviewers pick out similar statements. Analyze these statements to see if the respondents tended to agree in what they thought the character would do. On the basis of this analysis, have the interviewers make some generalizations about how real and predictable the character apparently was to the children who were interviewed.

Primary grade children could do a simplified form of the activity with the problem of a found dog in *Somebody's Dog* by Miles.

Sociological Criticism

1. *Construct:* Select portions of the literature that are propagandistic in tone.

Persuade children to prepare a debate on the issue of the character of General Henry Hamilton, a British officer during the time of the American Revolutionary War who has been defamed in most historical accounts. Have children turn to an encyclopedia, history books about the Revolution, particularly about the "Year of the Bloody Sevens," and the biography of Hamilton by Havighurst, *Proud Prisoner*. Encourage children to find facts to support their cases. Urge them to find examples of misrepresentation or untruths in the accounts about Henry Hamilton in historical studies. Have a group of peers judge the debate and note which side made the more convincing argument. Younger children might contrast books that tell of the long-suffering bravado of the American Revolutionary War soldiers with the more humanly portrayed soldiers in *This Time, Tempe Wick?* by Gauch.

2. *Construct:* Confirm that certain segments of the literature are truly representative of the social, political, or economic views of the time depicted in the tale.

Direct children to work in pairs in order to research the actual information concerning social, political, and economic influences of the times. Historical fiction books and biographies are appropriate types of literature for study in this assignment. Children might compare several biographies of Christopher Columbus, for example, to note the type of statements and actions attributed to the man. Dalgliesh's *The Columbus Story* differs in tone from the D'Aulaire's *Columbus*. Third and fourth grade children could find opposing points of view and then read further in other sources to note other interpretations of the man's actions. The finished form of their project could be a list of statements about the life of the times, documented from their nonfiction sources. Other books that might be researched in this way are biographies of Daniel Boone, George Washington, and other persons of long ago who have been almost idolized in children's books. *Poor Richard in France* by Monjo and *Me and Willie and Pa* by Monjo are good examples of biographies of Franklin and Lincoln written from fictional point-of-view of a child. These might be unique forms to study. Historical fiction books that might be interesting studies are *Sing Down the Moon* by O'Dell and *Me, Cholay and Co: Apache Warriors* by Schellie.

3. *Construct:* Make judgments concerning whether the responses of the characters to issues, problems, and events were in keeping with the norms of the time and place.

The book, *Amos Fortune, Free Man* by Yates has been acclaimed and decried. Those who praise the Newbery Award winning book believe that it gives a warm personal study of a black man rising from slavery to become a free man making a contribution to his community. Others believe that the book portrays an invalid picture of a human, especially in the instances where the character is offered his freedom and rejects it, saying he is not ready. Have a child study some recent histories of life during slavery, such as Lester's *To Be a Slave* and other factual accounts. Encourage the child to share the findings with a group, emphasizing that the nature of the times had a great deal to do with the actions of people who lived then.

The book, *Carolina's Courage* also by Yates, could be studied by second and third grade students for the reality of the responses of the characters concerning the norms of the time and place.

4. *Construct:* Identify traits of characters depicted as ideal heroes.

Arouse children's interest in making word profiles of characters who might be considered ideal heroes. This term might be more relevant to children if they thought of the hero not as a political or social hero, but as a hero of childhood. Sobol's Encyclopedia Brown, to cite one hero, exemplifies many ideal characteristics that young children aspire to attain. Nancy Drew, another series character by Keene, holds a kind of aura for her fans. Children might find it interesting to list those character traits they admire in her. These written lists could be turned into artistic lists by using the words to actually draw the outline or profile of the character. Other fictional characters that could be identified in this way are characters from classics, such as *Heidi* by Spyri or *Robin Hood* as told by Pyle, or picture book heroes such as Peter in *The Snowy Day* and other books by Keats, or Henry in *Henry the Castaway* by Taylor. Projects such as this might provide more depth for summer reading programs in public libraries.

5. *Construct:* Point out items within the story that add to its realism.

A learning station might be developed to help children become aware of the instances of realism within a story. A student could be asked to itemize the realistic problems, responses to problems, and eventual outcomes. The completed list could then be discussed with a peer who had read the book, while the child supported the realism of each of the items. Books appropriate for this project would be *Zeek Silver Moon* by Ehrlich, *Watch Out for the Chicken Feet in Your Soup* by DePaola, and *Donald and the Fish that Walked* by Ricciuti. Intermediate grade students might enjoy using *After the Goat Man* by Byars, *That Crazy April* by Perl, and *Trouble on Treat Street* by Alexander.

6. *Construct:* Identify groups of characters that are relegated to certain social classes.

Encourage children to do a simple content analysis of the characters within books. They might make a chart that classifies paired groups of characters, such as:

Indians and Pioneers

	Low		Average		High	
	Indians	Pioneers	Indians	Pioneers	Indians	Pioneers
Type of Job						
Wealth						
Trust						
Attitude toward Peace						

In historical fiction books, the groups of characters might be immigrants and Americans or patriots and British soldiers. In realistic fiction the groups might be blacks and whites, men and women, etc.

Books that might be used for comparisons are *The Matchlock Gun* by Edmonds, *Small Wolf* by Benchley, *Only Earth and Sky Last Forever* by Benchley; *Our Country's Story* by Cavanah, *And Then What Happened, Paul Revere?* by Fritz, and *Two If by Sea* by Fisher; *Black Folk Tales* by Lester, *Teacup Full of Roses* by Mathis, and *Charlie and the Chocolate Factory* by Dahl.

Have children work on their charts for several weeks, then take time to discuss in a larger group the evidence they have collected.

7. *Construct:* Judge whether the author portrays different classes with equality.

Encourage a group of children to compare the treatment given to various classes among books that differ in the class to which the main character belongs. For example, how do the authors treat differing classes within these books: *Migrant Girl* by Laklan, *Ox Goes North: More Trouble for the Kid at the Top* by Ney, *Then Again, Maybe I Won't* by Blume and *Sidewalk Story* by Mathis. After the study of the class treatment within each book, have the children make comparisons of the treatment among the books. Does the author tend to treat a higher socio-economic class character better, worse, or with equality when the main character is from a low socio-economic class? Urge the students to support their judgments with passages from the books.

8. *Construct:* Point out how the social, economic, or political forces of the time affected the lives of the characters.

M. C. Higgins the Great by Hamilton is especially usable for noticing how the environment—social, economic, and political—affected the lives of the characters. A group project such as the following would create discussion and exchange of ideas. Make a chart listing the various kinds of problems that plagued the families in this book, such as pollution, weather, money, etc. Then have the children give instances of how these things affected the various family members. Students may want to differentiate the problems in the categories of money problems, people problems, or problems of nature. An extension of the chart would be to find other books that show how other families coped with similar difficulties.

ARCHETYPAL CRITICISM

1. *Construct:* Recognize examples from contemporary literature that draw on archetypes from Greek and Roman mythology.

Students might develop an ongoing collection of references from contemporary writing that use archetypes from Greek and Roman myths. One theme current today that has many ancient referents is the cyclic pattern of the seasons. Children might read some of the many poetry books based on seasons, such as *The Seasons of Time* by Baron, *Hello, Year!* by Jacobs, and *All for Fall* by the Kesslers. Some of the children may want to read aloud or tape poems that show cyclic changes. Others may want to begin with a large chart listing many Greek and Roman referents concerning the seasons. As poems are read and the referents are noted, they might be placed on the chart in pictorial form. This would be a usable individualized project for a public library.

2. *Construct:* Explain the allegorical references in selected literary works.

Lead a small group of students to select allegorical references in contemporary works and show their relationship to religious stories and symbols.

Books appropriate to this assignment are the Narnia books, beginning with *The Lion, the Witch, and the Wardrobe* by Lewis, *Dorp Dead* by Cunningham, *The Real Thief* by Steig, and *Two Brothers* by Schwarz. The children might want to make a booklet of comparisons, using one side of a page to show contemporary references and the other side to note the religious referent. An activity such as this might lead into the study of Bible literature or even a comparative study of the literature of many religions.

3. *Construct:* Show relationships that could be considered universal among characters in various works of literature.

Primary grade children can point out universal characters as they note a character who is similar to or who "reminds them of" a character in another book. For example, the character of the lovable oaf is developed in the main characters of *Lyle Finds His Mother* by Waber and *Veronica* by Duvoisin. Wise beasts who surmount problems are found in *Anatole* by Titus and *Crictor* by Ungerer as well as in folk tales about Anansi, such as in *A Story, A Story* by Haley and stories about Rabbit, as in *Jambo, Sungura* by Heady. Children who can do strong feats and manage well in an adult world are the main characters in *The Plant Sitter* by Zion, *The Real Hole* by Cleary, and *Send Wendell* by Gray. A storyteller can stimulate oral discussion of similar characters by mentioning a pair that seem to be similar and asking for support of that similarity if children agree.

4. *Construct:* Point out elements from literature that are suggestive of basic archetypal themes: Birth.

Focus attention on one of the basic archetypal themes and plan an activity suitable for several ages around it. For example, the birth archetype is present in a great deal of children's literature. Bring together primary grade and older age children prepared to share their current literature on this topic. Some may want to speak about the archetypes in their book, others may show pictures and some might want to dramatize the unfolding of a bud or the scrambling to its feet of a newborn calf. Some books that contain this theme are *A Firefly Named Torchy* by Waber, *April's Kittens* by Newberry, and *Miracles on Maple Hill* by Sorenson.

5. *Construct:* Point out elements of literature that are suggestive of basic archetypal themes: Journey.

Many children's books use the journey archetype. Encourage children to chart the journeys their characters take. When several books are noted, students may want to categorize the stories according to whether the characters met with harm or success, whether they returned home, or whether they had to be helped by other characters. Books for primary grade children that deal with journeys are *Anton the Goatherd* by Carigiet, *Looking for Something* by Clark, *Chester the Worldly Pig* by Peet, and *The Camel Who Took a Walk* by Tworkov. A library discussion group of intermediate grade children might benefit from doing this activity with *Journey from Peppermint Street* by DeJong or *The Endless Steppe* by Hautzig.

6. *Construct:* Point out elements of literature that are suggestive of basic archetypal themes: River.

Urge a group of children to select a common theme of literature and find examples of it used in various books. They might select, for example, the river.

Books such as *Journey Outside* by Steele and *The River at Green Knowe* by Boston would provide interesting studies. Encourage the students to determine if the symbol was used as a theme or was simply an environmental or plot addition to the story. The group might make a presentation explaining these uses to another group of students. A montage of filmed river scenes or a tape-slide show would be intriguing and would be likely to hold the attention of other students during the explanation of the archetypes.

STRUCTURAL CRITICISM

1. *Construct:* Discern the structural form of a literary work.

Help children understand the author's purpose in developing the unique structure of the stories. Encourage them to determine if structure tells any more of the story than is told in the text alone. The book *Sam* by Scott, for example, tells of four extremely similar encounters that the hero has with members of his family one after another. One incident alone would carry little meaning, but if children experienced through creative drama the frustration of the character after having been rebuked <u>four</u> times, they could sense the purpose behind the author's use of repeated incidents. Other books that would be adaptable for role playing are two with pyramid structures: *Tell Me a Mitzi* by Segal and *Brian's Secret Errand* by Lonergan. These two works offer interesting contrasts.

2. *Construct:* Discern the structural form of a literary work.

The visual structure of picture story books can be a helpful source for children's understanding of the author's purpose. In *Bird Boy* by Wende the hero tries to fly in his pair of home-made wings. All the pictures that tell of making the wings are drawn against a white background. When the inevitable crash comes, Bird Boy is transformed into a bird-sized creature. The pictures in the dream sequences are framed all in a water color rectangle. Enlist the children's aid in pointing out the visual clues to the textual meaning. *The Old Dog* by Abbott is another book that uses the picture structure to show the difference between real and imaginary. A book that shows step-by-step happenings—many on a page—is *Robin in Red Boots* by Herzka and Steiner.

3. *Construct:* Differentiate the various shades of meaning of particular words, phrases, and metaphors used in literature.

Use the book *Peter's Chair* by Keats to point out to children the shades of word meanings in the following portion of the text where Peter notices that his old baby furniture is being painted pink:

> Peter <u>thought</u> that the cradle was his cradle.
> Peter <u>whispered</u> that it was his high chair.
> Peter <u>muttered</u> that it was his crib.
> Peter <u>shouted</u> that they hadn't painted his old chair yet.

Have the children role play this scene as Peter looks at various pieces of his furniture. Then discuss the different meanings of the words and how they build in intensity.

Rosie's Walk by Hutchins and *Mr. Gumpy's Outing* by Burningham use forms of words in ways worthwhile for children to notice. The first uses numerous prepositions and children can have fun while differentiating among the words by role playing the story after reading the book or viewing the film. *Mr. Gumpy's Outing* uses verbs in a similar fashion and children enjoy telling and describing with actions these verbs when the story is retold as a flannelboard tale.

4. *Construct:* Define the meanings of certain words used in literature in order to determine the meaning that seems most appropriately to fit the author's intent.

Use the form of paraphrasing to initiate thinking about the meanings of titles and other especially significant words. For instance, the title, *When Hitler Stole Pink Rabbit* by Kerr has various meanings for different persons. Ask children individually to write brief essays about titles or certain words in the books that they have read. Collect the essays until a sizable group is available, then have a group discussion of the meanings and encourage differences of opinion.

5. *Construct:* Identify sound patterns in the literature.

Use picture books with primary children to point out sound patterns within books. *Parakeets and Peach Trees* by Kay Smith is filled with alliterations, *Crash! Bang! Boom!* by Spier is a whole collection of onomatopoetic words, and *Plink Plink Plink* by Baylor builds suspense about sounds. Provide opportunities for children to listen to these words and to say them, allowing them to make tapes of the books if they choose.

6. *Construct:* Identify sound patterns in the literature.

A number of books that have been recorded contain especially fine sound combinations of words. Have children listen to a recording of Henry's *Misty of Chincoteague*[10] for example, to note the use of alliteration and assonance or view and hear the filmstrip recording of *Charlotte's Web*,[11] noting the unique phrasings that E. B. White gives to his own book. Discuss these sound combinations following the use of the media and then encourage children to read aloud passages that they find particularly pleasing to the ear.

7. *Construct:* Point out differences in literal and figurative meanings of phrases.

Whet children's interest in adding some original incidents to the adventures of the hero of *The Phantom Tollbooth* by Juster. In this book figurative language abounds and many puns are used. Children might want to create the new incidents artistically through puppet shows for their peers or they might find it more enjoyable to write the incidents, savoring their newly created puns as they create. *Amelia Bedelia* by Parrish is another book that might be used in this way at an easier reading level.

8. *Construct:* Recognize the use of irony.

Engage intermediate grade children in discussing the use of irony in a panel discussion. During the panel planning session, urge the participants to consider such questions as: Why would an author want to use irony? What effect does it have on the reader? Is the element of irony lessened when it is foreshadowed?

---

10. Marguerite Henry, *Misty of Chincoteague,* Newbery Award Record No. 3043 (New York: Miller-Brody Productions, Inc.).

11. E. B. White, *Charlotte's Web,* filmstrips and recordings (Santa Monica, California: Steven Bosustow Productions, 1974).

Books such as *Good Ethan* by Fox, *Push Kitty* by Wahl, *The Aminal* by Balian, *The Mystery Beast of Ostergeest* by Kellogg, and *All the Lassies* by Skorpen would lend themselves to this discussion. The points made about irony might be taught effectively by the discussant through contrast with books that do not contain irony.

9. *Construct:* Compare the relationship of a particular poem with the traditional body of poetry.

Haiku is a form of poetry frequently used with children. Some of the poetry is published in the 5-7-5 syllable form while many of the original Japanese writings which are translated into English lose the 17 syllable pattern. Have children compare the poems in the two forms, noting whether the structural differences create any feeling of difference between the poems. Examples of books containing these forms are *In a Spring Garden* by Lewis, *More Cricket Songs* by Behn, *Birds, Frogs, and Moonlight* by Cassedy, and *Haiku, the Mood of Earth* by Atwood.

10. *Construct:* Point out the contradictions in metaphors.

A number of poetry books based on the use of color in metaphors have been used to inspire children's creative writing. Prompt children to study what is said in the poetry and notice if contradictions are apparent. Encourage the children to determine if the poets used these contradictions intentionally. Books that could be used effectively here are *Black Is Brown Is Tan* by Adoff, *Hailstones and Halibut Bones* by O'Neill, and *Green Is Like a Meadow of Grass* by Larrick.

11. *Construct:* Analyze the effect of certain words and phrases on the emotional tone of the literary work.

Compare several books that use very satisfying refrains with books that tell a good story without the use of the refrain device. Books with refrains such as *Millions of Cats* by Gág, *Journey Cake, Ho!* by Sawyer, and *Horton Hatches the Egg* by Seuss are quite usable. Encourage children to respond emotionally to the tone set through the refrain. How do they feel after hearing the stories? What do they want to say? Do books such as these leave them with a different feeling than books such as *Under Christopher's Hat* by Callahan with no set refrain? Encourage the youngsters to think about and share orally the effect of the books.

A Word of Encouragement

The suggestions above are provided only as brief examples to support the point that the critical approaches described in this book are quite possible and very workable for using children's literature in the classroom and the library. These suggestions are not intended to be all-inclusive, limiting, or overpowering. People who work with children have great acuity for using just exactly the right approach for their particular group of children when they receive some stimulation—a new focus for an idea, a unique approach, a slightly altered process for organizing a learning experience. The intent of this book was to offer that stimulation. Its fruitfulness will lie in the reader's adaptation of the ideas to individual children and their books.

REFERENCES

Abbott, Sarah. *The Old Dog*. Illus. George Mocniak. New York: Coward, McCann and Geoghegan, 1972.

Adoff, Arnold. *Black Is Brown Is Tan*. Illus. Emily McCully. New York: Harper & Row, 1973.

Alexander, Anne. *Trouble on Treat Street*. Illus. John Jones. New York: Atheneum, 1974.

Alexander, Lloyd. *The High King*. New York: Holt, Rinehart and Winston, 1968.

Armstrong, William H. *Sounder*. Illus. James Barkley. New York: Harper & Row, 1969.

Atwood, Ann. *Haiku: The Mood of Earth*. New York: Charles Scribner's Sons, 1971.

D'Aulaire, Ingri and Edgar Parin. *Columbus*. Garden City, New York: Doubleday, 1955.

Balian, Lorna. *The Aminal*. Nashville: Abingdon Press, 1972.

Baron, Virginia Olsen (ed.). *The Seasons of Time: Tanka Poetry of Ancient Japan*. Illus. Yasuhide Kobashi. New York: The Dial Press, 1968.

Baylor, Byrd. *Plink Plink Plink*. Illus. James Marshall. Boston: Houghton Mifflin, 1971.

————. *Sometimes I Dance Mountains*. Illus. Bill Sears and Ken Longtemps. New York: Charles Scribner's Sons, 1973.

Behn, Harry, trans. *More Cricket Songs*. Illus. with pictures by Japanese Masters. New York: Harcourt Brace Jovanovich, 1971.

Benchley, Nathaniel. *Only Earth and Sky Last Forever*. New York: Harper and Row, 1972.

————. *Small Wolf*. Illus. Joan Sandin. New York: Harper and Row, 1972.

Blume, Judy. *Then Again, Maybe I Won't*. Scarsdale, New York: The Bradbury Press, 1971.

Bonham, Frank. *Viva Chicano*. New York: E. P. Dutton, 1970.

Borland, Kathryn and Helen Speicher. *Good-by to Stony Crick*. Illus. Deanne Hollinger. New York: McGraw-Hill, 1975.

Boston, L. M. *The River at Green Knowe*. Illus. Peter Boston. New York: Harcourt Brace Jovanovich, 1959.

Brink, Carol Ryrie. *Caddie Woodlawn*. Illus. Kate Seredy. New York: The Macmillan Company, 1935.

Burningham, John. *Mr. Gumpy's Outing*. New York: Holt, Rinehart and Winston, 1970.

Byars, Betsy. *After the Goat Man*. Illus. Ronald Himler. New York: The Viking Press, 1974.

————. *The Summer of the Swans*. Illus. Ted CoConis. New York: The Viking Press, 1970.

Callahan, Dorothy M. *Under Christopher's Hat*. Illus. Carole M. Byard. New York: Charles Scribner's Sons, 1972.

Carigiet, Alois. *Anton the Goatherd*. New York: H. Z. Walck, 1966.

Cassedy, Sylvia and Kunihiro Suetake, trans. *Birds, Frogs, and Moonlight*. Illus. Vo-Dinh. Calligraphy by Koson Okamura. Garden City, New York: Doubleday, 1967.

Cavanah, Frances. *Our Country's Story*. Illus. Julia Keats. New York: Rand McNally, 1962.

Clark, Ann Nolan. *Looking-for-Something*. Illus. Leo Politi. New York: The Viking Press, 1952.

Cleary, Beverly. *The Mouse and the Motorcycle*. Illus. Louis Darling. New York: William Morrow, 1965.

————. *The Real Hole*. Illus. Mary Stevens. New York: William Morrow, 1960.

Cunningham, Julia. *Dorp Dead*. Illus. James Spanfeller. New York: Pantheon, 1965.

Dahl, Roald. *Charlie and the Chocolate Factory*. Illus. Joseph Schindelman. New York: Alfred A. Knopf, 1964.

Dalgliesh, Alice. *The Columbus Story*. Illus. Leo Politi. New York: Charles Scribner's Sons, 1955.

DeJong, Meindert. *Journey from Peppermint Street*. Illus. Emily Arnold McCully. New York: Harper and Row, 1968.

DePaola, Tomie. *Watch Out for the Chicken Feet in Your Soup*. Englewood Cliffs, N.J.: Prentice-Hall, 1974.

Duvoisin, Roger. *Veronica*. New York: Alfred A. Knopf, 1961.

Edmonds, Walter D. *The Matchlock Gun*. Illus. Paul Lantz. New York: Dodd, Mead, 1941.

Ehrlich, Amy. *Zeek Silver Moon*. Illus. Robert Andrew Parker. New York: The Dial Press, 1972.

Fisher, Leonard Everett. *Two If By Sea*. New York: Random House, 1970.

Fox, Paula. *Good Ethan*. Illus. Arnold Lobel. Scarsdale, New York: Bradbury Press, 1973.

Fritz, Jean. *And Then What Happened, Paul Revere?* Illus. Margot Tomes. New York: Coward, McCann and Geoghegan, 1973.

Gaeddert, LouAnn. *Too Many Girls*. Illus. Marylin Hafner. New York: Coward, McCann and Geoghegan, 1972.

Gág, Wanda. *Millions of Cats*. New York: Coward-McCann, 1928.

Gauch, Patricia Lee. *This Time, Tempe Wick?* Illus. Margot Tomes. New York: Coward, McCann and Geoghegan, 1974.

George, Jean. *Julie of the Wolves*. Illus. John Schoenherr. New York: Harper and Row, 1972.

————. *My Side of the Mountain*. New York: E. P. Dutton, 1959.

Gray, Genevieve S. *Send Wendell*. Illus. Symeon Shimin. New York: McGraw-Hill, 1974.

Haley, Gail E. (reteller). *A Story, A Story*. New York: Atheneum, 1970.

Hamilton, Virginia. *M. C. Higgins, the Great*. New York: The Macmillan Company, 1974.

Hautzig, Esther. *The Endless Steppe*. New York: Thomas Y. Crowell, 1968.

Havighurst, Walter. *Proud Prisoner*. Illus. Leonard Vosburgh. Williamsburg, Virginia: Colonial Williamsburg; New York: Holt, Rinehart and Winston, 1964.

Heady, Eleanor B. *Jambo, Sungura: Tales from East Africa*. Illus. Robert Frankenberg. New York: W. W. Norton, 1965.

Herzka, Heinz and Heiri Steiner. *Robin in Red Boots*. Trans. Elizabeth D. Crawford. New York: Harcourt, Brace and World, 1969.

Hinton, S. E. *That Was Then, This Is Now*. New York: The Viking Press, 1971.

Hoban, Russell. *Harvey's Hideout*. Illus. Lillian Hoban. New York: Parents' Magazine Press, 1969.

Hutchins, Pat. *Rosie's Walk*. New York: The Macmillan Company, 1967.

Ish-Kishor, Sulamith. *Our Eddie*. New York: Pantheon, 1969.

Jackson, Jacqueline and William Perlmutter. *The Endless Pavement*. Illus. Richard Cuffari. New York: The Seabury Press, 1973.

Jacobs, Leland B. (comp.). *Hello, Year!* Illus. Frank Aloise. Champaign, Illinois: Garrard Publishing, 1972.

Juster, Norton. *The Phantom Tollbooth*. Illus. Jules Feiffer. New York: Random House, 1961.

Keats, Ezra Jack. *Peter's Chair*. New York: Harper and Row, 1967.

————. *The Snowy Day*. New York: The Viking Press, 1962.

Keene, Carolyn. *The Clue in the Old Stagecoach*. Nancy Drew Mystery Stories. New York: Grosset and Dunlap, 1960.

Kellogg, Steven. *The Mystery Beast of Ostergeest*. New York: The Dial Press, 1971.

Kerr, Judith. *When Hitler Stole Pink Rabbit*. New York: Coward, McCann and Geoghegan, 1972.

Kerr, M. E. *Dinky Hocker Shoots Smack!* New York: Harper and Row, 1972.

Kessler, Ethel and Leonard. *All for Fall*. New York: Parents' Magazine Press, 1974.

Konigsburg, E. L. *From the Mixed-Up Files of Mrs. Basil E. Frankweiler*. New York: Atheneum, 1968.

————. *A Proud Taste for Scarlet and Miniver*. New York: Atheneum, 1973.

Laklan, Carli. *Migrant Girl*. New York: McGraw-Hill, 1970.

Larrick, Nancy (selector). *Green Is Like a Meadow of Grass*. Illus. Kelly Oechsli. Champaign, Illinois: Garrard Publishing, 1968.

Lester, Julius. *Black Folktales*. Illus. Tom Feelings. New York: Grove Press, 1970.

———— (comp.). *To Be a Slave*. Illus. Tom Feelings. New York: The Dial Press, 1968.

Lewis, C. S. *The Lion, the Witch and the Wardrobe*. Illus. Pauline Baynes. New York: The Macmillan Company, 1965.

Lewis, Richard (ed.). *In a Spring Garden*. Illus. Ezra Jack Keats. New York: The Dial Press, 1965.

Lonergan, Joy. *Brian's Secret Errand*. Illus. Cyndy Szekeres. Garden City, New York: Doubleday, 1969.

Loree. Sharron. *The Sunshine Family and the Pony*. New York: The Seabury Press, 1972.

Mathis, Sharon Bell. *Sidewalk Story*. Illus. Leo Carty. New York: The Viking Press, 1971.

————. *Teacup Full of Roses*. New York: The Viking Press, 1972.

Miles, Miska. *Somebody's Dog*. Illus. John Shoenherr. Boston: Little, Brown, 1973.

Monjo, F. N. *Me and Willie and Pa: The Story of Abraham Lincoln and His Son Tad*. Illus. Douglas Gorsline. New York: Simon and Schuster, 1973.

————. *Poor Richard in France*. Illus. Brinton Turkle. New York: Holt, Rinehart and Winston, 1973.

Mowat, Farley. *Owls in the Family*. Ilius. Robert Frankenberg. Boston: Little, Brown, 1961.

Newberry, Claire Turlay. *April's Kittens*. New York: Harper and Row, 1940.

Ney, John. *Ox Goes North: More Trouble for the Kid at the Top*. New York: Harper and Row, 1973.

O'Dell, Scott. *Sing Down the Moon.* Boston: Houghton Mifflin, 1970.

O'Neill, Mary. *Hailstones and Halibut Bones.* Illus. Leonard Weisgard. Garden City, New York: Doubleday, 1961.

Parish, Peggy. *Amelia Bedelia.* Illus. Fritz Siebel. New York: Harper and Row, 1963.

Peet, Bill. *Chester the Worldly Pig.* Boston: Houghton Mifflin, 1965.

Perl, Lila. *That Crazy April.* New York: The Seabury Press, 1974.

Pyle, Howard. *The Merry Adventures of Robin Hood of Great Renown in Nottingham-shire.* New York: Charles Scribner's Sons, 1946.

Ricciuti, Edward R. *Donald and the Fish that Walked.* Illus. Syd Hoff. New York: Harper and Row. 1974.

Sawyer, Ruth. *Journey Cake, Ho!* Illus. Robert McCloskey. New York: The Viking Press, 1953.

Schellie, Don. *Me, Cholay and Co.: Apache Warriors.* New York: Four Winds Press, 1973.

Schwarz, Eugene. *Two Brothers.* Trans. Elizabeth Reynolds Hapgood. Illus. Gabriel Lisowski. New York: Harper and Row, 1973.

Scott, Ann Herbert. *Sam.* Illus. Symeon Shimin. New York: McGraw-Hill, 1967.

Segal, Lore. *Tell Me a Mitzi.* Illus. Harriet Pincus. New York: Farrar, Straus and Giroux, 1970.

Seuss, Dr. *Horton Hatches the Egg.* New York: Random House, 1940.

Skorpen, Liesel Moak. *All the Lassies.* Illus. Bruce Martin Scott. New York: The Dial Press, 1970.

Smith, Kay. *Parakeets and Peach Pies.* Illus. José Aruego. New York: Parents' Magazine Press, 1970.

Sobol, Donald J. *Encyclopedia Brown Takes the Case.* Illus. Leonard Shortall. Camden, New Jersey: Thomas Nelson, 1973.

Sorenson, Virginia. *Miracles on Maple Hill.* Illus. Beth and Joe Krush. New York: Harcourt Brace Jovanovich, 1956.

Spier, Peter. *Crash! Bang! Boom!* Garden City, New York: Doubleday, 1972.

Spyri, Johanna. *Heidi.* Illus. Leonard Weisgard. New York: World Publishing, 1946.

Steele, Mary Q. *Journey Outside.* Illus. Rocco Negri. New York: The Viking Press, 1969.

Steig, William. *The Real Thief.* New York: Farrar, Straus and Giroux, 1973.

Steptoe, John. *Train Ride.* New York: Harper and Row, 1971.

Taylor, Mark. *Henry the Castaway.* Illus. Graham Booth. New York: Atheneum, 1972.

Titus, Eve. *Anatole.* Illus. Paul Galdone. New York: Whittlesey House, 1956.

Tworkov, Jack. *The Camel Who Took a Walk.* Illus. Rogert Duvoisin. New York: Aladdin Books, 1951.

Ungerer, Tomi. *Crictor.* New York: Harper and Row, 1958.

Waber, Bernard. *A Firefly Named Torchy.* Boston: Houghton Mifflin, 1970.

————. *Lyle Finds His Mother.* Boston: Houghton Mifflin, 1974.

Wahl, Jan. *Push Kitty.* Illus. Garth Williams. New York: Harper and Row, 1968.

Ward, Lynd. *The Biggest Bear.* Boston: Houghton Mifflin, 1952.

Wende, Philip. *Bird Boy.* New York: Cowles Book Company, 1970.

Yates, Elizabeth. *Amos Fortune, Free Man.* Illus. Nora S. Unwin. New York: E. P. Dutton, 1950.

_____. *Carolina's Courage.* Illus. Nora S. Unwin. New York: E. P. Dutton, 1964.

Zion, Gene. *The Plant Sitter.* Illus. Margaret Bloy Graham. New York: Harper and Brothers, 1959.

Zolotow, Charlotte. *The White Marble.* Illus. Lilian Obligado. New York: Abelard-Schuman, 1963.

Index